SOLDIER OF FORTUNE 5

ACTION IN THE ARCTIC

SOLDIER OF FORTUNE 5

ACTION IN THE ARCTIC

Peter Leslie

22

First published in Great Britain 1994
22 Books, Invicta House, Sir Thomas Longley Road,
Rochester, Kent

Copyright © 1994 by 22 Books

The moral right of the author has been asserted

A CIP catalogue record for this book is available from the
British Library

ISBN 1 898125 28 7

10 9 8 7 6 5 4 3 2 1

Typeset by Hewer Text Composition Services, Edinburgh
Printed in Great Britain by Cox and Wyman Limited, Reading

Prologue

A few minutes before the explosion, a streak of jade green separated the icy waters of the Barents Sea from the slate-coloured Arctic sky. The 'perpetual daylight' of the extreme north was only weeks away: the sun was about to reappear after its short-lived nightly dip below the horizon.

As the band of light deepened, shading through orange to an angry pink, the masts and upper works of the ships in the convoy assembled themselves in silhouette above the steely slopes of the swell. The convoy was an important one: twenty-seven merchantmen, with an escort of six destroyers, two submarines and three anti-aircraft vessels. Two British and two American cruisers lay in close support to the west; three more British and two Russian submarines lurked offshore along Norway's northern coast; and the main covering force – two battleships, three cruisers, a carrier and a flotilla of destroyers – was steaming on a parallel course between Bear Island and the southern limit of the pack ice.

Apart from its size, this particular convoy had a special importance. It was the spring of 1942. North Africa was in flames and Rommel was about to take Tobruk. Malaya and Singapore had fallen to the Japanese. The Royal Navy's resources were stretched to the limit, protecting the Atlantic convoys vital to Britain's continued existence and ensuring the survival of Malta. But Stalin, dismayed by the Allies' inability to relieve pressure on him by opening a second front in Europe, was screaming for an increase in the supplies sent to him via the perilous Arctic sea route to Murmansk, so that he could better contain the Nazi thrusts deep into the Russian homeland.

Convoy PQ-13A – codenamed out of chronological sequence to confuse any German radio cryptographers intercepting Allied naval traffic – was part of Whitehall's initial response to this Soviet plea. The twenty-seven freighters had been selected as those with the most useful cargo among more than a hundred, already loaded and waiting for escorts in Iceland.

The sea paled quickly that early morning: high clouds blowing up from the west, teased out into long streamers, glowed now in the radiance of the approaching sun, gilding the wave crests as they crumbled into foam.

The officers on watch aboard the escorting destroyers were hoping, for once, that it was going to be a quiet, uneventful day, even if, as usual, it was a very long one. They were out of range of the twin-engined Heinkel bombers flying from Nazi airfields at Elvebakken and Lakselv, 400 miles south on the wild Norwegian coast near the North Cape. No U-boats had been reported in their sector. And Hitler's *Tirpitz*, the world's most heavily armed battleship, mistakenly reported at large, was in fact safely berthed in Trondheim with the cruisers *Hipper* and *Scheer*.

Nothing, therefore, prepared them for the colossal detonation which erupted without warning from the forward well-deck of the last ship in the convoy – a thunderous explosion hurling a column of black smoke marbled with flame hundreds of feet into the air. It was followed, before the blazing debris spewed out by the blast splashed into the sea, by a curious diminishing rumble like a distant mutter of thunder.

Then the most extraordinary thing of all happened. It was as if the stricken merchantman had been cloven in two by a giant axe. The forecastle and bows rose abruptly into the air, pointing skywards; at the same time the rusty stern, with its twin screws, rose clear of the water. The guard rails of the well-deck sank beneath the waves. The wheel-house and bridge were no more than a tangle of buckled plates and twisted steel through whose jagged edges the rim of the sun was visible hoisting itself above the horizon. And all at once the ship simply vanished: both halves slid smoothly, quietly, effortlessly into the deep. One moment, crippled, shattered, but still afloat, she was there, a skeletal shape against the sun's glare; the next, there was nothing beneath the billowing tower of black smoke but a mill-race of raging foam, a welter of waves punctuated by crates, casks, eddying planks, and the heads of survivors dwarfed by the immensity of the sea.

An underwater explosion, muffled, stirred the swell; a huge bubble, filmed with oil, broke surface and burst. On the port wing of the flotilla leader's bridge, the lieutenant on watch had been hurled against the canvas dodger by the blast. He struggled upright and bellowed orders through his megaphone. The destroyer heeled over as the man at the wheel spun the lean craft through a 180-degree turn; behind the creaming double-U of her wake, other escort ships were racing towards the wreckage.

A tall, lean senior officer, huddled into a duffle coat and oilskins, left the chartroom to join the lieutenant on the bridge wing. 'My *God*,' the young man exclaimed. 'What sort of a tinfish was that? Did you *see* it, sir? Christ, I've watched enough ships go down; I've seen enough U-boat hits, sometimes with more than one torpedo. But, Jesus, I *never* saw a single strike produce an explosion like that. The whole bloody ship was gone in seconds! I mean, God, I never . . .' He shook his head at a loss for words.

The senior officer screwed his eyes shut against the icy wind. 'The ship was not torpedoed,' he said.

The lieutenant stared at him. 'Not . . .?'

'I was in the chartroom. I happened to have my glasses on the ship. There was no water-line hit, nothing under water; no exterior plates were damaged.'

3

'I don't understand,' the lieutenant said. 'To go down that fast . . .'

'The vessel sank immediately because the bottom was blown out of her by an enormous charge,' the officer said. 'I was watching. The explosion came from *inside* the hull, not from a surface hit that smashed inwards – from something down in the hold that burst *out*.'

'Good God! You don't mean . . . sabotage, or something like that?'

'I don't think so. Did you notice that odd rumbling noise just after the hit? Quite loud at first and then dying away?'

'I don't think so, sir. What with the waves and the spray out here . . .'

'Never mind. I was going to say I believe the ship was hit from the air. By some kind of projectile.'

'But there's no EA for hundreds of miles, sir! Besides, we'd have *heard* a plane, even at a high altitude. It would have shown up on . . .'

'I didn't say a bomb, my boy. A projectile. Possibly with a one- or two-second delayed-action fuse, so that it penetrated well before it went off.'

'Do you mean,' the lieutenant said slowly, 'that it was something *fired* at the ship? All the way out here? And that it was a direct hit?'

The senior officer was looking out over the hissing crests as the destroyer smashed through the waves. Whole continents of cloud revealed by the flaming dawn now dimmed and vanished as the direct rays of the sun fanned out. The red light drained through bronze and silver to a livid blue against the glare of which only the mushroom of oily smoke marking the freighter's grave remained sharp and distinct. 'I'm afraid that's what I do think,' he said. And then, almost apologetically, with a wave at the smoke: 'Torpedoes and shells fired from surface craft chuck up a great column of water and steam and foam when they explode. There was none

4

of that here: the blast actually *flattened* the sea for an instant!'

'What do we report, sir?' the lieutenant said. The nearest escort craft were lowering nets towards the blast-concussed, wounded, oil-grimed and desperate survivors in the water. Several boats had been launched to pick up those carried further away by the swell. Immersed in the freezing tides of these northern latitudes for more than two and a half or three minutes, a weakened man risked dying of hypothermia.

'Report?' the senior officer echoed. 'I'm only aboard on a watching brief, young man. You're the skipper – and the flotilla leader. If I were you, I'd simply report one ship lost by enemy action. With the exact co-ordinates, of course: time, position, weather, number of survivors, so forth. But nothing more; the details can wait.'

'Yes, sir. Thank you, sir. But . . . but won't there be questions asked? I mean to say, in the circumstances . . .?'

Commander Archie Lang smiled bleakly. 'You bet there will. But they can't ask them, for security reasons, until we're in port. You'll have to stall them off until then.' He shook his head. 'Whether or not there'll be any answers is another matter.'

'Yes, sir.'

'In the meantime,' Lang said, 'we must do a bit of homework ourselves. Sound out every single person, on every ship in the convoy, who actually saw the hit. Time can alter a witness's recollection, so the sooner we collect and collate these statements the better. If you can organize me a launch, I'll check with the cruiser captains and get on to that right away.'

'Very good, sir. Willco,' the lieutenant said.

The destroyer was hove-to. Crew members were helping the bedraggled, exhausted survivors swarm up the nets. Some were already in a bad way. Others seemed to have great difficulty forging their way through the water to safety. The surface of the sea, for hundreds of yards around, was clogged with bales and bundles and sodden individual examples of floating debris as dun-coloured as the swell itself – a heavy layer of flotsam impeding the strokes of swimmers, clinging to their limbs and sometimes threatening to drag them underwater.

'Hell, if that isn't Sod's law at its ironic bloody best!' There was a touch of hysteria in the lieutenant's laugh.

Commander Lang raised surprised eyebrows.

'Do you know what cargo that ship was carrying, sir?' Lang shook his head.

The lieutenant pointed over the rail. 'Dozens of blokes out there freezing to death in the icy water,' he said, 'and what's stopping them climbing out into the warmth? One hundred thousand heavy woollen greatcoats destined to keep away the cold from Uncle Joe's troops in the Ukraine!'

1

'The official report,' the admiral in charge of the inquiry said, 'will be that the ship struck a mine.'

'Four hundred miles out in the Barents Sea?' the flag-officer responsible for convoy co-ordination said incredulously.

'A floating mine . . . broken loose from its moorings . . . carried northwards over the months by wind and tides. An unhappy coincidence.'

'And the real reason?'

'Haven't the foggiest,' the admiral said frankly. 'It's a real teaser. From the point of view of the convoy itself, everything there is to know is here in Commander Lang's report.' He tapped a buff folder on his desk. 'No enemy aircraft in the vicinity at the time of the hit. No U-boats. No surface craft within several hundred miles. The operation as a whole lost eleven out of twenty-seven merchantmen and one destroyer. Eighty-six thousand tons of war materials went to the bottom. Nine of the merchant ships were sunk by submarines and one by aerial attack. The destroyer was the victim of an aerial torpedo. No other incidents were observed of the type concerned in this inquiry.'

'What about the testimony of survivors? And those in the convoy who actually saw the explosion?' the flag-officer asked.

The admiral opened the folder. 'I'll summarize it for you,' he said. 'Thirteen individuals in the entire convoy happened to have their eyes on the ship at the exact moment of the impact. Many more, of course, turned their heads as the blast wave and the sound of the explosion reached them. From two of the thirteen, Commander Lang and the flotilla leader, Lieutenant Townsend, we have already heard the most valuable accounts. The remaining eleven agree, except in minor detail, that the initial thrust of the discharge was upwards – and presumably downwards – from the centre of the ship, rather than inwards from an exterior strike. Milliseconds later, of course, it had fanned out with the normal spreading of debris. Three of these witnesses recall hearing the diminishing rumble mentioned by Commander Lang. One, a petty officer aboard the destroyer *Wallflower*, swears – and will not be shaken from his story – that he had an instantaneous vision of what he terms 'a finned shape' streaking from the sky a heartbeat before the detonation.'

The admiral closed the folder and looked around the room. Twelve men, high-ranking officers and civilians, sat in a rough semicircle in front of the desk. Some carried folders similar to the admiral's own, with the red Top Secret seal on the top right-hand corner. One civilian had set a bulging briefcase by his feet; another nursed a long, tightly scrolled cylinder of cartridge and tracing paper. They included representatives from Naval Intelligence, the War Office, the Home Office, the American Embassy, the Norwegian branch of the Special Operations Executive, Military Intelligence and the office of Winston Churchill's scientific adviser, Professor Lindemann. Outside the long windows, criss-crossed with adhesive anti-blast paper, rain fell on the traffic trundling down Whitehall.

'Nothing useful from the survivors?' the man from the US Embassy asked. The ship had been one of seven American vessels in the convoy.

The admiral shook his head. 'It was a huge explosion. The first thing many of them remember is the shock of being in icy water. Others were still too dazed to be coherent when they were questioned. And "after the event" recollections can be seriously misleading.'

'So what are we left with?' the American asked.

'To answer that,' the admiral said, 'I'll call upon Dr Williams from the boffin factory run by Lindemann.'

The man with the bulging briefcase unbuckled the flap, took out some papers, shuffled them, and rose to his feet – a thin-faced, freckled young man with a shock of sandy hair and horn-rimmed spectacles. 'Gentlemen,' he began, 'in the light of such evidence as we have, there's only one conclusion to be drawn. If we rule out a torpedo, a bomb, a floating mine, a shell and a deliberate act of sabotage . . .'

'Is that wise – to rule out sabotage completely?' someone interrupted.

'Oh, I think so,' the flag-officer said. 'There are plenty of Axis agents around capable of it. But look at the cargo – army greatcoats! Who would bother when the other ships were loaded with tanks, APCs, radar apparatus, bomb-sights and munitions? Please continue, Doctor.'

'Ruling out all those things,' the scientist resumed, 'we're left with the inescapable conclusion – shared by Commander Lang – that the vessel was hit by some other kind of projectile; a missile as the term is now.'

'Four hundred miles out to sea?' the SOE man said. 'Fired from where?'

'On the evidence we have, it has to be land-based.'

'But, good God, man . . . I mean, the distance! Fired from Norway?'

'If fired is the right term,' said the scientist. 'No gun on earth, not even one that's still on the drawing board . . .' He shook his head. 'An engineer-artificer aboard the American freighter nearest the wreck is something of an explosives expert. He's also one of the thirteen witnesses. He reckons' – the young man took a sheet of paper from the sheaf in his hand and glanced at it – 'he reckons it would take at least a ton of high explosive, maybe a lot more, to sink a ship of that size that quickly, even after a direct hit amidships.'

For a moment there was silence in the room. The rain drummed on the windows.

'With that weight,' Williams said, 'the trajectory of a missile over that distance would have to be enormously high – personally, I'd incline towards at least a measure of self-propulsion. Dropping from such a height, the projectile would certainly have reached its terminal velocity. Assuming that was in excess of the speed of sound, this would explain the express-train rumble heard by the Commander and other witnesses after the detonation of the warhead.'

'What's terminal velocity?' the Home Office representative asked.

'The point at which a falling object has attained its maximum acceleration. It varies with the mass of the object, the gravitational pull and the resistance of the atmosphere in which it falls – as Galileo found out, dropping a stone and a feather at the same time from the top of the leaning tower of Pisa. But however heavy the object, once that point is reached, it cannot drop any faster.' The young man smiled. 'Remember what the petty officer saw,' he added.

The admiral leaned his elbows on the desk, steepled his fingers, and rested his chin on them. 'What you are saying, Williams, is that Hitler does in fact have one of these blasted secret weapons he's always threatening us with?'

'Yes, sir. I'm afraid that's about the strength of it.' Williams sat down.

'How do you account for this 100 per cent accuracy – a direct hit over four hundred miles of sea?' the man from Naval Intelligence demanded.

The man with the roll of paper answered. He spoke without getting up, in a lazy drawl that went with his whipcord trousers, suede jacket and the lock of dark hair falling over one eye. 'Only two alternatives,' he said. 'A: yes, there really is a secret weapon Jerry's testing in this area, and this poor bloody ship happened to stray into an experimental firing range or something, and got pranged by chance. A million to one chance – a hundred million to one according to our statisticians – but it could happen. B: yes, there is a weapon, and it's equipped moreover with a magisterial rangefinding device which guarantees first-time accuracy over huge distances. In which case we have something of a problem!'

'You mean,' the flag-officer said, 'either the ship was a deliberate target, hit deliberately. Or it wasn't.'

'Well, yes, you could put it that way, if you wish.'

'It's shorter,' the flag-officer said.

'Which alternative do you guys root for?' the American Embassy man asked.

It was Williams who replied. 'Long odds were never my choice. Nevertheless, B seems even less likely than A. For a start, assuming there *was* such a rangefinding device, how the devil, over four hundred miles of the earth's curved surface, did they know *precisely* where their moving target was in the first place?'

'A hit,' the Military Intelligence man murmured. 'A very palpable hit!'

'All right then.' The admiral was suddenly brisk, even a trifle testy. 'Whatever this damned thing is, wherever it is, I take it we're agreed something drastic has to be done about it. The firing base must be located, the installation evaluated. We must find out how the bloody thing works, if necessary pinch the idea, then destroy the whole place, eliminate it.' He glared around the room. 'Any of you people got the least idea where we should look? Bonham-Charvet – what's that roll of bumph you have there?'

The young man in the suede jacket rose to his feet. He walked across to the desk, unrolled the paper cylinder and spread his arms to hold down the stiffly curling ends. 'Vectors, triangulation, interacting variables,' he drawled. 'Much of the area rules itself out automatically. If we're looking for a land-based installation – and if we assume the target was at the present maximum range of the weapon – more than 280 degrees of the 360 centred on that target are open sea.'

Bonham-Charvet looked up from his paper, which was a transcribed chart representing the northern half of Scandinavia and the surrounding oceans, with the site of the hit indicated by a red cross. 'Bill? If you wouldn't mind . . .'

Williams hurried to the desk and held down the edges of the chart; the others left their chairs and crowded around.

A circle had been drawn on the cartridge paper with the red cross as its centre. 'The scale radius of the circle is a shade over four hundred miles,' Bonham-Charvet said.

'Aren't we jumping the gun a bit, assuming that *is* the maximum range?' the flag-officer asked.

'One of my variables,' the young man said. 'And, yes, of course, you're right. But it's the only finite figure we have: the nearest ship-to-shore distance. If we don't use that in the equation, X can equal literally anything from four hundred upwards.'

He tapped the chart. 'As you can see, the lower or southern circumference of the circle passes through this extraordinary indented upper fringe of Scandinavia, roughly from Tromsö, in the west, to Petsamo, on the Russian side of the frontier. The only other land masses within the circle are Bear Island, which is too small for any kind of military base, Spitzbergen – still frozen up – and Nova Zembla, which is Soviet territory.'

'So what it amounts to,' the officer from SOE said, 'is that we're looking for some kind of secret base in what used to be called simply Lapland?'

'Right. We can narrow down the area, though.' Bonham-Charvet laid a sheet of tracing paper over the chart. With a soft pencil, he reproduced the arc of the circle cutting through the Scandinavian land mass, and the serrated coastline above. He drew two straight lines linking the outer points of this arc to the red cross showing through from the chart below, then laid a finger on the left-hand side of the narrow segment thus produced. 'The intelligence wallahs who evaluate data supplied by our overseas agents reckon that the country from Tromsö to the airfield at Lakselv, beyond the Alta Fiord, would be unsuitable for a secret installation: too much German military traffic, too much naval activity in the fiords. It seems Jerry expects us to attempt a landing there any day!' Bonham-Charvet chuckled. 'Some hopes! Anyway they think nothing secret in that sector would remain secret very long.' He drew another line from the centre, past Lakselv, to the arc. 'So we'll ignore everything west of this.' He cross-hatched out the area bounded by the two radii.

'Much the same story on the other side,' he said. 'The intelligence analysts are convinced nobody would construct a top-secret installation within a hundred miles of Petsamo. Too near the Russkis for comfort – Jerry comfort anyway!' A fourth line joined the arc to the centre, and once again the space between that and the right-hand radius was blocked out.

Bonham-Charvet looked at the remaining, very narrow triangle. 'Theoretical area of ops, you see, is substantially reduced. Broadly, I'd suggest looking for your base on the desolate highlands between two mountain lakes: Petsikko, on the northern tip of Finland, and Mollišjok, on the other side of the Norwegian frontier.' He nodded to the admiral, flipped back the lock of hair over his eye, rolled up the chart and returned to his chair. It was only when he was settling himself into it with special care that they realized one of his legs was artificial.

'Battle of Britain,' the SOE man whispered to the American. 'He was in the drink for eighteen hours before they picked him up.'

'Thank you,' the admiral said to the young cartographer. He placed his hands palm down on his desk and looked slowly at each member of the group. 'Well, gentlemen?'

There was a chorus of comments.

'They could blast hell out of us from across the Channel with such a weapon,' the Home Office man said.

'To say nothing of an actual battle.'

'We have to find that bloody base and neutralize it.'

'I'll see if we can organize a photo overflight of the area by carrier-based aircraft,' the Naval Intelligence man said.

'We need more data. Warn all naval patrols in the area to watch out for similar explosions and report any PDQ.'

'I'll alert all our chaps in Norway to keep their eyes skinned,' the SOE representative said. 'They're already on to some ultra-high-security Nazi factory built on a fiord near Narvik.'

'Once the place is located,' the officer from Military Intelligence said, 'we'll go into it really seriously. I'll sound out Dickie Mountbatten on the chances of a combined-ops raid or a parachute drop.'

The admiral shook his head. 'No,' he said. 'Don't do that. Winston's already vetoed anything of that sort.'

'Why not, for God's sake? The place has got to be destroyed, dammit. Christ, we can't expect the boys in blue to steam up the nearest fiord and lob over a few rounds of sixteen-inchers!'

'Sensitivity, Colonel, is the name of the game,' said the admiral.

'Sensitivity?'

'The area itself is highly sensitive. It lies, as we have seen, midway between occupied Norway and our Russian ally, a hair's breadth away from neutral Sweden – and largely in Finland, an Axis satellite since the Soviet invasion and subsequent annexation of Karelia in 1939. But on that subject I think our ambassadorial friend has something to say.'

'Why, yes,' the American said. 'It seems there's a possibility – no more than that – that the Finns would like to negotiate a separate peace through the – ah – good offices of our embassy in Moscow. Needless to say, any overt Allied incursion on their territory at such a time would be embarrassing in the extreme. It could lead to a breakdown in the negotiations.'

'In addition to which,' the admiral said, 'we are about to sign a treaty with Russia stipulating that *none* of the Allies may conclude a separate peace with any Axis power except by mutual consent. Any military action of ours near the Russo-Finnish border could very well anger Stalin and affect that also.'

'The Foreign Office is also concerned over the question of Sweden,' the flag-officer put in. 'If forces engaged in any operation to put this base out of business happened to cross their frontier – that is to say, violated their neutrality – there'd be hell to pay. They might even offer, after all, to grant Hitler the Baltic bases they've been denying him for the past two years.'

'And finally,' said the SOE man, 'there's Norway itself. 'No problem if the frontier is crossed. They'd jump for joy. But if anything went wrong, if there was any kind of cock-up and Norwegian property was destroyed or lives lost . . . well, the flow of vital information on German movements that we get from there might diminish or even dry up. Dammit, the whole bloody thing's too delicate for words!'

'So what's the answer?' the man from Military Intelligence enquired.

'There's only one answer,' said the admiral. 'I take it we're all agreed that *something* has to be done? We're equally agreed that the situation all around is too sensitive for us or any of our Allies to do it. Or be seen to do it.' He leaned back in his chair. 'Very well then: we'll get somebody else to do it.'

'Somebody else?'

'Someone totally unconnected with any of us, neutral or whatever, uncommitted anyway.'

'I'm not sure I'm with you, sir,' the man from Military Intelligence ventured.

'I'm talking of professionals. Soldiers who can be hired. Mercenaries, if you like.'

'You mean hire a band of . . . of *outsiders* . . . and get them to do the job for us?'

'That's exactly what I mean.'

'But . . . do you think it would work? Could such a group do it?'

'If we got the right fellow to lead them, yes. It's a simple seek-and-destroy operation, basically. Brief them well enough, train them well enough, pay them enough, and of course they could do it.'

'Suppose they were captured?' someone said.

'That's the beauty of it,' the admiral said. 'Captured, interrogated, tortured even, they won't be able to give anything away because they won't *know* anything. They won't even know for sure who's paying them. Hitler will know bloody well, of course, but he won't be able to *prove* it; he'll have no witnesses, no evidence.'

'But, Admiral, sir,' the American protested, 'even assuming such an idea was valid, how in hell would you propose setting up such a unit?'

'For that,' the admiral said genially, 'we need specialist advice.' He pressed a key on his intercom and called: 'Would you come in a moment, please?'

A tall, dark girl in the blue uniform of the WRNS knocked on the door and entered. 'Ah, Molly,' the admiral said, 'I think it's time we all had a cup of tea. Could you cope? . . . Oh, and would you please ask Commander Lang if he'd join us?'

2

Commander Lang walked north along Whitehall as the air-raid sirens wailed over the roofs of the city. Nobody took any notice: traffic was light; off-duty soldiers and civilians with their gas-mask cases were hurrying to an early lunch, hoping to find a table and something edible before it was 'off'; passengers in the red buses heading for Victoria, Liverpool Street, East Acton, continued to read their newspapers. It was only Jerry sending over the usual high-flying reconnaissance plane to photograph the destruction caused by last night's raid.

A building near the corner of Northumberland Avenue had received a direct hit. Smashed glass littered the pavement for a hundred yards on either side of the great slant of rubble cascading into the street from the pulverized façade. Most of the rooms had been used as offices, but tin-helmeted salvage workers were still picking over the chaos of fallen masonry and beams and smashed furniture in the hope of locating possible survivors. Brick dust lay heavy on the humid atmosphere, and wisps of smoke curled here and there among the wreckage.

The road was steaming too. The rain had stopped and shafts of sunlight warmed the wet macadam and gleamed on the three gold bands circling Commander Lang's uniform sleeve.

He skirted the roped-off debris which blocked the pavement and spilled halfway across the street, waiting for a honking taxi to pass before he crossed to the far side. He passed glassless shop fronts and the blank windows of blast-damaged houses, then turned the corner leading to Admiralty Arch and the Mall.

Beyond the arch there was a sandbagged brick-and-concrete air-raid shelter. And fifty yards from this, sunk deep into the ground of the park, was that strange, equally windowless, concrete fortress known as 'the Citadel'.

Lang showed his special pass to the armed sentry at the entrance. Sixty feet below the surface, he stepped out of a lift and strode along a rubber-tiled corridor to a grey steel door on the frosted-glass upper panel of which was the announcement:

Combined Operations (Security) Executive,
Capt. S. McP. O'Kelly, R.N.

In the small operations room on the far side of the door, a telegraphist with earphones sat in front of a complex switchboard controlling a battery of radar screens covering one wall, a row of monitor speakers above the map-stand, and a transmitter-receiver installation racked beyond the huge central desk. Behind the desk was the room's occupant: a large man with a pink complexion and silver hair.

'Archie!' he said. 'That must have been a hell of a briefing; they certainly took their time! *We'll* only have time ourselves for a single snort of pinkers before we push off to Scott's for lunch.'

Lang smiled. A large bottle of gin and a small bottle of Angostura bitters already stood, together with two glasses, on O'Kelly's desk. The captain had politely awaited the return of his number two before drinking himself. Now he dribbled a few drops of the bitters into each glass, swirled the thick fluid around, and then tipped what remained into a small sink beside the radio console. He added a generous measure of gin to each glass, critically examining the faint rose-coloured tinge lent to the clear spirit by the dash of bitters still clinging to t.ie glass before he drank. 'Cheers!' he said. 'Now what have those buggers in Whitehall dreamt up for us this time?'

Lang sipped his pink gin. 'Bit of a tall order,' he said. 'They want us to organize a hell's own complicated operation . . . and then not do it ourselves.'

'Oh, God!' O'Kelly said. 'You'd better keep it for lunch, Archie. Drink up and we'll scramble up the Carlton House steps and breeze along Haymarket for that lobster.'

Many top-level planners, tacticians and strategic experts were summoned by the Prime Minister to high-security conferences in the bomb-proof Citadel. But the existence and real purpose of CO(S)E – irreverently dubbed 'Cosy Corner' by those courageous and foolhardly enough to work for it – was known only to three men: the heads of Naval and Military Intelligence and Churchill himself. The Sovereign too could have been privy to the exploits of O'Kelly's cloak-and-dagger operatives had he so wished. But he was a wise man, and knew when not to ask awkward questions. O'Kelly in fact was handed the undercover 'dirty work' which even the Secret Intelligence Service would have been loath to own up to.

Seated at one end of the counter in the famous fish restaurant opposite the Prince of Wales Theatre, O'Kelly listened without comment to Lang's low-voiced account of the morning's deliberations. 'Three more things have come up since I submitted my original report,' Lang concluded. 'Four similar explosions, complete with rumble, have been recorded since the original ship was hit. None of them was remotely near any of our vessels, although the area in which they fell was within twenty miles of that first explosion. Two: carrier-based recce flights show no evidence of any kind of experimental station in the area of Finland under discussion. And lastly: SOE operatives in Tromsö nevertheless report a marked increase in heavy military traffic heading in an east-south-easterly direction from the town – which is to say towards the region we're talking about.'

'This Newburg's uncommonly good,' O'Kelly said, probing for a final sliver of flesh inside a hot lobster claw. 'Those bloody Bretons, I bet – landing half their catch in Cornwall again, because the prices are higher!' He signalled the barman for two more glasses of Chablis.

'You're right, of course,' he continued, laying down the claw in the remains of the sauce, 'it's got to be some kind of a firing range. The ship you saw go down just happened to be in the wrong place at the right time. Unhappy coincidence.'

'Coincidence with an arm four hundred miles long!' Lang said mildly.

'Do any of the other theories make more sense?' O'Kelly demanded. 'Don't tell me the Boche have developed a rangefinder capable of pinpointing a ship-sized target that far over the curvature of the earth! That's complete bosh!'

'Very droll,' Lang said drily.

O'Kelly glared. He was not in the habit of making deliberate puns. 'And they expect us to dig up some damn scallywag of a gun-runner, some desperado with allegiance to nobody who'll do anything for money . . . and then brief him and train the blighter and baby him along until he's earned his filthy lucre? Is that what you're telling me, Archie?'

'That's about the size of it,' Lang said.

'I never heard anything so damn silly in all my life,' O'Kelly growled. He held out his hand for the bill. 'Come on: we'd better get back into the cage and start writing bloody minutes!'

Unkind Whitehall tongues wagged to the effect that Seamus McPhee O'Kelly had never been nearer the Emerald Isle than Mooney's pub in Piccadilly. In fact he was born in Kinsale, a small fishing port in County Cork, joined the Royal Navy in 1915, served with distinction in a cruiser squadron until he was wounded in the Battle of Jutland, and was subsequently transferred to a strategic planning department at the Admiralty. His present position was directly due to a friendship formed when Churchill was First Sea Lord. Apart from his intelligence and determination, O'Kelly possessed in full two of the most important qualities required in a successful leader of men: he knew when to delegate; and, whatever the circumstances, however grim the story, he invariably backed up his subordinates, defending them to the end. It was because of the trust engendered by this that those seconded to CO(S)E would go to lengths for him far beyond the call of duty and frequently in excess of those available in any other command.

'Do you think we've a ghost of a chance of pulling this off, sir?' Lang asked when they were back in the operations room at the Citadel.

'Depends,' O'Kelly said. 'Given the time and the facilities and the right leader, there's no reason why we shouldn't train a unit – even a group of bloody misfits, if you like – point them in the right direction, and have them locate this damn experimental base – if it exists.'

'I'm pretty sure it exists all right,' Lang said.

'Frankly, old boy, so am I. But once it *is* located . . . well, what happens then's in the lap of the gods. Or the lap of the poor sod we pick to lead this unit!'

'I don't suppose you have the foggiest idea of how in hell we're going to find such a man – an uncommitted military leader in the middle of a world war?'

O'Kelly permitted himself a grin that could almost be described as crafty. 'Funny you should say that, Archie,' he drawled. 'But as it happens there *is* a chap I think might fill the bill. But before I know for sure, you'll have to pull strings, wangle me a fast passage to Lisbon, and organize an onward flight from Lisbon to Geneva . . .'

'Is that all?' Lang asked.

3

Riordan sat alone at a pavement café halfway along the Champs-Élysées. He was reading that day's edition of Hitler's gift to the newspaper readers of Occupied Paris, the German-language *Pariser Zeitung*. Crumpled on an empty chair beside him were copies of the French collaborationist dailies, *Le Petit Parisien* and *Paris-Soir*.

Next door to the café, two Wehrmacht soldiers with machine-pistols stood guard over double doors above which the street number 114 was picked out in white figures on a blue enamel plaque. The building was the headquarters of AFIP, the Agence Française d'Information et de Presse. Once the Paris home of the German news agency DNB, it was now the official channel through which the victors funnelled selected items of information to newsmen, foreign as well as French.

Riordan was foreign. He was also a newspaper correspondent, or at least posing as one. His accreditation as a neutral confirmed him as a contributor to news magazines published in Zurich, Helsinki and Madrid, and he did from time to time file stories to those cities in English, Finnish or Spanish. The Finnish – an unusual language for an Irishman – he had picked up three years previously, fighting for General Mannerheim when his country was invaded by the Russians; he had learned Spanish in Mexico, working for Pancho Villa and Zapata – enough anyway to enable him to lead one of the International Brigades during the Spanish civil war. For Riordan's real profession was military: he was a soldier of fortune, a mercenary (a term he himself repudiated). As an adviser he had worked with the Chinese at the time of the Sino-Japanese conflict in Manchuria in 1931, and for Haile Selassie during the Ethiopian Emperor's courageous but vain resistance to Mussolini's Italians in Abyssinia.

His reasons for being in Paris in the spring of 1942 were twofold. One was a curvaceous and enthusiastic redhead named Aline. The other was the belief that, if he hung around long enough, in the right places, the French capital was the likeliest city in Europe to come up with what he privately thought of as 'something interesting': even under the iron hand of the occupiers the climate of international intrigue remained ripe for action.

Riordan admired the ruthless efficiency of the Nazi war machine, and applauded the resolve of the British and the American ideal of liberty. But he himself was totally uncommitted: his loyalty was reserved for those who paid for his special talents. A man who lived for action, he was prepared to accept anything, from the smuggling of gold bullion to the storming of a stronghold, from the hijack of an arms shipment to the organization of a *coup d'état* in Africa . . . if the price was right. He would never under any circumstances, however, accept a contract for individual assassination. Soldiers got killed: that was part of the game; the moral line between this and the extinction of bystanders or those who didn't know they were in the game was a faint one, but for Riordan it was there.

He had talked his Swiss, Finnish and Spanish contacts into appointing him as their Paris stringer because it gave him a valid reason to remain in France – while he waited for that 'something interesting' to show up.

The work was not always as easy as it looked. The AFIP was geared to provide journalists with the story, omitting no detail, however slight, of each and every German victory; it would supply information on anything and everything Adolf Hitler did or intended to do; it would catalogue the medals worn by Hermann Goering and explain what they were awarded for. It was the sole supplier of news to the French press and the organism controlling radio news bulletins – in German, of course – from the Paris broadcasting headquarters in the sixteenth *arrondissement*. It arranged fact-finding tours for foreign newsmen in Riordan's category.

But it was not an ideal source for human interest material, for reports on how the population reacted to the occupation, or for investigative work on dissatisfaction or the Resistance. Such stories had to be submitted to the censors at the Greater Paris Propaganda-Staffel, just up the street at number 52, or smuggled out via Switzerland under a fictitions byline if they were likely to get the writer in trouble with the Propaganda Abteilung at the Hôtel Majestic.

Riordan sighed. He folded the paper and added it to those on the vacant chair. It was one of the three days per week on which it was forbidden to supply alcoholic drinks. From a small, leather-covered hip-flask, he discreetly added a dash of calvados apple brandy to the coffee in front of him – an unappetizing ersatz brew made from acorns and chickpeas and known as *café national*. He swallowed the mixture with a grimace of distaste, left money on the table and pushed back his chair. He had a noon date with Aline at the Café de la Paix. There were no taxis; the Métro was closed every working day from eleven in the morning to three in the afternoon; it was virtually impossible to fight your way on to a crowded bus – if you could find one. He would have to walk the mile and a half to the Place de l'Opéra.

In fact he ran the last half mile, partly because he relished any excuse to supplement a rigorous personal keep-fit routine, mostly because an attractive woman sitting alone at the Café de la Paix risked being mistaken for a *fille de joie*, and he made a point always of being there first when he had an outdoor date with Aline.

Barney Joseph Riordan, son of a County Wicklow farmer, had been known to his family and schoolfriends as Barry-Joe, to his intimates later as Barry, and to those with whom he came into professional contact simply as Riordan. So far as he could recall, nobody in his life had ever addressed him as Mr Riordan.

He had been obliged to leave Ireland after a misunderstanding with the British during the Easter uprising in Dublin in 1916 – groundwork in urban-guerrilla tactics which had proved useful after he worked his passage to the Gulf on an oil tanker and ran across one of Zapata's lieutenants in a Galveston whore-house.

In the spring of 1942 he was an arresting figure: a lean six-footer in matchless condition, with curling, iron-grey hair and craggy good looks. A glance at Riordan's weathered features and bright-blue eyes revealed nothing about his age: he could have been anything from forty to sixty.

The auburn-haired Parisienne who drew a wicker chair up to his table five minutes after he arrived was, at twenty-seven, a good deal younger and was what Riordan's father would have called a stunner.

Aline Pacquot, a Lyonnaise, worked as a saleswoman in the exclusive couture salon of Lucien Lelong, where many of the customers, and even more so their husbands, considered her prettier than any of the highly paid mannequins showing off the clothes.

Riordan had met her at a press reception at Maxim's in the Rue Royale – or, to be more precise, their eyes had met in one of the gilt-framed mirrors above the red-plush banquettes in that famous restaurant – and if it wasn't love, it was most certainly lust at first sight. Riordan took her back to his apartment in the Rue Clauzel, two blocks below the Moulin Rouge in Montmartre, and they didn't get out of bed for three days. Her slim-waisted but fleshy enthusiasm was a perfect foil for Riordan's rangy masculinity: they moved together with the precision of a Swiss watch.

There was the fact, too, that, as a girl from the

gastronomic centre of France, Aline could do more culinary magic with their meagre ration tickets – and what black market produce she could find – than anyone he had ever met. She kept her own small studio near the Place St-Sulpice, on the Left Bank, but spent most of her non-working time in Riordan's larger flat, outside which she installed, like thousands of Parisian housewives, a rooster, half a dozen hens and a hutch full of rabbits between two slopes of roof.

It was forbidden to make or sell croissants, brioches or the creamy pastries for which the Café de la Paix had been renowned. Coffee was out of the question. It was a non-alcoholic day. So they toyed with insipid water-ices while they scanned an entertainment guide, trying to decide which film to see.

Smart women clacked past in the wooden-soled plat-form shoes that were all the boutiques were permitted to sell. A tide of pedalled traffic swirled around the forest of German-language signposts and the concrete pillbox sunk into the roadway in the middle of the wide square. Cycles towing delivery trailers, rickshaw-style taxis drawn by bicycles, private landaulets with pedal power joined the flood of ordinary riders and the occasional military vehicle or police van circling the central subway entrance and then peeling off down the Boulevard des Capucines, the Rue du Quatre Septembre or the Avenue de l'Opéra like sparks from a Catherine wheel.

They decided finally to walk up to the Gaumont Palace in the Place Clichy and see the new Marcel Carné – Jacques Prévert gothic fantasy *Les Visiteurs du Soir*, with Arletty – a film about which most of Paris was talking, and many were laughing behind their hands.

It was only a ten-minute stroll, afterwards, to the Rue Clauzel.

'Crazy, isn't it?' Riordan said as they climbed the stairs to his sixth-floor apartment. 'With all their efficiency the Nazis are sometimes such idiots!'

'What do you mean, *chéri*?' Aline asked.

'The film. All scenarios have to be submitted to German censorship before a single foot can be shot; the edited film has to be passed before it can be publicly shown. Yet here's this medieval romance that they don't even see as an allegory: they haven't twigged that when the lovers are turned into statues by the Devil – but their hearts continue to beat inside the stone – this is a metaphor for the spirit of France still alive under German domination!'

'Perhaps they are a more literal-minded people than we are,' Aline said.

'Perhaps. Who was the actor who played Satan?'

'Jules Berry.'

'Bloody good, I thought. Sinister as hell – but at the same time with touches of the comic. I'd like to see him in *Faust*!' Riordan turned his key in the lock, ushered Aline into the hallway . . . and froze.

The man facing them through the open door of the living-room was sitting in an armchair. He was pink-faced and silver-haired, and he wore a Norfolk jacket and breeches in heavy brown tweed. He held on his lap a green felt hat with a feather tucked into the band.

Aline gasped and clung tightly to Riordan's arm. 'Relax,' he murmured. 'He wouldn't be sitting down if he was hostile.'

'Correct,' O'Kelly said. 'I assure you, Madame, that there is no weapon concealed beneath this headgear.' And then, lifting the hat: 'Mr Riordan, I presume?'

'Oh, God!' Riordan said. 'I suppose there has to be a first time for everything!'

'I beg your pardon?'

'Nothing. Just . . . well, just a private joke. So who the hell are you? What the devil do you think you are doing, breaking into my home? And what do you want anyway?'

O'Kelly rose to his feet, laying the hat on the arm of the chair. 'Huefer,' he said. 'Alexis Alexander Huefer. From Geneva.' He held out his hand.

Riordan ignored it. 'Well, Herr Huefer, give me one good reason why I shouldn't seize you by the neck and throw you out of here.'

'*Monsieur* Huefer, please,' O'Kelly corrected. 'I am originally from the French-speaking part of Switzerland.'

'So?' Riordan scowled. 'I am still waiting for that reason.'

'I give it to you in one word: money.'

'Ah. You are here to offer me employment? You want a story written? You represent a magazine or a newspaper in search of features from a country designated as part of the New Europe?'

'I have a proposition.'

'You have an eccentric way of introducing yourself to a possible client,' Riordan said with a glance around his living-room.

'I apologize. The train from Geneva is slow; it is a long walk from the station; I am not as young as I was and I needed to sit down. Nothing is damaged, I assure you. I happened,' O'Kelly added deprecatingly, 'to have a key that fitted your door.'

'How convenient. And what a coincidence. Well, now that you *are* here, make your proposition. I might be interested if the story is good enough.'

'Oh, it's a good story all right,' O'Kelly said.

Riordan glanced at the girl. She knew about his press work but not about the military side of his life. She knew that once, in some way, he had been connected with the oil business in Texas. She had asked a lot of questions, of course, about the period in between, but she was intelligent enough to be content with evasive answers. For Riordan, work and play were not different sides of the same coin; they were from different currencies. The press work came in between, but he regarded it more as a pastime, a means to a private end, than as work in itself.

Was this uninvited visitor connected with the real work or the play?

Judging from the unconventional entry, Riordan suspected the former, but he had to find out without Aline
knowing.

'Do sit down again, Monsieur . . . Huefer,' he said. 'I
will not insult your palate by offering you what we are
obliged to drink instead of coffee, but perhaps after your
tiring journey you would care for an aperitif? Aline, *chérie*,
if you would be kind enough to see if there is any Dubonnet
in the kitchen?'

The glamorous redhead nodded, but before she could
leave the room, O'Kelly tugged a small package from the
pocket of his Norfolk jacket. 'A cup of coffee would be
delicious,' he said, 'if you would be so kind.' He handed
her the package, on the waxed paper of which were the
words in gold lettering: 'Torrefaction Helms, Zurich.
100% Pure Arabica.'

'Real coffee!' Aline cried. '*Zut!* You are an angel from
the Swiss heaven! I will grind some at once.' Her wooden
soles clattered down the corridor to the kitchen.

As soon as he heard the handle of the machine grinding,
Riordan turned towards O'Kelly and said: 'Quick! You're
not press, are you? What do you want with me?'

'A military operation. Small group of experts. As of
now,' O'Kelly said promptly.

'Where?'

'The far north.'

'Money?'

'Not quite unlimited, but getting on that way.'

'We must talk,' Riordan said. 'But not here.'

'Perhaps you would care to call by my Paris office,
when we can discuss the matter in more detail,' O'Kelly
said smoothly. Aline had come back into the room with a
tray bearing cups, saucers and sachets of artificial sugar.
'This evening, preferably, because time, as the British say,
is short.' He handed Riordan a small slip of pasteboard.

Riordan stuffed the card into his pocket. It was only
after the coffee had been exclaimed over, drunk and

appreciated, and Aline was showing the visitor out, that he had an opportunity to look at it.

There was no printing, no name and no address on either side of the card. It was blank except for a single line of handwriting in pencil which read: 'Wepler. 10.45 p.m. Tonight.'

Riordan tore it into very small pieces and flushed it down the lavatory pan.

Wepler's, the famous seafood brasserie across the road from the Gaumont Palace in the Place Clichy, was thinning out by the time Riordan arrived. Curfew was at midnight and few Parisians liked to risk being caught out after that time. Those netted by the German military police could spend the rest of the night shining Feldgendarmerie boots; if there had been an attack on occupying soldiers, they could be taken as hostages and shot in reprisal.

'I apologize for the late hour,' O'Kelly said, sitting alone on a padded leather bench in one of the booths. 'It is easier to talk privately when one is not jammed in with a dozen chattering French men and women. I trust you can eat skate: I bribed the waitress to keep us two portions.'

'Skate is fine,' Riordan said. Anything remotely edible was fine in a city where the rationing was so severe, and the meat allowance so small that it could be wrapped – so the joke went – in a Métro ticket – provided it was unused. If the ticket had been used, they said, the ration could fall out through the hole clipped by the collector's punch.

'I understand that you know Finland, and that you speak the language,' O'Kelly said, once they were eating.

'I have been there,' Riordan said.

'I am informed further that you have guerrilla experience, urban and otherwise, in places as far afield as Manchukuo, Mexico and Eritrea.'

Riordan forked in a mouthful of fish. He made no comment.

'You led one of the International Brigades in Spain,

but you yourself are uncommitted, either to the left or the right.'

'You appear to be well informed,' Riordan said.

'Information on an expert is always available, provided one knows where to look,' said O'Kelly. 'The dossier on your good self is ample.'

'So where does it get you?'

'It is advisable to make certain that one is talking to the right person before one commits oneself on one's own side. The proposition I have to make concerns a situation in a northern European war zone that needs urgently to be . . . remedied.'

For the first time Riordan showed interest. 'You mean some kind of raid?'

'Yes and no.' O'Kelly was wearying of the heavy, supposedly Swiss, style of stilted English he had adopted. 'I will be as brief as I can,' he said.

He detailed the unexpected sinking of the American merchantman in convoy PQ-13A, the manner in which it occurred, and the conclusions which had been drawn from that. Without revealing where it had taken place or who had been involved, he summarized the findings of the Whitehall conference and the decisions which had been taken.

'Let me get this straight,' Riordan said in a low voice, glancing cautiously around to make sure none of the few remaining customers was within earshot. 'You want me to locate this dump with a reliable bunch of mercs . . . and then destroy it?'

'Once you have discovered what is in it, and how it works, yes. If you are interested, that is.'

'I'm interested,' Riordan said. 'What kind of money are we talking about?'

'What kind of money would interest you?'

Riordan named a sum that was twice what he would have been prepared to accept.

To his astonishment, O'Kelly agreed at once.

SOLDIER OF FORTUNE 5

'Payable in Swiss francs, into a numbered account of a bank in Zurich?'

'Exactly.'

'Payable how?'

'In four quarters: twenty-five per cent immediately; a further twenty-five when you have recruited your team and we consider it suitable; the third quarter when we receive news that you have located the base; and the remainder when its working parts, shall we say, have been evaluated and destroyed. The remuneration of your ... soldiers ... is naturally to be your own responsibility.'

'We're in business,' Riordan said. He held out his hand. 'Tell me now: who am I working for? The British? The Americans? Surely not the French?'

'It is not necessary for you to know in detail. Let us say a consortium of industrialists are unwilling to see their products continually ... wasted.' O'Kelly shook his head. 'All you need to know is that your loyalty is due solely to those of us paying the bill. And the men's loyalty due solely to you.'

'That's the way I work,' Riordan said.

'Any feeling you have for any one, or any group, of the belligerents in the war, you must put from your mind. Forget it. The mission is all ... and it's a one-off job. Do I make myself clear?'

'Understood. You didn't have to say it.'

'My principals,' O'Kelly smiled. 'They expect me to say it. What kind of a group do you have in mind?'

Now that the preliminaries were over, Riordan's speech became crisp, decisive. 'On this kind of operation – reconnoitre, go in, do the job, get out – the fewer the better.'

'Something like a dozen?'

Riordan shook his head. 'Six. That's half as many possible fuck-ups. I'll take an explosives expert, an engineer, a locksmith and safe-breaker, two specialist marksmen and what the Americans call a forage master. That's a logistics

32

technician – a guy who can act as pathfinder, map reader, cook, doctor, my number two when necessary. Above all someone capable of enabling seven clandestines to live off the land. One of them must be a forger.'

'And you know of such experts who'd be willing to work for you?'

'I do. Take a few days to round them up, though.'

'When could you start? As I said, it's . . . kind of urgent.'

'For myself, tomorrow morning. For the unit, say a week – except for the explosives man. I've got to have him: he's the best . . . and he's also the forger. As important as the locksmith. I don't suppose,' Riordan said with a sarcastic smile, 'that even your own so . . . convenient . . . key ring is loaded enough to open every door in northern Europe!'

O'Kelly grinned. '*Touché!*' he said. 'So what's the trouble with your explosives man cum forger?'

'Unfortunately,' Riordan said, 'he's halfway through a seven-year prison stretch in Burgundy. Before we can start, I'll have to organize a jailbreak and get him out.'

4

The prison was built in the form of a Maltese cross, with a central tower and four radiating cell blocks, each with its own exercise yard, which varied in design according to the category of the convicts in the block. Entrance to the prison was through an arched, fortified gateway, and the blocks were linked by a twenty-foot wall topped with barbed wire. The place dated from the mid-nineteenth century and was certainly conceived as a punishment – rather than a rehabilitation – centre.

It lay on a slope of barren hillside overlooking the triangle of vineyards between Beaune, Nuits-St-Georges and Bligny, six miles from the nearest village.

'You'd need a squadron of motorized cavalry, with artillery and air support, to break in there,' Riordan told O'Kelly the day after their meeting at Wepler's. 'Fortunately, our man, Frenchie Delorme, can get outside the walls on his own: it's getting a message *in*, telling him he's going to be sprung, that's the problem. That and smuggling him *out* of the country, fast, once he's free.'

'What do you mean, he can get outside?' O'Kelly asked.

'He's what they call a model prisoner – that's a laugh for a start! – with hopes of remission for good conduct; he goes out with other trusties on working parties.'

'He'll lose the remission if they recapture him,' O'Kelly said.

'They won't recapture him in Finland,' replied Riordan.

It took three days to set up the break. Riordan told Aline that he had to go south, near the demarcation line separating Vichy France from the Occupied Zone, because his new Swiss client wanted inside information for a Geneva magazine on networks set up by the Resistance leader Jean Moulin, who had recently been flown back to France from London. Beaune, the Burgundy wine capital, was the nearest big town to the prison. He went there with an ex-con who had contacts in the region, travelling on a misnamed *rapide* which stopped at every station and spread the 175-mile journey over nine hours.

The first step was to check the prison rules on visits, the sending of letters and the inmates' right to receive parcels. An evening with the ex-con in the bars and cafés around the ramparts of the old walled town produced enough underworld know-alls to answer some of the questions. Letters were out: prisoners were allowed one a month, from a wife or next of kin only, in the first week of the month – a date already past. One visit a week was permitted: fifteen minutes with a wife or near relative, and on one visit each month, the visitor could bring a parcel: foodstuffs only, subject to a rigorous search. A barmaid and her prostitute friend in a waterfront dive by the River Bouzaise gave them the most useful lead: the name of a drunken GP who was also employed three days a week as one of two prison doctors. He was, the brassy-haired whore told them with a laugh, 'eminently bribable'.

They found him in a late-night brasserie near the railway station, a bearded giant with a pot belly and a white napkin tucked into his shirt collar. He was forking in huge mouthfuls of spaghetti, washed down with red wine from a carafe that was nearly empty. Riordan sat down facing him and ordered a bottle of the best wine on the list. He came straight to the point: he wanted a message, a single sentence, nothing compromising, passed verbally to one of the convicts during the weekly medical parade. There would be a fee involved of so many hundred francs for each word of the message transmitted.

'And supposing I was to agree to this ... this most improper suggestion,' the doctor said, 'what manner of message would I be passing? What kind of intrigue would I be associating myself with? Apart, of course' – he glanced at the expensive wine – 'from doing a small favour for a friend?'

Riordan had come provided with a lot of money. He slid an envelope containing a small bundle of high-denomination banknotes across the table. 'An earnest of good faith,' he said. 'You would be involved in no kind of misconduct inside the jail – nothing *inside* the jail at all, in fact. The prisoner in question still has certain financial interests – investments, shall we say? – outside. The message is simply to inform him that one of them is going well.'

'Why can't he be given the message by his weekly visitor?' the doctor said craftily. He was beginning to slur his words.

Riordan poured him more wine. 'Time is vital in business matters. If he has the message *first*, he will be able to reflect, and then tell the visitor whether to buy or sell on the next occasion.'

The doctor had opened the flap of the envelope and taken a swift and unobtrusive look at the contents. He stowed it now in an inner pocket. 'And the message itself?' he asked.

'A line from an old Scottish song – with one word changed. A marching song, usually with bagpipe music, of the Campbell clan. The words you pass on are: "The Riordans are coming, tra-la, tra-la." Just that.'

'The ... Reedons?'

'Riordans. Ri-or-dans. It's important to get it right, because it's the name of the ... of the stock. *Riordans.*'

The doctor repeated the line reasonably correctly, improving at a second attempt.

'Right,' Riordan said. 'You can just slip it in as part of a casual conversation, if you get a chance to talk. Or sing

36

it to yourself as if it was a song on your mind if you're only passing along a line of men. I shall telephone you tomorrow with the convict's cell block and number.'

'Do I get paid for the tra-las?'

'Both times,' Riordan said solemnly. 'And you can count each as two words!'

The doctor erupted into a great gust of laughter, his huge belly rocking the table. 'Tra-la, tra-la,' he wheezed. 'I will do my best, tra-la.'

Riordan paid for the wine and the doctor's dinner, and left the brasserie.

The following day he spent an excessive sum persuading a local taxi driver to take him and his ex-con companion on a tour of the countryside around the prison. They travelled in what the French called a *gazogène*. This was a device invented to counteract the crippling shortage of petrol, severely rationed and reserved in practice for the occupiers, essential services, doctors and those with a special *Ausweis*, or pass – usually collaborators, black-marketeers or officials with strings to pull. The gas powering the engine was obtained from the burning of charcoal or wood in a heavy boiler installed in the boot of the vehicle. *Gazogènes* were difficult to start, extremely noisy, and limited in range because of the need constantly to refuel the boiler.

There was a civil airfield on the northern outskirts of Chalon-sur-Saône which had been requisitioned by the Germans, and a pre-war gliding school taken over for the training of paratroops. Nearer the prison, the mines near Le Creusot produced raw materials for the German war effort and were thus vulnerable to sabotage. Because the presence of occupying troops in both areas was therefore likely to be heavier than usual, Riordan decided to approach his target from the west by way of Arnay-le-Duc and the network of minor roads linking the villages of St-Pierre-l'Église and Roquefort. Even so, they were flagged down by a military

patrol in the hilly, wooded country twelve miles north
of Montchasseur.

A Hanomag half-track scout car was drawn up under
the trees on the verge. Four steel-helmeted soldiers in field-
grey, two in the back with Mauser rifles, two standing by
the roadside with Bergmann-Schmeisser machine-pistols,
accompanied the young Feldgendarmerie officer who
stopped the *gazogène*.

Riordan flicked a glance at the Hanomag. The driver
remained at the wheel behind his armoured windscreen.
There was a Madsen machine-gun slung between the
spare wheel and the nearside front wing. The men with
the Schmeissers stationed themselves front and rear and
the officer approached the taxi driver's window, curtly
demanding papers.

The driver handed over his licence, his *Ausweis*,
his French work permit and his ID, explaining that
he had been hired to drive two foreigners, neutrals,
around. The officer inspected the documents carefully
and returned them.

The ex-con, whose name was Zabrisky, had been
furnished with a forged Swedish passport and accreditation identifying him as Riordan's photographer. The
officer flicked through the pages, turning back twice.
Sweat trickled between Riordan's shoulder-blades. 'What
camera do you use?' the German asked.

'I'm afraid he speaks neither German nor French,'
Riordan replied. 'But he is a good photographer.' He
unzipped a canvas holdall and held up a weathered 35mm
Agfa which he had bought for just such an eventuality.

'Ah! A good German make,' the officer said approvingly
to the ex-con.

Zabrisky used the only English phrases he knew. 'Oh,
yes,' he said with a smile he tried to keep from trembling.
'Very much so.'

The officer examined Riordan's papers and asked: 'Why
are you in this area, Herr Riordan? Where are you going?'

'Autun, if we can find enough fuel for this . . . machine,' Riordan said with a contemptuous look toward the boot. 'My Scandinavian employers are running a feature on churches in this part of Europe, and there are extraordinary capitals in the cathedral there, carved in the twelfth century by a local monk.'

'Very well.' The young officer handed over the papers, stepped back and saluted. 'But I must caution you not to stop in this area. There is a high-security French prison near Mont St-Vincent, and sightseers are discouraged.'

'Understood,' Riordan said. 'And thank you.'

The German motioned his men back to the verge and waved the taxi on. The *gazogène* spluttered protestingly and lurched forward.

'Shit!' Zabrisky said with feeling. 'I could practically see the gun barrels of the firing squad!'

Riordan grinned. 'I must teach you another English phrase,' he said. 'You must learn to say: "Fuck off, you Nazi pig."'

'Oh, yes? This is an interesting, a useful form of words?'

'In certain circumstances,' Riordan said.

They used all thirty-six frames of the film in the camera approaching, passing and driving away from the forbidding red brick fortress of the prison. Armed French gendarmes stood guard outside the huge arched gates; two riders of the CRS – the Compagnie Républicaine de Sécurité, or riot police – smoked cigarettes beside their parked motorcycles.

The quarry where the work parties broke up stones was three miles from the jail, hewn from a granite outlier in the undulating landscape. In quick succession, Riordan photographed corrugated-iron shacks, stone-crushing machinery, a slant of bucket carriers feeding the installation, and hopper trucks on a network of rails leading to and from the face where the prisoners were working. Twelve warders, equipped with carbines and side-arms, stood guard in strategic positions.

The granite chippings taken away from the crusher in lorries were used as a dressing in resurfacing and other roadworks. 'We'll have to make it from above the face,' Riordan said. 'Maybe with a diversion behind that line of buckets.'

Back in Beaune, they made the final arrangements. Frenchie Delorme was unmarried, but he had a girlfriend he had passed off as a cousin and it was she who visited him each week. Zabrisky used his contacts to locate her, and she agreed to smuggle him a message the following week.

The young woman, a big, busty brunette called Marie-France, furnished the ex-con with Frenchie's number and details of his cell block, which Riordan phoned through to the doctor as arranged. That message would be delivered the following day, he was promised.

Marie-France worked in a bakery. The second communication would be concealed inside a currant cake she would take him. Conversations on visiting days were strictly monitored, so she would say nothing whatever about the cake, once she had handed it in to the authorities, not even that she hoped he would enjoy it. Warders' suspicions were easily aroused. But Riordan hoped the doctor's enigmatic tra-la would alert Frenchie enough for him to take his gift apart very carefully once it was handed over.

The message would be written in indelible ink on a fragment of paper which could be swallowed once the communication itself had been digested. Tightly rolled into a tiny cylinder one inch long and no thicker than a matchstick, the paper was to be pushed into the cake where a currant had been removed, and the small hole sealed with a slightly larger currant. In such a position, Riordan hoped, the message would remain undetected, even if – as frequently happened – searchers transfixed the cake with bodkins before it was given to the prisoner.

He prepared the paper himself before he left Beaune to return to Paris, making several attempts before he was satisfied the miniature scroll was sufficiently tight. Finally he fixed each end of the cylinder with a minute blob of glue. He had written, in the smallest characters he could manage: 'Face it, and be prepared to be hoisted on somebody else's petard' – and the time and date of the planned jailbreak the following week.

When he returned to the apartment in the Rue Clauzel, Aline told him that the mysterious Monsieur Huefer had called and left a number he was to ring.

Riordan went to a café in the Rue St-Lazare, paid for a *jeton*, and dropped it into a phonebox beside the toilets. He dialled the number.

O'Kelly told him that four more explosions of a similar type had been reported in the area under discussion. None had been near a ship. 'But,' he added, 'in each case, this time, it was noticed that the sea around the burst was stained by a vivid, different-coloured dye – presumably to allow a spotter plane to pinpoint each explosion and distinguish it from the others. This confirms, beyond any doubt, that what you are looking for is some kind of experimental firing range.'

5

Aline rolled her fleshy hip against Riordan's lean, hard frame. 'Just who is this Swiss, this man Huefer?' she asked. 'I hope he pays you well, the amount of hours you waste running around for him. You spend more time stomping up and down the stairs to this apartment than you do in bed with me!'

'He pays very well,' Riordan said. 'The magazine he works for specializes in revelations, a little on the sensational side – preferably connected with revolutionaries, the underworld or anything, you know, clandestine. Unearthing the facts for him requires a lot of running around, as you put it, often in somewhat . . . well, kind of dubious places.'

'Sounds exciting. Couldn't I come with you? Couldn't we run around together sometimes?'

'I'm afraid not. My shady contacts would clam up at once if there was anyone they didn't know with me. Even anyone as sexy as you!'

'What's the name of this magazine then?'

'*Echoes of Europe*,' Riordan improvised. 'It's a glossy. Very expensive.'

'I must get hold of a copy. It would be nice to see your name in print.'

'It's not imported into France: mainly for the American market.' Riordan laughed. 'As for *wasting* time, what about you, *mon amour*? You spend more hours clothing bodies for other women than you do unclothing your own for me!'

Aline reached for him. The pressure of one splendid

breast against his arm had already stiffened him to awareness. 'It's always more agreeable to serve a masculine customer,' she said. 'Provided, of course, that he can find the time.'

Riordan muttered something she didn't catch. Then, kissing her savagely on the mouth, he rolled over and penetrated her at once. It was always like this with them: immediate and total; the instant the spark of desire was ignited, it blazed into action. But Riordan was a skilful lover: the rapidity of the start was not reflected in the lovemaking that followed.

'That's my man,' Aline said breathlessly, scissoring her thighs over his back.

The mercenary leader had in fact been intensively occupied, assembling as far as he could the remaining recruits for his six-man team. Two of them were in Paris – if he could find them. A third was in Spain and could probably be persuaded to come to Paris, provided Riordan was able to locate him. For the remaining two, he would himself have to visit Amsterdam and Basle, on the Franco-Swiss frontier.

The last couple were the gunnery experts and marksmen he was determined to have with him. Pieter Van Eyck, the Dutchman, was a world champion small-arms competitor, who had once won the King's Prize for rifle shooting at Bisley. The second sharpshooter was a young Englishman. 'And you won't believe this,' Riordan said to O'Kelly before the latter returned to Geneva, 'but his name is Beverley Hills; it really is!'

'Just so long as he shoots straight,' O'Kelly said.

'He can do more than that,' Riordan said. 'Before the family moved to your country, his father was a director of Woolwich Arsenal. The boy was apprenticed to Husqvarna in Sweden – and he knows about automatic weapons too.'

'Perhaps, when the team's complete, you can assemble them all in Switzerland before I give you a final briefing and the latest gen on our range,' O'Kelly said.

'I wouldn't care to risk such an assembly here in Paris!' Riordan said.

It was in Paris nevertheless that the recruiting started.

He had already sounded out the ex-con Zabrisky, the only one of the six who was not basically a soldier, a fighter . . . but who had one specific talent Riordan rated as essential, especially if there were to be plans stolen, records examined or high-security premises secretly entered. For Zabrisky was a peterman, a safe-breaker. He had been jailed for his part in a multimillion-dollar jewel robbery from the holiday home of a Hollywood film boss on the Riviera in the early 1930s. He also had an invaluable knack of getting on with people, of ingratiating himself and obtaining information – as Riordan had already discovered in Chalon.

Born Zigmund Zanussi in Marseilles, the safe-breaker had delighted his underworld cronies when he came to Paris by changing his name officially to Zabrisky, because 'in a chauvinistic country like ours, Zanussi sounds so *foreign*. And anyway I can still keep the double-Z on my suitcase, wallet and razor case'.

He had been dubious about accompanying Riordan and his companions to a country where he would be even more foreign – and illegal as well – but the sum the mercenary leader had mentioned had at length won him over.

Riordan's second Parisian prospect was even more of an oddity. Zanussi-Zabrisky had two names, both of them legal; the man who was known as Art Daniels had no official name at all, because he had no papers, had never had any. In the eyes of the authorities he didn't exist, which was probably just as well, for he was a prominent member of the Paris Resistance, the FTPF (Franc-Tireurs et Partisans Français), the activist arm of the outlawed Communist Party.

Daniels was a genuine Romany, member of a circus family which had moved west from Hungary soon after the First World War. He was an acrobat, an escapologist, a knife-thrower and a wire walker. But Riordan wanted him because, with his knowledge of landscapes and country lore, his familiarity with flora and fauna, he would be the ideal forage master for the expedition.

Daniels was a compact, muscled man, middle height, middle age, with – oddly for a gypsy – bristly red hair and pale-blue eyes. Riordan found him in a run-down bar in Belleville, a poor, cosmopolitan quarter in the north-east of Paris, where Arab immigrants from North Africa rubbed shoulders with Negroes from the French colonies, the homeless and needy, and members of *les bas fonds* – the dregs of the underworld. It seemed a strange choice for a stateless person belonging to an outlaw organization – the German military presence was noticeable, not just off-duty Wehrmacht men looking for a cheap lay but MPs and black-uniformed SS – but Riordan supposed the noisy, brawling street life, which turned the district into a kind of surrogate kasbah, was as good a cover as any in a city of enemies.

Art Daniels accepted his proposition immediately, even before the question of payment was mentioned. 'I'd do it for free,' he said. 'Almost. Especially if it gives me the chance to get back at these bastards on something like even terms. In any case, even if the Finns have turned fascist now, they don't regard my people as non-existent or expendable, to be eliminated like surplus hogs on a pig farm.'

Riordan pushed an envelope across the marble tabletop. 'Be in this bar at noon on Saturday,' he said, 'and I'll brief you on the initial muster. Lie low until then. Relax. And take care.'

'Low is the only way to lie in this goddam city now,' Daniels said. 'Be seeing you . . . *et merci, Chef!*'

Allied air raids on the Antwerp docks, on factories outside Brussels and subsequently on the huge Dutch electrical plant in Eindhoven, slowed the overnight express from Paris to Amsterdam to an infuriating degree. 'I could go faster,' the engine driver told Riordan during one of the halts, 'but I'm not allowed to leave the fucking train!'

It was raining in Amsterdam when the train finally eased into the central station. Outside the arched spars where the canopied glass roof had been, the street, the sky, the wet slate roofs and the still water of the inner harbour were the same sullen grey. On the far side of the Afgesloten Ij basin, a fire-fighting float was hosing the smouldering upper works of a freighter which had been hit during the night's raid.

As a neutral and a press correspondent, Riordan had been allotted a seat in a compartment reserved for German officers. He expected nevertheless to be questioned by military police when he handed over his ticket; he knew he would be ordered to report to the Propaganda Abteilung, halfway along the Damrak, once his papers had been checked and his accreditation confirmed; he expected, when he got there, that the officials would ask why he had asked the AFIP in Paris to organize permission for his trip to Holland (supposedly to research a piece showing how life had returned to normal in the Dutch capital under the guidance of friendly German occupiers).

What he had not expected was the tail they put on him.

Normally foreign journalists were left pretty much on their own, so long as they kept their noses clean and stayed away from military installations: after all, anything they wrote or wished to cable abroad would pass through the hands of the official censors. So why should he be singled out for special attention? Did the Germans in Holland consider themselves more at risk from hostile reports?

Riordan had been booked into a small hotel a couple of hundred yards from the propaganda headquarters. The first tail was already sitting in a writing-room opposite the reception desk when he checked in. Probably he would have paid no attention – a thin man in a long leather overcoat and a slouch hat nursing a stein of beer – but he happened to have noticed this one before: in the next compartment of the night train from Paris.

Coincidence? Possibly. But it made him even more watchful. For the first time in many months, his fighter's awareness, sharpened, honed to register the slightest hint of danger, prickled the hairs on the nape of his neck.

He left his suitcase in his room – unlocked so that the fasteners wouldn't be damaged when it was searched – and went out to look for a meal.

The bodega on the next corner could only offer raw herring with a potato salad, washed down with weak beer. Riordan took it; he was hungry. He sat at one of the dark oak tables – half covered, as is the curious custom in the Netherlands, with a strip of carpet – and fought his way through the herring. The salad was passable.

His earlier suspicion was confirmed when the man in the leather coat walked in, spoke to the woman behind the bar and walked out again. That would be to check that there was no back way out. Then he could wait outside until Riordan emerged: if he bought himself a drink, he would have to pay for it out of his own pocket; organizations like the Gestapo – and Riordan was becoming convinced the man *was* Gestapo – were sensitive on the subject of expenses.

But why should the Gestapo suddenly become suspicious of *him*?

He swallowed the remainder of the beer, paid his bill and left.

There were in fact two of them, he realized when he was out in the rain again: the one who had followed him from Paris, and another in a car. He was sure of that because the car was disguised as a taxi, and although he was carrying no fare, the driver ignored three prospective passengers who attempted to flag him down. Probably a local Gestapo colleague, Riordan thought, or an operative from Mussert's NSB, the Dutch Nazis.

Whatever the reason, he was under surveillance. And both tails must be shaken off before dusk, because the only lead he had to the man he wanted to see was a club owned by a friend of Frenchie Delorme's, and he was determined not to be followed there: it could lead them too close to the man himself.

He decided to lose the man in the car first – not too difficult in Amsterdam.

Bending his head against the rain, which was now driving in from the sea, he walked back past the hotel in the direction of the station. Leather coat followed about a hundred yards behind, on the other side of the street. The taxi made a U-turn and kerb-crawled behind Riordan. Apart from cyclists, there was no other traffic.

The wide square outside the station, with its spider's web of tramway tracks, was deserted. The trams wouldn't be running again for another hour. A policeman in a shiny black raincoat stood among wide pools pitted with rain, waiting for traffic to direct.

Riordan turned right and crossed the bridge spanning the Afgesloten Ij. Beyond the dock basins and the deep-sea merchantmen berthed along the waterfront, two oil tankers had been backed off a refinery wharf where firemen still moved among the embers of a gutted warehouse.

There were two hot quarters in Amsterdam, one of them, nearer the city centre, where the high-class trade plied for hire in a nest of nightclubs, call-girl bars and strip shows. The other was on the far side of the bridge – a network of narrow streets and alleys, criss-crossed by minor canals, where the professional women of the port displayed their charms to sailors in the windows of narrow little houses giving on to the street. For Riordan, the charm of the district was that most of the alleys were barred to wheeled traffic. Increasing his pace, he turned sharply down the first of these. That disposed of the taxi man: even if he junked his car and joined his confederate, two would be as easy to lose as one if the plan Riordan had formed worked out.

The houses were old and shabby. A rowdy beer hall on the corner of the lane showed the first sign of life Riordan had seen since he left the bodega: a shouting, brawling throng of seamen, dockers and German soldiers.

The alley itself was fairly crowded too, despite the rain. Off-duty Wehrmacht men mingled with local civilians window-shopping along its two-hundred-yard length. It was almost dusk. Through the downpour, the pink-lit interiors of the houses appeared inviting . . . until the shoppers took a closer look. Many of the women on view were haggard and raddled, some were fat and flabby, and all of them were over-painted, though few could be called overdressed. The rooms on view had an almost homely air. Some were decorated with artificial flowers, others sported framed proverbs worked in tapestry, or a cat asleep in a wicker basket. One good-looking whore was actually knitting.

Riordan threaded his way between potential customers, past two houses reserved for German soldiers and members of the Kriegsmarine and another, in much better condition, with prettier girls, for officers. He had to gamble on finding the right kind of woman. The hard-boiled ones, the obvious sexpots, the money-grubbers were out: he needed someone he could trust. At least for the time it would normally take to turn a trick – maybe twenty minutes.

The one he settled for was in the last block before the Zeedijk. A middle-aged woman with Asiatic features and a dusky skin. The face was a lived-in face, but despite the shiny black mackintosh she wore, the glimpse between its unbelted edges of flesh corseted in leather, despite the laced, knee-high black boots, she looked – he thought – like someone's mother. He assumed she would have been from the Dutch East Indies, despised therefore by the Nazis as 'inferior', and thus more inclined to help another non-German. He tapped on the picture window and raised enquiring eyebrows.

The woman got up from her chair and slid aside a pane. 'Thirty guilders,' she said.

'I'll give you twice that if you'll do what I want,' Riordan said.

She opened the front door of the house. 'Come in, dear,' she said, and then, when the door was shut again: 'What exactly did you want, darling? Klisterotherapy? Rubber? A whipping?'

'Does this place have a back door?'

She was with it almost before the words were out of his mouth. 'Gestapo?' she whispered.

He nodded, ushering her back into the room, where they would be visible from outside. It was convenient to let her think he was on the run. His ploy – derived from a tip passed on by a Chicago newspaperman on the run from a Mafia hit squad – was based on the fact that whores in Holland didn't take their clients upstairs once a figure had been agreed upon; they stayed right there in the front room, simply pulling a curtain across the big window to shut out the public and indicate that they were occupied.

'What I'm buying,' Riordan said, 'is for you to keep the curtains drawn for at least fifteen minutes after I've gone. That's what I'm trusting you to do. So that the man, or men, shadowing me – somewhere out there watching us at this minute – won't know I've slipped the net until you draw back those curtains and set up shop once more. Are you with me?'

'A pleasure,' she said, the voice already hoarse with the pleasures of Dutch gin and Willem II cheroots. 'It will give me a chance to enjoy a quiet drink and a smoke on my own.' She eyed his spare, muscular figure with approval. 'Just the same, there's no reason why I shouldn't keep the curtain closed for *half* an hour if you'd like to relax a little before you go. I've been paid for it after all!'

Riordan shook his head. 'I'd appreciate that. But, thanks just the same, I think it'll have to be another time.'

She smiled. Under the make-up her skin was the texture of old parchment. 'Turn right at the end of the corridor,' she said, 'through the kitchen and out into the yard. Dustbins will help you over the wall. And good luck, whoever you are.'

She tucked the banknotes into her brassière and drew the red velvet curtains across the window. The raindrops and the faces staring in from the dark vanished. Riordan thanked her and left.

Five minutes later he was striding down the street that led to the Nieuwbrug. So far as he could see, nobody was following him. He crossed the bridge and turned east.

The trams were running again and there were people staring into the masked windows of expensive shops along the Kalverstraat. He passed through the arch beneath the Munttoren tower and hurried along Rokin towards the Rembrandtsplein – the centre of the city's higher-class hotspot. The rain had stopped, but a chill wind rippling the surface of the Amstel was still laden with moisture.

The Rembrandtsplein, pre-war oasis of neon lights and nakedness, of legitimate lesbians and fetishist floor shows, was a dismal backwater after dark in occupied Amsterdam. Once a rival in sexual excess to the notorious Reeperbahn in Hamburg, the small square was now deserted. The pavement cafés, under whose awnings even in winter drinkers could bask in the warmth of overhead electric heaters, were shuttered and silent. Lights from a German patrol car cruising the western and northern sides of the square momentarily revealed a vast heap of rubble where a bombed building had collapsed into the street. But behind the dark façades, Riordan knew, the wild night-life of the stricken city roared crazily on.

The club run by Frenchie Delorme's friend was archly called the Trick 'n' Treat. It was a ruse simply to get around the occupiers' ban on *public* dancing. Membership was a formality, a joke: a couple of guilders slipped to the bouncer when the entrance fee was paid ensured the delivery of a valid card to the client's table before the first drink was ordered.

Two young women were standing by the reception desk when Riordan braved the blackout curtains and went in. One, wearing a tightly belted, shoulder-strapped raincoat and a felt hat with the brim pulled down, looked like a cut-price Marlene Dietrich; the other sported a tweed jacket, riding breeches and polo boots. Riordan grinned. Aping the famous British racing tipster, Prince Monolulu, he barked: 'I gotta *horse*!'

The girl turned her back on him.

The bouncer-receptionist, a muscular, Charles Atlas type, was heavily made up. He wore a black bow-tie with his dinner-jacket, but no shirt. Furnished with a membership card, Riordan was installed at a small table on a crowded balcony overlooking an even more crowded dance floor. The trio at the entrance had given him an idea what to expect, but the reality was nevertheless surprising.

Jazz, of course, was banned by the occupiers and instigators of the New Europe as 'decadent', so the eight-piece band below – mostly brass and violins – was blaring out a selection of Viennese waltzes, Bavarian folk tunes and 'acceptable' foxtrots; but the frantic throng on the floor were defiantly *dancing* jazz: despite the stodgy rhythms of the music, the lower level was a stomping, whirling, hip-swinging phalanx of jitterbugs.

Eighty per cent of the dancers – and of the drinkers jamming the tables around Riordan – were female. It was only when he had been served with a glass of inferior sparkling wine and had time to look around, that he realized his error: eighty per cent of the club's clients were *dressed* as women. Many of them were transvestites – and the minority of males included a number of beefy, deep-voiced ladies wearing trousers and mannish jackets with their cropped hair.

Frenchie Delorme's friend, the owner of the club, was Dirk Eilers. He joined the mercenary leader at his table soon after a card on which Riordan had scrawled a few words had been taken into an office behind the reception desk. And whatever the sex of his clientele, there could be no doubt whatever of the Dutchman's own gender: the hair on his chest – as Frenchie had once quipped – practically showed through the stiff white shirt below his black tie. A stocky, swarthy character with a five o'clock shadow all day long, Eilers compensated for his sombre appearance with the glitter of a gold watch, gold cufflinks, a gold cigar-cutter and a selection of gold teeth.

'Any friend of Frenchie's,' he said. 'The boy done me a big favour one time; tip-off that saved me being put away for five, Stateside.' And then, seeing Riordan's glass: 'Hey, you don't want to drink that shit. Have a glass with me.' He signalled a waiter.

Riordan looked around the club while the bottle was uncorked and the wine poured. The noise had increased. A group of German girls from one of the women's army corps cavorted with scantily dressed dancers from the floor show. Some of them were singing. Off-duty policewomen and Dutch lady ticket collectors in uniform danced with blondes and brunettes in cocktail dresses and platform heels while the band blasted out a selection from *Der Rosenkavalier*. And around the jammed floor, down from the balcony, predatory eyes gazed hungrily at the buttocks and breasts swivelling and bouncing below the band.

'Prost!' Riordan raised his glass. The wine was genuine champagne, from a good year. 'This is quite a place you have here!'

Eilers drank. A gold identity bracelet winked from among the black hairs on his wrist. 'I had a classier one once,' he said. 'Called it The Tuxedo. But the Royal Air

Force found it last January.' He shrugged. 'Our Teutonic friends allow me to run this dump because they believe that if all the so-called "degenerates" are encouraged to forgather under the same roof, then automatically they'll be able to lay hands on dissidents or Resistance elements simply by knocking on the door.'

Riordan nodded. He was thinking of Aline's remark: 'Perhaps they are a more literal-minded people than we are.' He said: 'And no doubt the dissidents take care never to come near the place?'

'Check. If they go anywhere in public, they make it to one of those gloomy, fumed-oak businessmen's luncheon clubs overlooking the Amstel.'

'Any special reason?' asked Riordan.

'Yeah. Two, in fact. First of all, because German officers go there, and neither the Gestapo nor the NSB would think of looking under their own noses, among their own top brass. Second, because they imagine folks they themselves have dubbed "terrorists" and "inferior" would never dare do anything that intelligent. They're victims of their own propaganda there: call a man a *Dummkopf* often enough and you'll begin to believe he'll act and reason like one.'

Eilers poured more wine. 'Of course, in return for the permit, the Krauts expect me to level with them and pass on any info on newcomers, strangers, any suspicious clients outside of the usual faggots and dykes. What do I tell them about you?'

'That I'm a neutral newspaperman writing a piece featuring all the improvements in life brought by your friendly occupier. That's what *my* permit is for; that's what it says on my papers.'

'And the real reason for your visit?'

Riordan smiled. 'I was looking for a shooter, a gunnery expert called Pieter Van Eyck. I was hoping, maybe, that you could point me in the direction of whichever gloomy, fumed-oak club he might be lunching in.'

Eilers stiffened. At the mention of the marksman's

name, his eyes had suddenly narrowed; the gold teeth vanished behind compressed lips. 'There, you kind of put me in a spot,' he said tightly. 'The word . . .'

He broke off in mid-sentence. A male transvestite with a red wig and crimson lips had lurched up to their table. Beneath a low-cut evening dress fringed with beads, loose flesh from a flabby chest had been pinched up with sticking plaster enough to form breasts half-filling a small lace brassière. 'A *man*!' this apparition shrieked into Riordan's face. 'A gorgeous, genuine, manly man! Where have you been all my lonely life, dreamboat? I positively *insist* that you trip below and dance with me.'

'Fuck off,' Eilers said.

'Oh, but darling, surely you wouldn't *deny* me . . .?'

'Beat it!' the club owner growled. 'Can't you tell the difference between a punter and a business associate? Can't you see what we're drinking?'

'You were saying . . .?' Riordan prompted when the transvestite had stumbled away, muttering something uncomplimentary. 'I put you in a spot, you said.'

Eilers sighed. 'Sensitive material,' he said. 'Frankly, I'd rather not know. The number in question, you see, has put a foot – several feet if the truth is known – wrong. The word is that the word has gone out: urgently wanted for questioning. Mussert's gang, the cops, the Gestapo and the Feldgendarmerie – the whole bazaar on the strict lookout.'

'I was aiming to take him away with me,' Riordan said.

'I owe Frenchie,' Eilers sighed, 'otherwise I'd have to say no. Do you know this person? Are you familiar with the way he looks?'

'We know each other.'

'You may be too late already. He'll be in some kind of disguise anyway. The faster you go, the more chance you have.' It was clear that, now the mercenary leader's cards were down, Eilers wished to be rid as soon as possible of a possible embarrassment.

Riordan pushed back his chair and rose to his feet. 'Which club do I go to?' he asked. 'I shall forget where I heard the name.'

'No clubs any more. All I can tell you,' Eilers said awkwardly, 'is that you should maybe look around a small hotel on Sintpieterstraat. The Grote Gavioli. Not far from the Prins Hendrik Kade. That is all I can say.'

'You have been very kind, very helpful,' Riordan said. 'I thank you, too, for your company and the pleasant drink.' He turned away from the table. 'Oh,' he said over his shoulder, 'just one more thing. You wouldn't, I suppose, happen to know what kind of disguise our friend favours when he goes to a fancy-dress ball?'

Eilers laughed, giving the reply he always gave when he was asked a difficult question. 'How would I know? I run a night-club for screaming queers, don't I?' he said.

The hotel, two tall, narrow canal-side houses fused together, was easy enough to find. A large nineteenth-century barrel-organ on wheels stood by the entrance steps. The organ case – of the kind suggesting a monkey on top with a red cap and a tin held out for contributions – was covered with painted flowers and golden swags framing the words 'Grote Gavioli'. Riordan approached the place cautiously. He had no particular reason to doubt the word of Frenchie's friend, but he was certain that his 'levelling' with the occupiers must involve more than routine reporting of non-*habitués*; otherwise he would never be permitted to run the club – unless, of course, Riordan reflected with a grim smile, it reminded them of Berlin between the wars and its decadent *Blue Angel* cabarets. There was, too, the club owner's use of the word 'punter' – rather than 'client' or 'customer'– when he bawled at the transvestite. It almost certainly meant that Eilers (and the occupiers?) permitted the place to be frequented by male as well as female prostitutes. Clearly there were complexities in the Dutchman's character which were not at first evident.

Riordan was a great believer in the tell-tale content of the speech used by people with whom he had business connections – especially if the business verged on the clandestine. He had noted with interest, for instance, the careful distancing from the Allies employed by the enigmatic Monsieur Huefer. From Geneva, naturally. Where else?

He had noted too the studious reliance on the third rather than the first – person plural every time the French or the English were mentioned: it was always 'they' and never 'we'. He had noted the artful inclusion of the phrase 'as the British say' when Huefer had quoted an Anglo-Saxon proverb.

All of which led Riordan to believe that he was in fact dealing with someone secretly from the Allied camp, almost certainly one of the British intelligence services. Doubtless they had their reasons; indeed, he could imagine some of them. What the hell: it was all the same to him so long as the bill was paid.

Somebody was leaving the hotel. The door opened and a man hurried down the steps. Riordan was standing beneath the trees which bordered the canal. Below him, the dark water, pitted with drops of the rain which had begun to fall again, was strewn with last year's leaves. He moved behind a tree.

The man was tall, with a straggly blond beard, a wide-brimmed, floppy felt hat, and ill-fitting clothes. He circled the barrel-organ, picked up the shafts and trundled the unwieldy machine across the sidewalk.

Riordan waited. Cold drops falling from the wet branches needled his bare head. He was not sure yet.

The wooden wheels of the organ thumped over the kerb and clattered across the cobbled roadway. Swinging it heavily around, the bearded man began wheeling it north, away from the dock area.

It was the walk, allied to the height, that convinced Riordan. Nothing could disguise that long, loping stride, the particular set of the shoulders. It was Van Eyck all right.

Imprudently, for once, Riordan darted out from under cover. 'Pieter!'

The tall man swung around. His eyes widened beneath the hat brim; a broad smile flashed from the beard. 'Barry Riordan, by all that's holy! What the hell do you do here, man? How did you . . .?'

'Looking for you,' Riordan cut in. 'I have a job. But you're hot, Piet: there's an all-stations call out for you, and it seems . . .'

'Don't I know it!' Van Eyck interrupted in turn. 'I was maybe a little too careless with the radio, but someone . . .'

He broke off, staring back past the hotel. A very large, upright limousine, black with a huge chromed radiator, had swung into view around a corner at the far end of the street. 'Shit!' Van Eyck exploded. 'Is Mussert's blackshirts. One must make a stand. You have a gun?'

Riordan shook his head. The Dutchman swept off his hat and plucked a tiny pistol from a leather pocket inside the crown. 'Beretta 22,' he announced, tossing the weapon towards Riordan. 'Small, but good enough over eight, maybe ten metres.' He opened a panel in the decorated face of the organ and removed a long-barrelled Walther P-38 recoil-action automatic from a shelf inside. 'Maybe we get the car,' he said.

Riordan caught the Beretta and checked the slide. The two of them swung the organ around until it was broadside-on to the street, and crouched down behind the frame. The car, a Belgian-built Minerva weighing almost two tons, advanced towards them, fat tyres spraying water from the glistening cobbles.

'No questions,' Van Eyck said. 'But wait until they stop, yes?'

'OK.'

The Minerva stopped outside the hotel, perhaps fifty feet away. Through the perpendicular windscreen, they could see that there were several people inside. Three of the four doors swung open. Four men leapt out, leaving the driver behind the wheel. Two of them wore the black uniform of the NSB; the others, long leather coats, felt hats, dark glasses – obviously Gestapo. One of the Germans carried a Bergmann-Schmeisser machine-pistol. The remaining three were armed with automatic pistols.

It was not clear whether they intended to raid the hotel, rush the barrel-organ so impudently blocking the street, or both. Van Eyck in any case pre-empted whatever plan they had. Coolly, steadying himself with an elbow on top of the instrument, he fired a single shot at the car. The windscreen shattered. The driver slumped over the steering wheel. Blood-sprayed shards of glass glittered on the road.

The action that followed was over very quickly.

At the sound of the shot, the four men whirled towards the barrel-organ and opened fire. The tearing-calico rasp of the machine-pistol, punctuated by heavier single reports from the Germans' handguns and Van Eyck's Walther, shattered the silence of the deserted street.

Heavy slugs thudded into the body of the organ, splintering the panels, smashing the spokes from one wheel. The machine careered drunkenly over to one side as the two men flung themselves to the cobbles. Ricochets screamed into the trees; Riordan felt the hairs on his head stirred by a near miss while he was falling. He rolled to one side, loosing off three quick shots aimed just below the flaming muzzle of the machine-pistol.

The gunner, hit in the belly, folded forward, his finger tightening convulsively on the trigger. The weapon, which had been firing very short bursts at a rate of 500rpm, spewed out the remaining 9mm slugs in its thirty-two-round magazine. Riordan's small automatic finished the man with a whip-crack single shot to the head before he hit the ground.

Van Eyck meanwhile had calmly picked off the second German and one of the uniformed blackshirts, dodging around the end of the stricken barrel-organ to enfilade them as they blasted away at Riordan.

The remaining Dutchman, who had taken refuge behind the big car, was standing on the luggage grid and firing over the roof.

At that moment there was a strange whirring from inside the organ. The final burst from the Schmeisser, slamming high up into the upper part of the frame, had disturbed part of the mechanism. The pierced music rolls within started to turn and, slowly at first but then groaning into the right key, the damaged machine started to wheeze out the strains of the Victorian romantic tune 'It's Time To Say Goodbye'.

The shock of that final burst had also stirred the barrel-organ itself into movement. Limping on its broken wheel, it lolloped down the camber of the road, lurched over the kerb, and came to a halt on the edge of the canal bank, still churning out the sentimental melody.

Van Eyck had scrambled along behind the organ, on hands and knees, using it as cover until he could leap behind a tree and menace the NSB shooter from the flank. Riordan rolled to the opposite sidewalk, levered himself up and began to advance, crouched low, towards the limousine.

The man, perhaps from self-respect, fired a round into the tree behind which Van Eyck was concealed. Then, faced with a pincer movement and the need to reload, he gave up. Raised hands appeared above the Minerva's roof, followed by a frightened face and black-uniformed shoulders.

'All right,' Riordan shouted. 'Throw down your weapon.'

A pistol fell to the roadway and slid away along the cobbles.

'Shit,' Van Eyck called in English. 'One cannot take him too – and now he is weaponless one cannot shoot him down in cold blood . . .'

Riordan was level with the front wheels of the car. 'All right,' he said again. 'Jump down from that carrier, turn your back on us . . . and *run*!'

Boots skidded on the wet road, followed by pounding footsteps. There had been a slight hesitation to begin with, but once he had gained confidence, the man displayed a good turn of speed. Riordan fired two shots at the ground to encourage him, striking sparks from the cobbles on either side of the Dutchman, steepening the curve of his acceleration.

Together, the two friends dragged the dead driver from the car and tipped him into the canal; Van Eyck pushed the remaining fragments of bloodstained glass from the windscreen frame and swept them to the ground. Then it was the turn of the man with the machine-pistol, the other German and the first NSB operative to find a watery grave. 'Thank God you were here, Barry,' Van Eyck gasped when the last body had been dumped. 'I don't know how one could have coped, carrying the four of them over there, without your help.'

Riordan laughed. 'Nothing like a guy with confidence in his own power to succeed,' he said. 'You conceited bastard!'

'I think maybe we better now go,' Van Eyck said. He looked back down the road. The gunman had disappeared around the corner. 'You drive. Once that man has reported, it may be necessary for one to shoot a little before we get through the blocks they set up.'

'Where do I drive?'

'I will direct you,' the Dutchman said. He clambered into the front passenger seat and slammed the heavy door. Riordan eased himself behind the outsize wheel and thumbed the button, whirring the starter. He powered the lever into the first slot of the three-speed gearbox.

In the whole length of the street, not a window had opened, not a curtain had twitched during the three and a half minutes the action had taken. In occupied cities, in the spring of 1942, it was wiser to behave like three of the monkeys which might once have sat on top of the barrel-organ, seeing nothing, hearing nothing and saying nothing.

The instrument itself proved to be equally reticent. It might have been the slight vibration as the huge car sped silently past; it might have been an interior jerk in the savaged mechanism as 'It's Time To Say Goodbye' jangled to a halt and the next music roll was slotted into place – but whatever the reason, the Grote Gavioli shuddered forward a final six inches, teetered on the stone lip, and then tipped forward to sink beneath the waters of the canal with scarcely a splash.

6

Pieter Van Eyck's hair was a blond so pale as to be almost albino. The eyes which could steady gunsights with such deadly accuracy were a very pale grey. His complexion too, especially when he was angry, paled to the point where it was virtually colourless. The one colourful thing about him, so far as Riordan was concerned, was his speech. His English was fluent but idiosyncratic, notably in his choice of pronouns. 'One better can cram on a spot more speed,' he said as the Minerva traversed a network of canal-side streets in the north-eastern corner of the city. 'As one is already the subject of an all-stations alert, one fears the report that fellow we released will make shall increase vigilance all around the outskirts.'

'This is not exactly grand-prix steering,' Riordan said, his hands steady on the great wheel. 'It's a heavy old crate; she could slide straight off and slam into a building on a tight corner in these conditions.'

It was indeed as much as he could do to keep the car on the road at all at any speed over thirty-five miles per hour. The utterly silent, 6.5-litre, double-sleeve-valve engine pulled effortlessly in top, but with only three widely spaced gears, any attempt at fierce acceleration or high-speed manoeuvring on greasy cobbles made the limousine practically unmanageable. 'One turns right at the next intersection,' Van Eyck said, 'and then half to the left at the round-point beyond.'

'Where precisely is one going?' Riordan asked.

'To a pick-up.'

Riordan swung the big car around the corner, corrected

a slide, and lifted his foot as they approached a tangle of tramlines webbing a wide square. They were both drenched by the rain sucked in through the space where the windscreen had been.

'One was doing a spot of work for Naval Intelligence in London, you see,' Van Eyck explained. 'Dock information mostly. Imports, exports, ships berthed, German naval presence, that kind of thing. Then there was this unfortunate carelessness with the radio, and one was about to fly the coop when you showed.'

Riordan changed down into second and steered carefully past a two-horse dray piled high with rutabaga and sugar beet. Traffic was very light but the streets were getting narrower. 'Why the barrel-organ?' he asked.

'One had a rendezvous with friends, but one was . . . well, obliged to leave a little early. What better place to be waiting than outside the Doelen, the expensivest hotel in town, churning out the tunes for pennies from the rich guests? Mussert and the Germans would look for a guy running out in a hurry.'

Riordan laughed. 'You've got a bloody nerve, Piet,' he said. 'So where is this pick-up?'

'On the beach at the Ijsselmeer. A fall-back arrangement.'

'On the Ijsselmeer? But isn't that what used to be called the Zuyder Zee?'

'Correct.'

'Flat as a pancake? Every move visible for miles around? What do we do there? Build a sandcastle and dig ourselves in?'

'A boat shall be among the reeds. Like Moses – only this is a rubber dinghy in the bulrushes.'

'And we paddle across the Channel to Scapa Flow?'

'You joke, but one is serious. The dinghy is just to take us maybe four hundred metres to an island named Oost Marken. Reclaimed land. It lies to the north of a much larger reclaimed island, Oost Flavoland.'

Riordan frowned. 'Sometimes, Piet, you amaze me. What happens there?'

'Oost Flavoland is inhabited. A few fishermen. An agriculturist. Oost Marken, very small, very flat, is not. One has arranged with London that a Lysander shall land there at dusk and take one away,' the Dutchman said nonchalantly.

'Delete "sometimes". You amaze me all the time,' said Riordan.

'First we have to get there,' Van Eyck said, lapsing into the plural. 'Look!' He pointed ahead.

They were in a long street bordered by identical red-brick houses with steep, stepped gables. At the far end, a black police van was pulling out to block the roadway. They saw black uniforms, a squad of armed men in field-grey.

'The first roadblock,' Riordan said. 'Shit.' He spun the wheel, turning the Minerva into a side-street on the right.

'No!' Van Eyck shouted. 'No, this is a dead end. By a canal. You . . .'

'Don't worry,' Riordan said tightly. 'Just hold on.'

Tyres screeched on the wet granite as he hurled the limousine left into a narrow lane behind the houses, left again one block further on, and then right, back into the street they were on in the first place, but much nearer the patrol.

The blackshirts, seeing their prey apparently doubling back, had run towards three black Citroëns parked in the side-street from which the patrol wagon had emerged; the soldiers were hesitating; the police van itself was being manoeuvred into the beginning of a U-turn when the huge limousine reappeared and hurtled towards them.

'Get down beneath the dashboard!' Riordan yelled. Gritting his teeth, he wrestled with the wheel, wrenching the Minerva to the far side of the road, aiming the long bonnet with the silver goddess on top of the radiator at the narrowing gap between the police van and the kerb. He stamped the accelerator flat against the floor.

For an instant the car shuddered as the rear wheels spun, fighting for a grip on the slippery cobbles. Then it shot forward. The offside front wheel thumped up on to the pavement, scattering a row of galvanized dustbins with an alarming crash; the nearside of the heavy iron front bumper struck the police van with the full weight of the two-ton body behind it, just as the driver turned his wheels onto full lock. The impact, a thunderclap of tortured metal and buckled steel, lifted the van two feet off the ground and then slammed it over on its side.

Someone was shouting orders. A volley of shots cracked out. Three of the six side windows shattered and bullets thumped into the bodywork, gouging strips from the Bedford cord padding the inside of the roof. Then they were through and speeding away, Riordan crouching low, unhurt but minus a crease of sleeve where a bullet had narrowly missed his arm.

'Great stuff, man! That's marvellous!' Van Eyck cried, emerging from beneath the dashboard. 'Now I think one shall have some shooting to do. Those Citroëns very soon will be catching us up.' He knelt up on the bench seat and clambered over into the limousine's spacious tonneau.

The car was full of guns.

Apart from the two pistols Van Eyck had originally, they had taken three Walther automatics from the patrol – two from dead men and one from the man they let go – a .38 Magnum revolver from the driver, and of course the machine-pistol. There had been a spare clip in the dead Gestapo agent's pocket.

They had left the houses behind them and were speeding along an embankment that traversed a marsh, on the way to Muiden and the bridge that crossed the Gooimeer, when the three black cars appeared at the eastern extremity of the long, straight road.

The marsh thinned out and was replaced by strips of

polder planted with potatoes, turnips and sugar beet. Away to the left, a dull gleam of water was momentarily obscured by a squall of rain.

The Minerva thundered through a village. One single street with a domed Calvinist church off to one side and the roadway littered with huge clods of mud. Here, as in the open country, the road was still made up of rough cobbles – pitted and humped by subsidence and frost damage after nearly three years of war and no repairs. Riordan clenched his teeth, holding the limousine on the embankment by the strength of his hands and the quickness of his reflexes as it bounced and slewed, skidding through the depressions, crashing on its cantilever springs each time they hit a hump. Fortunately, the collision with the police van seemed not to have damaged the front suspension or the steering. But the risks of running out of road were so acute that he dared not coax more than forty-five – perhaps fifty – miles per hour from the heavy machine.

The black Citroëns, even in these conditions, even on a road like this, could easily maintain sixty or sixty-five, with their light, one-piece bodies and stable front-wheel drive. What had at first been no more than three black dots in the distance soon became a convoy of speeding machines, close enough for Van Eyck to distinguish the double chevrons on their radiator grilles.

When he could read the number-plate of the leading car, he knocked out the glass of the Minerva's oval rear window with the butt of the Schmeisser and then slammed the spare magazine into the weapon.

Riordan had begun to weave the Minerva from side to side, partly to stop the pursuers drawing alongside, partly to make a shot at his tyres more difficult.

Over the whine of the powerful engine, Van Eyck shouted: 'There's a bend half a kilometre ahead, just after that line of trees. Straighten up once we are around it, maybe for a hundred metres, OK? Time for one to have a shot or two.'

The leading Citroën was very close now. There were at least four people inside. A man in the back was leaning out of the open window with a heavy pistol in his hand.

The Minerva careered around the bend. Trees flashed past the side windows as Riordan straightened up and held the car steady. 'Stand by for the racket!' Van Eyck called. He poked the Schmeisser's muzzle through the shattered oval and fired a short burst. And then another.

The double roar, shatteringly loud in the confined space, momentarily deafened Riordan, but he sensed the car shiver as a volley from the pursuers thudded into the rear panels. Van Eyck had aimed well, however: in the rear-view mirror, the mercenary leader saw that certainly one of his bursts had gone home, pulverizing the Citroën's windscreen and cracking a lead whip across the chests of the two men in front. The black car swerved wildly, shrieking across the cobbles to jump a low grass bank and tip over the edge of the embankment. It rolled sickeningly down the slope and burst at once into flames – a puffball of oily smoke marbled with crimson which blossomed immediately into a blazing inferno.

'He must have been killing his engine for it to be hot enough to go up like that,' Van Eyck said. 'Pity. It's a nice car, the Light Fifteen.'

He knelt up again to peer through the oval. 'Time for another now?'

But the remaining cars had dropped back, waiting for the road to widen or a village square, so that they could use their superior acceleration and road-holding to outflank the Minerva and attack from either side. Van Eyck kept them at a distance with an occasional shot from the heavy-calibre revolver. One of the leading Citroën's headlamps shattered; for an instant a silver fountain played above the dark roof as the glass of the windscreen erupted.

Riordan was finding it increasingly difficult to see. The driving rain seemed to increase in force every minute, and the wind howling in through the empty windscreen frame and the three broken windows filled the inside of the limousine with a maelstrom of whirling drops. He dashed the back of one hand across his eyes. Heavy squalls gusted across the flat landscape like smoke, but through the moving curtain of moisture he could make out, beyond a long, looping curve in the road, the slate roofs and church spire of a village.

'This is the one,' Van Eyck said, peering over his shoulder.

'Which one?'

'The village I'm waiting for.'

As he threw the car round the curve, Riordan saw that this was a larger village than the first one: the road ran into a wide square with a fountain and war memorial, passed two side-streets and then divided to run either side of the white church with its stubby, onion-shaped steeple.

'The side-street on the left,' Van Eyck said urgently. 'Block it if you can. Broadside.'

Riordan hauled on the wheel, obeying instantly. He had been in enough tight corners with the Dutchman – and got out of them – not to question his judgement now.

Huge pools of water reflected the steely sky on each side of the square. The Citroëns had already increased speed to fan out and enfilade them. A ragged volley blazed out from each car. The Minerva lurched through the largest pool, spraying water wide . . . and then suddenly staggered, yawing and thumping alarmingly as first the nearside front tyre and then the offside rear were shot out.

Riordan fought the wheel, spinning the big saloon sideways towards the intersection, crunching the gear lever into first as the engine howled. The Minerva lost way like a crippled ship in a storm, slowing, slowing, and then hobbling to a halt.

Riordan couldn't make the side-street, but he managed

to place the car in such a way that no other vehicle could squeeze past into it. The Citroëns had stopped on the far side of the square. German soldiers and blackshirts were piling out, eight or nine of them, deploying on either side, running for the cover of the unused fountain basin. 'Smart,' Riordan panted. 'They have rifles: we're easy targets for them, but they're out of range for the stuff we have.' He ducked low, shoved open the passenger door, and crawled out on to the road on the far side.

Van Eyck stuffed two of the Walthers into the pockets of his ragged suit, scooped up the Schmeisser and dived through one of the shattered windows to join him as the pursuers started shooting again.

Prone beneath the Minerva's wide running-board, elbows steadied on the muddy cobbles, he took aim with one of the Walthers as a Dutch Nazi raced from the nearest car towards the basin.

Van Eyck fired a single shot. The black-uniformed figure halted in mid-stride, hesitated, then folded forward to a kneeling position. A split second later, the blackshirt slumped sideways with outflung arms. A slung carbine, sliding from his shoulder, skated away into a large puddle.

'A lucky shot,' Van Eyck said, scrambling back to squat beside Riordan. 'Waste of ammunition to try again.'

'So what do we do? Wait until we can see the whites of their eyes?'

'One runs,' the marksman said. Bullets from the rifles on the far side of the square punished the stalled Minerva, whined off the granite cobbles into the rain. He indicated the rear of the limousine.

Riordan was aware suddenly of the thin, aromatic stink of petrol. The forty-gallon bolster tank beneath the car's folding luggage grid had been punctured in several places. Beneath the distant shots and the pelting of the rain, they could hear fuel splashing to the ground. Van Eyck motioned his leader back. He took the revolver from the waistband of his trousers, held the gun low, almost parallel with the ground, and pressed the trigger.

The heavy, .38-calibre slug ploughed into the road beneath the fuel tank, showering granite chips. Van Eyck fired again. The third shot, flatter still in trajectory, struck the sparks from the stone that he wanted.

The petrol vapour ignited with a whump that blasted hot air past their rain-soaked faces. The Minerva was transformed at once into a raging fireball. Thick black smoke, seasoned with the smell of scorched rubber and charred upholstery, boiled across the square.

The two men were running down the side-street, between red-brick façades, white window frames and steep, shining slate roofs. Two hundred yards further on, the street turned sharp right and vanished.

Behind them, an angry voice was shouting in German. The roar of the flames was punctuated by the crackle of exploding ammunition from the guns they had left behind.

'They won't be able to get past the car into the street,' Van Eyck panted. 'Too much heat from the fire. They have to go all the way round the block before they can follow us.'

'Then what? What's around the corner? Another street?'

'Nothing. After fifty metres the road ends beneath a dyke.'

'Then what the fuck . . .?'

The Dutchman chuckled. 'Wait and see,' he said.

They turned the corner. The end of the street was as deserted as the first part. Any villagers who had been about had prudently vanished as soon as the shooting started. Most of the shutters were closed.

The steep, grassy bank barring the exit was half as high as the houses. Van Eyck led the way to the top of the dyke. Grey water thrashed by the rain stretched away on the far side to a long, low strip of land topped by the occasional ghost of a tree, half visible through the downpour. 'Two kilometres to the left, the bridge,' Van Eyck said. 'And then Oost Flavoland.'

Riordan frowned. 'Yes, but how . . .?'

Van Eyck seized his arm and pointed right. Fifty yards away, ten feet below the tow-path, a flat-bottomed, Carvel-built dinghy was tied to a weathered post. An outboard motor was tilted up over the little boat's stern. Riordan glanced over his shoulder before they scrambled down to it. Beside the church tower, a column of black smoke uncoiled slowly beneath the low clouds.

Standing in the dinghy, Van Eyck wound around his hand the cord that started the two-stroke engine. He hinged the motor down until the propeller and its supporting column could be lowered into the water.

A sharp jerk on the cord, and the engine spluttered to life.

Van Eyck sat down in the stern and took the tiller and its controls. The exhaust burbled and the screw churned the still water. He laid the machine-pistol on the central thwart as the dinghy headed out into the leaden expanse of the Gooimeer.

Riordan collapsed on to the forward thwart. 'Piet!' he raged. 'What the fuck's going on? How the *hell* did you know . . .?' He gestured towards the gunwale and the open water beyond.

The Dutchman chuckled again. 'Fall-back two,' he said.

7

The dinghy took them to the bridge. Hidden beneath the bridge were two bicycles. With these they rode to the northern coast of Oost Flavoland, a distance of just over twelve miles. On the long stretch of dyke running ruler-straight north-east and south-west of the hamlet of Swifterlad, Van Eyck searched for a wooden hut which was used to store nets and other fishing gear. The roof was half hidden among bushes below the level of the road running along the top of the dyke. It was about a quarter of a mile from the village.

'OK, one arrives!' Van Eyck said with satisfaction. He gazed right and left along the embankment. Between them and the plantation of trees half obscuring the roofs of Swifterlad there was nothing and nobody. In the other direction, the deserted road arrowed away until it vanished into the haze hiding the docks and city – a rampart separating the waveless water from the sodden green of the desolate flatlands below.

Van Eyck nodded. Leading the way, he slithered down the wet bank to the fringe of reeds at the water's edge. Oost Marken, featureless and flat, was perhaps a mile offshore. It was still raining, although a little less heavily.

The Dutchman looked back and up at the hut to check his position. 'Now we take seventy paces to the south-west,' he announced, striding along the marshy slope. Riordan followed, higher up the bank . . . and there, as Van Eyck was counting aloud the last three figures between sixty and seventy, he saw among a thick cluster of bulrushes the bulging yellow sides of a rubber dinghy.

'I am astounded,' Riordan said, sliding down to join his companion. 'For the second time, Piet, how the hell do you do it? I mean, the people who were to meet you outside the Doelen, this dinghy, the fall-back motor boat and the bikes, just *happening* to be at that particular village. What kind of routine is this?'

Van Eyck laughed, a little proudly. 'You must not think,' he said, 'that France is the only occupied country with an organized Resistance, or the only target for SOE. Naval Intelligence too has work to do inland – especially in a country with waterways.' He reached into the reeds to pull the dinghy closer. 'The bicycles and the outboard will be back with their owners before dawn. This dinghy one deflates and takes with one. One leaves no trace.'

'Bravo then – and good for one!' Riordan approved. There was nothing else to say.

As they paddled swiftly out to the uninhabited island, he filled the Dutchman in on the mission he had been entrusted with. As he had expected, Van Eyck agreed instantly to come in. 'So who does one work for?' he asked. 'Still the British, one supposes?'

'The contact could have been anyone,' Riordan said. 'Being, as you might say, from the same egg, I even suspected an Irish tinge. But he was very careful – perhaps a little too careful – to play the Swiss card. And once he used the word "gen", meaning information, which is a peculiarly British usage.' He shrugged. 'But officially, and for the others, we work for a Swiss industrial consortium – unlikely though that seems!'

The island, carpeted here and there with low bushes and clumps of grass, was little more than an extended sandbank or mud-flat. It was about a mile long and not quite as wide, never rising more than ten feet above the water. Originally it had been part of a plan to link Oost Flavoland with a broad promontory of reclaimed land known as Noord Polder, but work on the draining of that part of the old Zuyder Zee had been abandoned with the outbreak of war, and Oost Marken remained an isolated islet, a haunt of waterfowl and a reproach to the planners.

Light was already fading when Riordan and Van Eyck waded ashore, disturbing thousands of birds that were already settling for the night. Great clouds of them flapped angrily into the darkening sky, cawing and screaming as they wheeled above the island. They were still circling in separate flocks when the two men, sitting on the deflated and repacked dinghy, heard the distant wail of sirens from the direction of Amsterdam.

'This will be our chauffeur,' Van Eyck said. He rose to his feet and stretched, easing the sodden clothes away from his body. 'Right on time. Bloody good, eh?'

'Excellent service,' Riordan agreed. 'Did I hear a patter of anti-aircraft fire then?'

'Possibly. It has happened.' Van Eyck cocked his head, listening intently.

The cry of gulls and other sea birds, the faint drone of an approaching aero engine, the steady pelting of rain on their bodies, on the bare earth . . . and, yes, there *was* another, unexplained, noise intruding.

But it wasn't distant ack-ack fire. It sounded, now that it was nearer, much more like . . .

'Holy shit!' Van Eyck yelled. He had climbed to the top of a shallow bank. It's a motor boat full of Krauts in uniform! From the outpost on Noord Polder. Those *bloody* birds!' He shook his fist at the squawking flocks still noisily overflying their sanctuary.

The put-put of the boat had grown louder. Riordan joined Van Eyck on top of the bank and looked out across the water. It was a small vessel with the bow decked over, a wheel behind a windshield, and a kennel-shaped hutch covering the engine amidships. Half a dozen steel-helmeted soldiers with rifles crowded behind an officer with a peaked cap who was steering. Riordan assumed that Van Eyck was right: the patrol must have been alerted by the birds' uncharacteristic dusk display to the fact that something unusual was taking place on the deserted island.

The noise of the plane's engine was very loud now. It was visible as an enlarging speck against the dimming light in the dun-coloured western sky. The motor boat was perhaps three hundred yards offshore.

'You reckon he'll get here before they do?' Riordan asked.

'There's nothing we can do to stop him,' the marksman said. 'It's a regular run once a month, different days, different times. But there's no landing routine, no markers, no agreed signals. And of course no radio here. He just dumps her down, loads or unloads, and flies away.'

The Lysander was flying in very low above the water. Over the racket of its radial engine Riordan and Van Eyck could hear a commotion aboard the boat, now no more than a hundred yards away and increasing speed. The officer was bellowing orders; the men unslung their rifles. Two of them were armed with Bergmann-Schmeisser machine-pistols.

The yellow, high-wing monoplane, with its fixed under-carriage and spatted wheels, banked slightly, levelled out and touched down at the far end of the island. The pilot swung it around and taxied towards them, bouncing over the reclaimed land, the rudder swinging as he corrected to allow for the slopes and hollows of the uneven surface. On the other side of the island the boat had grounded and the soldiers were wading ashore.

Riordan and Van Eyck didn't see them: they had leapt down from the bank and were racing towards the plane. There were still ten or twelve rounds left in the Dutchman's Schmeisser. Riordan carried one of the Walthers.

A line of figures in field-grey appeared above the raised shoreline beyond the plane.

Van Eyck was waving his free arm wildly. He cut off

at an angle to intercept the machine and stand directly in the pilot's line of vision. Riordan followed. It was hard work, running: they were lashed by the rain, the soaked garments clung heavily to their bodies, the waterlogged ground sucked at their feet.

The soldiers were running too. Four of them dropped to one knee and started firing at the Lysander. The officer and the others fanned out to allow them a free field of fire and continued until they could shoot at closer range.

The plane juddered to a halt by Van Eyck, the throttled-down, three-bladed airscrew grumbling and whistling. The sliding hatch at the rear of the Perspex-canopied cabin had already been pushed back. Van Eyck swarmed up the lightweight ladder fixed to the fuselage beneath it, leaning in to shout some question at the pilot. He shook his head, climbed in, and motioned Riordan to follow. Strips of fabric, torn from the tailfin and the rear end of the fuselage by rifle fire, fluttered now in the airstream.

'No armaments on this agents' pickup version of the Lizzie,' Van Eyck shouted when Riordan was in the cabin. He thumped the pilot on the shoulder. 'Enough room for take-off if you keep straight ahead?' he asked.

The pilot swung around in his seat – a slight figure with fair tousled hair and an improbable moustache. He was wearing a blue sweater and a sleeveless, fleece-lined leather flying jacket. He looked about nineteen. 'Sorry, no go, old lad,' he called over the rumble of the 890hp Bristol Mercury engine. 'Not enough room on this soggy ground. And anyway there's a bloody tail wind. 'Fraid we'll have to about-face and leave the way we came in – over the boys in grey.'

A panel of Perspex splintered and starred as a high-velocity bullet zipped through the cabin. 'Here we go,' the pilot said.

A burst of the throttle and the Lysander surged forward, slewing left and right as he raced it to the far end of the island. When he turned back into the wind, they saw that the Germans were now all in the firing position, strung out to span the flight path he had chosen when he landed. 'Hope we're airborne before we reach the sharpshooters,' the pilot said. 'I'd hate to run those chappies down.'

He fed full power to the motor and the plane lurched into motion.

There was a small flapped door beside his seat. Van Eyck had fastened this back, squeezed himself into the space between the seat and fuselage, and poked the muzzle of the machine-pistol out into the slipstream. Riordan leaned out of the open hatch with his Walther.

The pilot kept as near the southern shoreline of the island as he could, but there were still four or five men well within range of the plane, including one of the machine-pistols.

It was a rough ride. The Lysander staggered over the marshy, undulating terrain, bouncing, thumping down hard, sometimes sliding, accelerating with what seemed agonizing slowness. Soon, it was evident that they would not be off the ground before they were level with the German patrol.

Riordan and Van Eyck prepared to shoot.

Seventy or eighty yards before the line of soldiers, the pilot started a complex routine with the throttle and flight controls, hauling the stick momentarily hard back at the last moment. The Lysander didn't have nearly enough air speed for take off, but it reared up like a startled horse, bounced over the patrol at a height of twenty feet, and then thundered back to earth with an impact that threatened to shake the wings from the body.

In those few seconds, there was action on all sides. The cabin was filled with the shattering racket of the Dutchman's Schmeisser, punctuated by half a dozen deeper reports from Riordan's handgun. Slugs ripped through the floor. The glass of a dial on the instrument panel shattered. The Perspex canopy was pierced several more times. And on the ground the man with the

Schmeisser fell; the officer keeled over and collapsed face down in the mud; a soldier immediately behind him was blasted backwards by the final burst from Van Eyck. Riordan thought he had winged one of the riflemen – the man had certainly dropped his weapon – but he couldn't be certain. The remaining members of the patrol swung round and continued with rapid fire.

'Oh, wizard show!' the pilot crowed. 'Jolly good shooting, that man!'

'That was a pretty smart manoeuvre of yours,' Riordan called. 'Rather like lifting the front wheel of a bike over the kerb.'

'Much the same principle,' the pilot agreed. He uttered a sudden gasp and sagged for an instant against his seat

'What is it?' Van Eyck demanded. 'You are hit?'

'Not to worry.' The pilot's face was pale. 'Parting shot from Jerry. 'Straight through the calf, I think. Probably a boot full of blood, but nothing permanent.' He boosted the tachometer to maximum revs and the Lysander raced ahead, skimming the mud-flats.

It was another thousand yards before the plane lifted off. 'Can't use the place again, now that Jerry's wise,' the pilot said, banking over Noord Polder to turn back west. 'Not really sorry. Bloody messy, putting a crate down and getting her up again on that sort of ground.' He straightened out and headed across the Ijsselmeer towards the coast. Over the roar of the engine, they could hear the thin whistle of air shrieking through the bullet holes in the fuselage.

'What about your leg?' Riordan asked.

The young man bit his lip. 'Shade uncomfortable, to be honest,' he replied. 'But it'll last as long as the fuel tank registers.' And then, turning to Van Eyck: 'Who's the stowaway, if you don't mind my asking?'

'Resistance comrade,' the Dutchman lied. It would be impossible to explain or excuse the presence of a mercenary on a Naval Intelligence lift-off. 'Too hot for him to handle, down there. So back to London for new orders.'

'Tally-ho,' said the pilot. 'Any friend of Pieter's. Welcome aboard, chum.'

'Talking of London,' Van Eyck said carefully, 'it would be much more convenient – and save an extra flight into the bargain – if you could make a detour and drop us in northern France instead. One has a network to catch up with there.'

'What?'

Van Eyck repeated his request.

'You must be joking, old boy,' the pilot replied. 'No chance.' They were flying towards the northern outskirts of Amsterdam, at a height of no more than two hundred feet.

'I guess they'll be expecting us by now?' Riordan observed.

'You bet. And they do have radar, but it's not as advanced as ours. At this height we'll be well beneath the screen.'

Riordan thought he detected tracer arching up against the dark western sky as they flew over the dock area, but nothing shook the Lysander, which continued its sturdy progress at just over two hundred miles per hour.

Over the sand dunes south of the Noordzee canal, Van Eyck returned to the attack. 'This is a Lysander III, isn't it?' he said into the pilot's ear. 'Without the armaments, and extra fuel tanks, you carry enough gas for eight hours, right? You could put us down anywhere – in the forbidden zone, in Picardy, on one of the beaches now that it's dark. Come on, it's hardly even a detour. Add ten minutes to your flight time, no more. One would hold oneself wholly responsible to NI. Unless of course you were simply to report that we didn't turn up at the RDV . . .'

'My dear old chap,' replied the pilot, 'this is a bus service, not a bloody taxi rank. There are schedules to be followed. I told you no – and that still stands. Next stop, Manston.'

The Dutchman whipped a Walther from his pocket and pressed the muzzle behind the pilot's ear. 'One hates to have to do this,' he said grimly. 'But one really does need to be in France this evening. Now . . . turn south at once.'

'Don't be bloody silly,' the young man said. 'A gun's useless unless you're prepared to use it. And you're not going to shoot me. Even if you knew how to fly this crate, at this height you'd stall and hit the drink before you even got my body out of the seat.' He raised a hand from the control column and pushed the gun away. 'I don't like to risk a prang when I'm driving a kite . . . so sit down like a good chap and swallow your medicine: next stop, fucking Manston. End of story.'

Van Eyck burst out laughing. He shoved the automatic away and sank into one of the canvas and tubular-steel passenger seats. 'Too bad,' he said to Riordan. 'But one has to try, no? Anyway,' he added, brightening up, 'at least one will be offered a drink in the officers' mess at Manston!'

8

The weather remained bad in central France. At dawn on the day that Frenchie Delorme was to be sprung, a thin drizzle veiled the heights west of Beaune and low clouds scurried fast above the huge, wide depression of the Saône valley. Further south, late-melting snows from the Alps had caused widespread flooding on either side of the river between Chalon-sur-Saône and Mâcon.

Riordan lay on the lip of the quarry between two clumps of broom, mentally checking for one last time the preparations which had been made.

The three vehicles they needed – a pickup with a tow-bar and a powered winch, and two identical black Citroëns – were in place. Zabrisky was thirty yards away, hidden beneath a gorse bush on his right. Van Eyck had concealed himself on the lower slopes of the hill from which the quarry had been blasted, with a clear two-hundred-yard view of the working area. Art Daniels, the circus Romany, was down below, hiding among huge blocks of granite near the stone-crushing plant.

The pickup was from a garage on the outskirts of Dijon run by José Manuel García, a contact of Zabrisky's. The Citroëns had been 'stolen' from a motor pool belonging to Darnand's Milice – the French Gestapo – and serviced by García's mechanics. One of them was parked in a spinney not far from Van Eyck; the other, attached to the pickup by a rigid bar, had been towed through the woods crowning the hill above the quarry along a grassy, unmetalled foresters' track. A three-quarter moon behind the clouds had allowed enough light to filter through to let them drive, yard by yard, without switching on the pickup's masked headlights. The black saloon was parked now on the edge of the forest, fifty yards from Riordan's position; the pickup itself had backed up almost to the quarry edge. Since the site was three miles from the prison, Riordan hoped that the noise of the engines — skilfully extra-silenced by García — would not have raised any suspicions among the night-duty warders.

He sighed, stretched out on the wet ground. All they had to do now was wait . . .

Riordan was, in truth, surprised to be in a waiting situation. So much had happened in the past few days that a period in which patience was required was a novelty.

At Manston, the RAF headquarters field in Kent, he had been kept a long time by the debriefing officer, sticking to Van Eyck's story that he had been working with the Dutch Resistance but refusing to give any details. Subsequently, he had been obliged to repeat the entire performance for a Naval Intelligence analyst from London. Fortunately, perhaps, he had given his own name to both men, for soon after midnight a high-priority message from Whitehall was transmitted to the Manston operations room. Messrs Riordan and Van Eyck were to be given every facility, including the provision of arms and immediate transport, if they so wished, to any part of occupied France within a Lysander III's range.

They were put down in a mustard field not far from Avallon. By dawn they had arrived in Saulieu, from where Riordan contrived to place a call to Zabrisky in Paris.

Since he himself, Riordan said, had been unavoidably delayed, the safe-breaker was to take his place and rendezvous with Art Daniels in the Belleville café. The two of them were then to go immediately to the station brasserie in Beaune, where the mercenary leader and Van Eyck would link up with them.

'Just as well you couldn't make the RDV,' Zabrisky said. 'You'd be holed up in Fresnes if you had come.'

'What do you mean?'

'Your pad in the Rue Clauzel. It's staked out. Permanent newspaper reader in the café on the corner. Fellow in a long leather coat. Gestapo Citroën parked around the corner in Rue Notre Dame de Lorette. The Milice have requisitioned the apartment across the courtyard from yours. Twenty-four-hour watch in three shifts.'

'Good God. But why . . .? I mean, what in hell . . .? What about the girl?'

'What girl?'

'My bird, the redhead. Aline Pacquot. She works with Lelong.'

'Haven't seen her,' Zabrisky said.

'Just as well. Let's hope she's in her own flat. If you should see her, tell her for God's sake to keep clear. I'll be in touch later.'

'It's unlikely. Don't call this number again. When I hang up, I'm clearing out, for good. For all I know, the number's bugged. I tell you, a trip down to . . . the town you mentioned won't so amiss.'

The news had worried Riordan. He had been tailed as soon as he got off the train in Amsterdam. And if his apartment was that well staked out, they must be waiting for him to come back. Why? Even if they had been tipped off by the Gestapo or Mussert's men in Holland, surely there was no way they could have tied him in with Van Eyck? Unless, of course, Eilers . . .

Whichever way he looked at it, this was disconcerting. It wasn't, after all, his war. At least not yet. So why should the security services of one belligerent be so interested – so lethally interested – in his activities? They couldn't conceivably, Riordan believed, be wise to a mission in an entirely different theatre of war – a mission that hadn't even got off the ground yet, that hadn't even assembled the full team that was to carry it out.

Or could they? It was not a train of thought he could afford to pursue: he was a day behind schedule, and he had to contact Zabrisky and Daniels and then arrange with Van Eyck the details of the jailbreak.

Now that the operation was about to begin, he banished all other considerations from his mind and concentrated on the events of the immediate future. It was full daylight now, or as full as it was ever going to be in these sombre weather conditions. He checked that the tailgate and winch of the pickup would be invisible from the floor of the quarry. The detachment of warders standing guard over the convicts while they worked would arrive at any minute.

Riordan double-checked the action of the two guns he carried: the Walther from Amsterdam and a Browning GP-35 automatic pistol. He was limiting himself to hand-guns because of the necessity for freedom of movement. Zabrisky, Daniels and Van Eyck were all armed with machine-pistols – the Dutchman with his Schmeisser (new clips courtesy of SOE at Manston), Zabrisky with a Swiss Steyr-Solothurn, and Daniels, astonishingly, with a Finnish Suomi. Van Eyck, in addition, was equipped with the new American Garand automatic rifle, for longer-range work.

The extra weapons had been parachuted into a field near Beaune under an arrangement agreed between Riordan and Huefer before the mercenary leader left for Holland. To maintain the fiction of his Swiss connection, O'Kelly had instructed that the container be dropped, not from a Lysander, but from an unmarked Hudson flying in from the East.

Riordan had smiled wryly. Events at – and after – Manston had convinced him beyond any reasonable doubt that he must be working secretly for the British. The fact that Van Eyck, unknown to him, had been furnishing information to Naval Intelligence via SOE was no more than a happy coincidence perhaps? The smile widened. What the hell – his not to reason why!

The snick of a metal safety-catch some way to his

right broke the early-morning silence. Behind the wheel in the pickup, José Manuel García, co-opted for this one operation, cleared his throat. A large bird flapped away from the trees behind them.

From beyond the quarry, they could hear the growl of a powerful engine grinding up the hill in low gear.

A grey Berliet motorbus appeared at the entrance, accompanied by two uniformed outriders on motorcycles. The convoy turned in through the gates and coasted down the ramp to the quarry floor. The riders dismounted. A dozen armed warders emerged from the bus and took up positions at each side of the rock-face, by the stone-crusher, at the entrance, and in strategic positions among the boulders littering the site.

Five minutes later, three dusty lorries, driven by civilians, arrived from the other direction. Checked in by the men on the gates, they backed up to the crushing machinery, awaiting the day's first delivery of granite chips.

Soon after that two more grey buses, each carrying thirty convicts, deposed their human cargo on the quarry floor. The warders accompanying them shouted orders; the men fanned out in different directions to start the day's work, even though the drizzle had turned to steady rain.

The crusher machinery grumbled to life. Picks started to ring. Hoppers, wheeled along the network of narrow-gauge railway tracks linking the rock-face with the plant, transported chunks of broken stone to the crusher. Half-way up the face, a pneumatic drill operated by a man on a ledge burst into a clattering roar.

Riordan assumed that his enigmatic message would have tipped off Frenchie Delorme that the rescue attempt would be at the rock-face . . . and Delorme, who had once worked as a quarryman in Canada, would probably be assigned to that part of the site, maybe even to lay charges once blasting began. But the prisoner would have no idea exactly when the attempt would be made. Riordan had therefore organized two signals: one to co-ordinate the actions of his own men, the other to warn Frenchie that now was the time to watch the rock-face like a hawk.

The action was to start immediately the first charge was detonated.

Parting the grasses beneath the clump of broom, Riordan inched forward and swept his binoculars over the toiling convicts. Fortunately the bad weather ensured that no tell-tale gleam of sunlight would reveal the lenses to the watchful eyes of warders below.

It was easy enough to pick out the squat, powerful shape of Delorme. He was indeed wielding a pick at the foot of the rock-face, not far from a fissure or 'chimney' separating two monoliths of granite. Twenty minutes after work started, the stutter of the drill died away, a whistle blew, and Delorme was escorted to the hut near the entrance to fetch sticks of dynamite and a length of fuse.

He returned to the rock-face and climbed to the ledge, exchanging a few words with the driller before he crouched down to lay the charges in the holes he had pierced.

Delorme stood up and waved his arms. Whistles blew again. Work stopped and both warders and their charges were withdrawn from the rock-face. The trolley-men stopped wheeling their hoppers.

Delorme produced a short, single-barrel horn and blew a single blast. He bent down to the fuse, straightened and retired to the far end of the ledge. The driller jumped down to the quarry floor. Delorme blew a second blast.

The ground beneath Riordan shook. He heard a flat, thumping detonation, and a section of the rock-face, neatly quartered from the neighbouring outcrops, crumbled and then collapsed to the ground in a towering column of dust and brown smoke. When the smaller rocks and stones had stopped pattering down, Delorme blew the same note for the third time, and work restarted at once.

But before the first hopper had tipped its load into a bucket on the chain moving up to the lip of the crusher, the mournful cry of the horn was followed, astonishingly, by the brassy, golden notes of a cornet. Van Eyck, who had once played with a forbidden jazz group called the Dutch Swing College, had produced the instrument in his hiding place off to one side of the quarry. With immaculate pitch, he blasted out the first ten notes, with an eight-note repeat, of the famous Scottish battle cry:

'The Campbells are coming, ta-ra, ta-ra ... The Campbells are coming, ta-ra!'

This was the signal to Frenchie Delorme.

For an instant the warders were too surprised to react. But in that moment Daniels appeared and leapt into the empty bucket, Van Eyck dropped the cornet and picked up the Garand, Riordan ran to the pickup and tossed 150 feet of climbing rope over the edge of the chimney, and García backed up the pickup until the winch, from which the rope had been uncoiled, was just inches from the drop. Riordan leaned over to yell: 'Frenchie! Here!' – and pulled back the slide on his Browning.

Delorme had frozen when he heard the cornet's first phrase, watchful eyes flicking right and left. At Riordan's call, he glanced up once, nodded, then raced to the far end of the ledge. He dropped down amid a wilderness of boulders waiting to be broken up, and ran for the chimney.

The guards, startled by the cornet, unsighted by the pall of dust and smoke lying heavily over the site beneath the rain, did not at first realize what was happening. By the time they did, he had reached the rope. A steeplejack's safety-belt was fastened to the lower end. Delorme eased himself into it, grasped the rope and tugged it to signal that he was ready.

Up above, Riordan swung around and gave the thumbs-up to García, waiting in the pickup. García started the motor, engaged the winch mechanism and slammed it into the lowest gear. Slowly, the drum revolved, coiling in the rope. Delorme allowed himself to be dragged into the chimney.

Pandemonium had broken out on the quarry floor.

The chief warder was bellowing orders. Half a dozen guards, shouting excitedly, herded the remainder of the working party into a corner. Others prepared to fire at the rescuers, so far unseen. One of the motorcycle outriders was in the hut, frantically twirling the handle of the telephone linked to the prison. A siren went into action with an ear-splitting wail.

Riordan had chosen the rough, jagged fissure as the escape route rather than the relatively smooth rock-face because once he was within the chimney, Delorme would be vulnerable only to marksmen directly behind him, whereas exposed on the face he could be shot at from all sides.

Necessarily, however, the ascent was slower. Belaying, 'walking' the vertical rock surface as he pulled himself hand over hand along a rope which was already being drawn upwards, the escaper had begun his perilous climb. And the chief was already waving armed warders in to cover the narrow field of fire open to them. Granite chips stung Delorme's face and drew blood from his forehead as the first shots came uncomfortably close.

It was at this moment that Zabrisky opened fire with three short bursts from the Steyr-Solothurn. The range was too great for the shots to be effective, but they scattered the sharpshooters menacing the chimney. At the same time Daniels, crouched low in the empty bucket nearing the top of the ramp feeding the crusher, loosed off a fusillade from his Suomi, scattering them further. The riflemen were now distributed in a rough semicircle, kneeling or prone behind individual boulders, trying angled shots at the occasionally visible figure now halfway up the granite shaft.

The chief had prudently taken shelter behind a loaded hopper. He waved in the second motorcycle guard, who remounted, gunned his engine, and weaved, skidding through clouds of dust, to the foot of the chimney. He braked and, still astride, unflapped his holster and removed his service revolver. Stretching out an arm, he sighted the heavy-calibre weapon up the interior of the fissure.

From the far side of the quarry, Van Eyck picked him off with a single shot from the Garand. The guard keeled over, capsizing the machine. The engine roared, spinning the rear wheel in the air.

Van Eyck dropped the chief with a second shot from the Garand.

Zabrisky and Daniels emptied their magazines. A warder fell, cursing as he grabbed a shattered knee.

For a moment the defenders were disorganized, attacked from above, from behind and from one side. They ran for cover behind a line of hoppers. At the top of the ramp, Daniels leapt away as his bucket inverted over the mouth of the stone-crusher. He landed on the roof of a prison bus parked on the far side of the plant, double rolled, and sprang to the ground. In front of the dusty installation, a loaded lorry stood, waiting for a signal to leave. Waving his empty Suomi threateningly, Daniels pulled the civilian driver from the cab and climbed in, started the engine and steered up the slope towards the gates.

The first motorcyclist ran out from the telephone in the hut, firing his revolver. The cab's rear window shattered; splinters flew as heavy slugs ripped through the wooden panel beside it. Daniels braked hard in the gateway and wrenched up the lever controlling the tip-up gear. The rear of the lorry canted slowly upwards, sliding out several tons of granite chips to fell the guard and block totally the exit from the quarry.

Daniels accelerated fiercely, forcing the lorry, still tipped up, out on to the road. He turned away from the prison and raced until he was a quarter of a mile from the quarry, finally broadsiding it across the road beside the spinney where the second Citroën was concealed. Van Eyck was already behind the wheel.

Daniels nodded, threw his Suomi on the back seat, and got in beside him.

The Dutchman started the engine and they drove away to play their part in the second – and perhaps the most important – phase of Riordan's plan.

On the lip of the quarry, things were not going so well. Delorme's face was a mask of blood. A ricochet had creased him just above one ear and he had lost consciousness. At the same time the winch motor had jammed. Riordan, Zabrisky and García were hoisting up his dead weight by hand.

Their burden was still twenty feet from the top of the chimney ... and they themselves were now targets for anyone with a rifle each time they allowed their heads and shoulders to appear over the lip, which was impossible to avoid now that Delorme was unable to steer the rope – or his own body – away from sharp outcrops in the rock gully.

Riordan was sweating. The operation was based on the single element of surprise. And after that, speed. From the first cornet blast to the getaway he had planned on a time-lapse of no more than four minutes, six at the outside – the time it would take for reinforcements to drive the three hilly miles from the prison. Now five minutes had already elapsed, and the man they were rescuing was still fifteen feet from safety. Daniels and Van Eyck, knowing nothing of the difficulty, would already have followed their allotted paths and left on schedule, so there could be no more covering fire from below.

Over the screaming of the quarry alarm, he could hear down the far hillside the ululating wail of approaching sirens.

'Come on,' he panted, 'one last almighty heave!' He leaned out over the edge and emptied the Walther at the warders 150 feet below. A volley of rifle fire crackled out.

91

Bullets whined overhead and screeched off the rocky lip
. . . but García had grabbed Delorme by the collar and
Zabrisky was pulling in the last of the rope.

'OK,' Riordan rapped out as the unconscious man was
at last manhandled on to the flat ground. 'Off with the
belt. Carry him to the car. Back out and start the engine.
You drive, García.' And then, as the mechanic raised
enquiring eyebrows: 'I'll be with you in thirty seconds.'

As the two of them hurried away with Delorme, he
leaned into the pickup's cab, eased off the handbrake,
rammed the gear lever into reverse and stabbed the starter
button. The engine coughed, jerked the vehicle's frame,
and stalled. He tried again. No luck: the gearing was too
high. Riordan bent down, picked up a long, flat stone and
leaned it against the accelerator pedal. This time when
he pressed the button the engine roared to life, the back
wheels spun, gripped and shot the pickup the few feet to
the chimney lip.

The back of the truck, with the winch, tipped over; the
whole vehicle reared up from the ground, hung in the air
for an instant with its sump and exhaust and silencer
exposed, then crashed backwards and somersaulted out
of sight.

The series of appalling metallic concussions that charted
its progress to the quarry floor seemed to go on for a
long time.

Riordan was sprinting the fifty yards to the trees. 'To
discourage pursuit up the chimney,' he explained when he
reached the Citroën. 'They might think we have another
pickup to throw at them.'

As García raced the front-wheel-drive saloon away
down the sodden forest track, his employer smiled
for the first time that day. Very quietly, he began
to sing to himself: 'The Campbells are going, ta-ra,
ta-ra . . .'

Escape and pursuit, thinking about it afterwards, seemed

to Riordan almost like one of the crazier chases by the Keystone Kops.

It wasn't like that at the time.

Confusion, admittedly, had been at the heart of the rescuers' plan. But at any moment it could have been confounded – with tragic results.

From the top of the quarry, there were only two directions a car could take: west and north, to a dead end and another quarry, now disused, higher up in the hills; or east, to join the main road to Beaune.

This was a wide highway, looping down to the plain. The corner where it was joined by the foresters' track was visible from a long way up the hillside. If Riordan's timing was right, the pursuers, knowing there was only one route they could take, would try and cut them off at that intersection . . . and would be coming into sight at the top of the straight as the Citroën turned into the main road. If they weren't in sight, García would be instructed to dawdle until they were.

It was then that the chase proper would begin.

At the foot of the hill, the road crossed a bridge and turned sharp right into a wood. Five hundred yards further on, in an area still densely packed with trees, there was a fork. Faced with a choice of two roads and nothing in sight the pursuers, Riordan reasoned, would split into two parties, each taking one of the roads. But whereas Party A would in fact continue following a black Citroën, registration number such and such, Party B would find itself faced, a couple of miles further on, by an identical black Citroën, with an identical number – but heading the other way, back towards the prison. Van Eyck and Daniels, having made a quick circuit of the area, would be back in the game.

After that, assuming the two parties to be in radio contact – with one another and with the prison – Riordan reckoned that the conflicting reports and different sightings of the two cars, some of them by local police alerted to the jailbreak, would so confuse the pursuers that they could be slipped altogether. Especially after a minutely worked-out crossing and recrossing of routes in a network of lanes five miles from Beaune.

Finally, the two Citroëns, stripped of their false numbers and showing genuine Milice plates, would drive sedately back in convoy to the motor pool in Dijon. After which a third Citroën, disguised by García as a taxi, was to return them to Beaune.

That, in any case, was the plan.

The most extraordinary thing was that, point by point, detail by detail, it worked precisely as Riordan had organized it.

Back in Beaune they holed up with the prostitute friend of Zabrisky's barmaid contact, where Frenchie Delorme, long recovered from his temporary KO, had his head wound dressed by the obliging prison doctor and was fitted out with a less noticeable suit of clothes.

All Riordan had to do now was spirit himself and four fugitives, one of them an escaped convict, clandestinely out of occupied France.

9

Frenchie Delorme was not in fact a Frenchman but a Québecois who had worked as a minder for the Purple Gang in Detroit during the 'booze wars' of the Prohibition era. He was a powerful, thickset man with long sideburns and gold teeth glinting among the stubble covering the lower half of his face. Grey hairs sprouted from the open neck of a lumberjack shirt Zabrisky had found for him in a local clothing store.

Marooned in Paris at the outbreak of war, Frenchie had soon found outlets for his multiple talents among the criminal fraternity of Belleville and Montmartre. Riordan had met him soon after the city surrendered to the Germans in the summer of 1940. At that time, soldiers from the Wehrmacht were paid in scrip, a government IOU which could be exchanged for French francs at an artificially high exchange rate, with the result that everything in France, even luxury items, seemed incredibly cheap. The most modest non-commissioned officer could live like a prince.

Sexy Parisian dresses and lingerie, unobtainable in Hitler's Germany for years, were among the most popular lines bought and sent home to wives and girlfriends by off-duty occupiers, even at the huge mark-ups slammed on the goods by profiteering shopkeepers. And it was here that Delorme first made his own mark.

Riordan met him by chance in a Pigalle bar. Along with his watered-down bock, Frenchie was minding a stack of shallow cardboard boxes emblazoned with the word 'Sexorama' in gold script. 'A snappy, fast-selling line in negligées,' he confided later. 'Manufacturers: F. Delorme Ltd. The material fell off the back of a lorry; the garments are rushed out by kids earning nought francs an hour in five sweatshops I have in Belleville and La Villette; and the guys in grey snap them up faster than I can shift the stuff in.' He grinned. "Course, the fact that I happened across a bunch of Schiaparelli labels may have helped some.'

Subsequently, Frenchie had branched out into the supply of illegal petrol, raided from German dumps; German small arms; and otherwise unobtainable foodstuffs. He became in fact one of the city's leading BOFs (the letters stood for 'Beurre, Oeufs, Fromage' – butter, eggs and cheese – the rationed items in shortest supply). But while his black-market activities appeared to leave him untroubled by the authorities, an aptitude for forgery was less kindly viewed. It was a matter of false passports for Jews and a production line of permits to cross the demarcation line into unoccupied France which had landed him in prison.

'Neither the Germans nor the French can conceivably connect the springing of Frenchie,' Riordan told his team, 'with a neutral reporter whose Paris flat is staked out by the Gestapo because he seems to have misbehaved in Holland. I reckon we can safely take it for granted they'll assume springing Frenchie was an underworld exploit.'

'For sure,' Van Eyck agreed.

'So what would they expect a freed ex-con to do?'

'Make it to the unoccupied zone as fast as possible,' said Zabrisky.

'Right. We're very near the demarcation line here; they'll treble security at every crossing post and double patrols all along the line – especially with Frenchie's history of phoney permits.'

'So what's the plan, mate?' Frenchie himself asked. 'Back to Paris and lie low until the heat's off?'

Riordan shook his head. 'That's the second thing they'd expect you to do,' he said. 'If there's no sign of you switching zones, they'll comb the capital from top to bottom: the Krauts won't like the idea of a brilliant forger on the loose.'

'And so?'

'So we don't go south to Vichy; we don't head north for Paris. We take a discreet trip in an easterly direction: we have a date in Switzerland.'

Frenchie's seamed, weather-beaten face wrinkled into a smile; the shrewd, dark eyes gleamed. 'Fine by me,' he said. 'I have some bank accounts there. I can draw myself some loot.'

'You won't need to use your own money,' Riordan told him. 'Not if you're coming with us to Finland.'

'Be your age,' Frenchie said. 'Of course I'm coming with you to Finland!'

Heavy rain continued throughout the day of the jailbreak. By the time it was dark, a chilly wind blowing in from the east had chased away the low clouds, but scattered showers fell occasionally from a bank of altostratus moving southwards at a higher altitude.

Riordan welcomed the breeze, but wished it was strong enough to blow away the upper layer of clouds too. For the meeting in Switzerland had to be preceded by another date, an arrangement made with Huefer before he left Paris, which couldn't be altered however late the schedule was running. And for this prior engagement to be successful a clear sky was necessary.

The final stage of the journey, in fact, was to be by aeroplane.

It was between seventy-five and eighty miles from Beaune to the Swiss border, and the last part of the route ran through the so-called 'Forbidden Zone' – the southern extension of Alsace, from which the entire French population had been expelled. The border between this strip and the rest of occupied France was policed as severely as the demarcation line, with an even stronger

German military presence to discourage the thousands of displaced persons who were trying constantly to creep back to their homes. And even if the zone could be secretly entered and crossed, there was still the frontier itself to be negotiated. Riordan and Huefer had decided that this double hazard, added to the uncertainty of finding a way through the Vosges mountains, would be asking too much of the group. An aerial leap-frog skipping the last few miles had therefore been organized.

The rendezvous was a farm including several large fields in the western foothills of the Vosges. The landing zone would be shown to them – and marked out for the pilot – by members of a local Resistance group. Riordan had stopped himself asking if they were local partisans or SOE agents parachuted secretly into France. Uncertainty about the identity of his employers was part of the 'need to know' routine: if he or any of his own group fell into German hands, the less they knew, the less they could tell. The airlift would solve a lot of problems – and, after all, getting the nucleus of his team out of France was no more than a preliminary to the actual mission – but there were still almost fifty post-curfew miles to cover before contact was made.

The first leg of the journey, to get them out of the sensitive area around Beaune, would in fact be after dark but before the curfew. Safety in numbers, Riordan felt, particularly if most of the numbers using the roads were ordinary citizens going about their business, was the most reliable choice for this initial sortie.

The invaluable García was once again able to supply suitable transport. 'I dare not risk a Milice Citroën a second time,' he told Riordan. 'And any petrol-engined car is sure to be stopped: the Boche will want to see an *Ausweis*, the local *flics* a permit for what they call essential use. We'll go the way the poor buggers living here go – by *gazogène*.'

García himself drove Riordan, Daniels and Zabrisky to St-Jean-de-Losne in an ancient *gazo* taxi. Van Eyck and

Frenchie were concealed – the first because he was foreign, the second because of the tell-tale dressing on his head wound. They made the journey – which was about the limit of a *gazogène*'s range – in a space beneath a stack of shallow crates laden with farm produce, in a relatively modern Berliet flat-bed lorry.

The taxi was stopped twice, once by a Feldgendarmerie patrol on the outskirts of St-Jean, and again by local police in the centre. Zabrisky and Daniels showed their own papers: they were going to see distant relatives at a wedding reception on the far side of town; Riordan – hoping he was far enough from Paris not to be on any local wanted list – produced his press card and accreditation. Once again he was a neutral journalist researching the way the French lived under the Occupation. The strategem appeared to lend credence to the story told by the others, for each time the taxi was waved on without comment.

The lorry with the farm produce was not stopped at all.

As it happened, there was a wedding reception – García was good on the details – on the other side of town, at an *auberge* on the road to Trouhans and Champdôtre. About forty guests were crammed into a small dining-room strewn with home-made paper streamers above a litter of empty bottles. Most of them, anxious to be home before curfew, were preparing to leave. But the groom, flushed and slightly drunk in a tight blue suit, his giggling bride, and half a dozen guests were still dancing among the crushed bouquets to the music of an accordion wielded by the *patron*. Riordan collected his companions together among the bicycles and carts and *gazogènes* in the car park behind the inn. They had a little more than a mile to walk before they reached the next stage on García's itinerary: a car dump from which a partisan would drive them, after midnight, to the farm in the Vosges.

This was the most dangerous part of the journey, because they would have to carry openly the arms which had been hidden with Van Eyck and Frenchie under the crates in the lorry. And they were very near the demarcation line, which veered sharply here towards Seurre and the north-east.

They tagged on behind a dozen departing guests, tipsily singing as they staggered away northwards along the country road. The rain had stopped again but the wind had freshened. One or two stars showed between the drifts of cloud.

The handguns were safely stowed in waistbelts and pockets, but there was nothing they could do with the three machine-pistols and the carbine but carry them slung or at the trail.

Three hundred yards from the *auberge*, when the strains of the accordion had faded and the singing of the party in front had died away to an occasional bawdy remark greeted by bursts of laughter, the road forked at the entrance to a wood. The wedding party turned left, heading for a hamlet on higher ground. Riordan and his men took the right-hand lane, calling out noncommittal replies as the guests shouted drunken goodnights.

It was on the far side of the wood that the trouble began.

The road sloped across a stretch of open grassland . . . and vanished.

As far as the eye could see in either direction, water covered the flat landscape in a leaden sheet. North of the confluence of the Saône and the Doubs, both rivers had overflowed their banks and flooded the tongue of country separating them. Fifty yards ahead of the fugitives, the road slid gently out of sight beneath the surface.

'Christ!' Riordan said.

What was left of the moon sailed out between two banks of cloud.

A breeze ruffled the water. Fleeting gleams from the minuscule wavelets rippled shorewards. In the wan light, they could see lines of trees, sentinel-straight above the

pewter flood water, stretching skywards like the spars
of sunken ships. Directly ahead, perhaps a mile away,
perhaps more, the land shook itself free of the inundation
and rose towards a line of low hills.

'That's where the dump is, at the foot of those hills,'
García said.

'How else can we get to it?' Riordan demanded.

The mechanic shrugged, then shook his head. 'You can
go south to St-Aubin and double back – if you don't mind
crossing the demarcation line twice, once in each direction
– or you can head for Auxonne, in the north. But by the
time you get back to the dump that means a detour of about
twenty kilometres. That's why I chose the place, because
it's on this isolated road, with no other access nearby.'

'And where exactly is the dump – from here?'

García pointed across the water. 'Straight ahead. At the
foot of those hills. It can't be more than a kilometre from
the far shore.'

'Very well,' Riordan said. 'We'll go across.'

'You mean swim? *Wade?* It can't be very deep, but one
can hardly . . .' Van Eyck began.

'We'll build a raft,' Riordan said.

'You want us to cut down one large tree or lash together
several small ones?' Zabrisky asked sardonically.

'You want to keep your eyes open,' Riordan said.
'Always. A hundred yards back, there was a stretch where
the road has been resurfaced – probably with chips from
Frenchie's quarry, spread on melted tar. There was a stack
of drums on the verge; they looked like oil drums, but
my money is on the tar. If the drums are empty, we're in
business.'

They hurried back. 'How long will your partisans wait,
if we don't show up on time?' Riordan asked García as
they neared the drums.

'Until an hour before dawn. No longer. They have to get
back under cover.'

'That should do,' Riordan said. 'The plane will come

at four-thirty. If no signals are showing, there's a fall-back flight an hour later. We'll try for that . . . if we're lucky here.'

There were a dozen drums in the stack. Five of them were empty. 'We'll take four,' Riordan decided. 'It'll be a near thing, with six of us aboard, but an odd number makes it twice as difficult to lash up.'

'If one can find something to lash,' Van Eyck said.

A dilapidated two-wheel trailer with a tow-bar had been left in the long grass at the far end of the roadworks. There was a coil of towing rope on the tarry floor, but it was only long enough to lash together two of the drums. 'We need a lot more,' Riordan said. 'To fasten together the other two, and then secure each pair to the other. Daniels, there's a broken-down gate at the entrance to the wood. The field beyond it looked unused, but there's probably a one- or two-strand wire fence around it. Take Piet with you and see if you can liberate a few yards.'

'You don't happen to have a pair of wire-cutters on you?' Daniels asked.

'No. You'll have to work it back and forth until it breaks.'

'And I thought I was going for a ride in an aeroplane,' the Romany complained.

'Don't beef,' Riordan said. 'Even in fun. It can be catching, and before you know what's happened, it's for real.' With Zabrisky, he took the rope and rolled two of the drums through the grass to the water's edge. Van Eyck and Daniels vanished into the darkness of the wood.

It was difficult work, and exasperating, manoeuvring the rope around curved surfaces in a near darkness only occasionally brightened by moonlight. Riordan swore as he barked his knuckles for the third time, and turned away from the drums. 'Frenchie,' he said, 'how's the head?'

'Throbbing like fuck, to tell the truth. Feels like there was a guy in there, trying to beat his way out with a sledgehammer.'

'You had a tough day. Especially mentally, not knowing what the hell was going to happen. Relax. Sit down and take a rest.'

'I don't want to cop out. That's not my style.'

'You won't be copping out: there's something you can do sitting down.'

'Tell me.'

'The trailer. Sit down beside it and deflate the tyres. Then roll them off the rims and take out the inner tubes. Blow them up again yourself as hard as you can, and we'll add them to the raft for extra buoyancy.'

'Good thinking,' Frenchie said. He walked, a little unsteadily, to the trailer.

Fifteen minutes later, Daniels and Van Eyck returned with two coils of fencing wire. 'Stiff as all getout,' Daniels said. 'You have to use both hands and both bloody *shoulders* to bend the bastard! There's an old hen run in the field: we unravelled some chicken wire too – for the tricky bits.'

Riordan approved. 'Now we can really get to work.'

'Now she be almost finished,' Van Eyck said later, 'how do we power her across? All paddling?'

Riordan shook his head. It was bright moonlight now, and the rising wind threshed the upper branches of the trees in the wood with a sound like rolling surf. 'We do like the kids in Oxford University,' he said. 'We pole her over.' He nodded towards the shadowed side of the road where it emerged from the wood. There was a temporary road sign there which they hadn't noticed before: a rectangular board, painted white, supported on a rounded stake driven into the ground.

Zabrisky walked across and began to wrestle the stake out of the earth, and as it came free he twisted it so that moonlight fell across the face of the notice. He laughed, turning it again so that the others could see the message.

In dark red letters on the white ground, they read: 'Warning: Flooding Ahead!'

'Now they tell us!' Zabrisky said.

When the unwieldy raft was lashed together to Riordan's satisfaction, with an inflated inner tube on either side, they carried it to the water's edge. It floated all right, but by the time the six of them had climbed aboard, together with the weapons, and huddled together on the quadruple curve of the drums, it had settled very low in the water, moving sluggishly as Riordan took the pole and punted them out.

The moon vanished behind a dark cloud mass, transforming the surface of the flood from silver to lead.

At first the water was very shallow, no more than two or three feet deep, and the pole separated easily from the sodden ground below. Then, suddenly, Riordan could no longer touch bottom, and they had to drift with the minimal current. It was then, as the moon reappeared, that the shooting started.

The first shots came from a knoll emerging from the flood water three hundred yards to the south – a crackle of rifle fire, followed by shouted orders in German that they were too far away to make out.

'*Merde!*' García whispered. 'They must be just this side of the line. They think we're trying to drift across under cover of darkness.'

'If only they knew,' Riordan replied. 'Crossing the line's the last thing we want to do!'

'They'll soon see we're going parallel to their damn line,' Zabrisky said in a low voice.

'Yeah, but they'll figure that's because *they're* there; they'll think we're going to try again further on – and alert patrols all the way along. Which won't help us at all, because we stick pretty close to the border for the next fifteen kilometres.'

'Stay as flat as you can,' Riordan ordered. 'Accurate shooting's difficult in moonlight.' Crouching low, he dipped the pole over the side, but the water was still too deep for him to touch the bottom. The raft, moreover, must have reached a position nearer the original river-bed, for now the current was perceptibly stronger, and they were was being carried directly towards the knoll. 'Hands over the side,' Riordan said, 'and paddle as hard as you can.'

Those of them able to reach the water did their best, but it was impossible to divert the course of the heavy craft, however hard they tried: caught in an eddy, they revolved several times and were then carried inexorably, and with increasing speed, towards the waiting patrol.

The harsh commands were repeated – 'What does he want us to do?' Zabrisky muttered. 'Put on the fucking brakes?' – to be followed at once by another volley of rifle fire. This time the gunners had the range. They could hear bullets hissing into the water; the raft boomed hollowly as two of the drums were hit; then something struck the top of Riordan's pole and wrenched it from his hand. He grabbed desperately, but it floated out of reach and was carried away by the current before he could close his fingers around the smooth shaft.

The moon slid out of sight behind a cloud.

'Over the side,' Riordan whispered in the semi-darkness. 'We're too good a target, hunched up here on top.'

'Too right!' said Daniels. 'Easy as ducks in a fairground sideshow!'

Moving as quietly as they could, they lowered themselves into the water, leaving the weapons in the centre of the raft. 'Grab the sides,' Riordan ordered, 'and kick out with your legs frog fashion, like in the breast-stroke. Piet, you stay up top and give them a couple of bursts next time the moon shows. Then we can use you down here.'

The water was unbelievably cold. 'Fucking *freezing*!' Zabrisky said. 'Christ, you'd think, at this time of year . . .'

'Of course it is,' García said. 'Only a couple of hours ago, it was snow!'

'No talking,' Riordan warned. 'Don't forget how voices carry over water.'

With five pairs of feet thrusting powerfully, the raft

wallowed at last in a direction across the current flow.
'Kick out together,' Riordan whispered. '*One* . . . and *two*
. . . and *three* . . . and *four* . . .!'

Slowly, they got under way. Soon they were free altogether of the drag from the invisible river, nearing the far
side of the flood with each surge.

The half-light brightened and a skein of cloud withdrew
from the moon.

At once the rifles opened fire. But the raft had slid off the
course the gunners were expecting, and the first volley was
wide. At the second, Van Eyck, kneeling up on the drums
with the Garand, loosed off two quick rounds, aiming at
the muzzle flashes. A cry of pain floated across the flood.
Something heavy splashed into the water.

The marksman dropped the carbine and picked up the
Schmeisser. He blasted two flaming bursts in the direction
of the distant patrol, then slid backwards into the water to
join the others.

For a moment there was no response from the Germans.
Seeing the raft stripped of its human cargo, they were
doubtless wondering whether the fugitives were swimming
– or whether, by some miracle, they had eliminated the
whole crew.

Then, quite clearly, Riordan heard the screech of a
field-telephone handle being twirled, and then a rapid-fire
torrent of German. Evidently the patrol commander was
alerting outposts on either side or reporting to base.

The raft was less than a hundred yards from the shore.
But it was becoming increasingly difficult to manoeuvre.
Several slugs from the last volley had pierced the drums
below the surface, and air was bubbling up as the water
gurgled in through the holes. Air hissed out too from one
of Frenchie's inner tubes which had been nicked.

Soon the raft, settling lower every second, would be too
waterlogged, too heavy for the swimmers to move.

Eighty yards from the flood-water limit . . . seventy . . .
slowing, slowing to sixty-five . . . sixty . . . their muscles

were groaning with the effort when Van Eyck, the tallest of them, shouted: 'Hey! Wait! . . . One's foot just touch something! I think . . . yes . . . she is shallow enough! One can walk.'

Gratefully, they lowered their feet and walked. The Dutchman's exclamation had warned the patrol that there were still escapers alive, and they opened fire once more. But Riordan's men were sheltered by the foundering raft, and they manhandled it along with renewed strength, crouched low behind the drums, until it grounded on a submerged tree root and they could grab the weapons and wade hastily ashore.

Seconds later they were in among the saplings of an acacia spinney, and the riflemen of the distant patrol gave up.

'Will they skirt the flood and come after us?' Riordan asked.

'No. They're not allowed to quit the line,' Garcî/fa said. 'Their job is to stop folks crossing it illegally, not to chase them back once they're in the occupied zone. But, like I say, patrols *inside* the zone will have been alerted.'

'OK,' Riordan said. 'Let's go.'

They had drifted quite a way south of the original crossing place. It took them fifteen minutes, hefting their weapons and heavy, sodden clothing across the marshy ground between occasional clumps of trees, before they saw the dull gleam of the road as it slid smoothly out of the water.

'How far?' Riordan asked García.

'Five hundred metres. No more.'

'Right,' said Riordan. 'At the double.' Carrying Van Eyck's machine-pistol, he jogged off along the country road.

Obediently, if a little reluctantly, Van Eyck, Zabrisky and the others followed on behind.

The car dump was at the end of a muddy track just off the road. It was surrounded by a thicket of elms. Skeletal in the light of the moon, stacks of rusty carcasses, saloons and tourers, lorries and vans, rose skywards in gaunt metallic heaps. Stripped bare of seats and doors, engines and wheels, the vehicles in their graveyard shared the anonymity of battlefield dead. There was even a war cemetery of salvaged radiator grilles – neat rows of them from Renaults and Citroëns, from Darracqs and Delages and Delaunay-Bellevilles, from Marendazes and Bugattis and Ballots, leaning like chrome gravestones against the high fence surrounding the yard.

Between two tangles of unidentifiable steel wreckage there was a wooden hut with a tar-paper roof and shuttered windows. A thin sliver of light showed the outline of a door. García approached it and lightly tapped out what must have been a code knock.

The door opened at once to reveal a small office, illuminated by a single oil lamp with a green shade. Riordan saw an unpainted deal desk littered with ledgers and sheets of paper, wooden walls covered by sheaves of bills and invoices clipped to boards hanging from hooks, a yellowing 1938 pin-up calendar advertising an Italian brand of petrol. A pneumatic drill leaned against an unlit iron stove in one corner.

'This is Marc, your chauffeur,' García said. He made no further introduction.

Marc emerged from a haze of pungent Gauloise smoke and shook hands. He was a stocky, bald man wearing workman's blue overalls, with a ruddy complexion and a large black moustache. Riordan guessed his age as about fifty. 'We'd best be going,' Marc said without preamble. 'Come outside and I'll show you the jalopy.' He led the way to the highest stack of wrecks, at the back of the yard. García stayed in the hut to make a phone call.

There was a standpipe, topped by a brass tap, against the tall fence. Beside the pipe, and attached to the wooden stake supporting it, an insulated electrical lead ran down and disappeared into the earth. At the top of the wire was a small button, which Marc pressed.

They heard a heavy click, followed by a whir of concealed machinery. To their astonishment, a whole section of the stack started to move: a dozen small saloons, a smashed delivery van and part of an iron traction engine had been artfully welded together into a single impenetrable mass, which swung out sideways to reveal a small garage housing just one car. The top of the garage was buried beneath another mound of wrecks and a heap of twisted chassis and crumpled mudguards buttressed each side.

'Took me damn near two years to build,' Marc said proudly, pleased with the exclamations of surprise and approval from Riordan's team. 'Had to be reinforced, you see, because of the weight.' He went into the garage and flickered a switch. The gasps were louder still when dazzling light from a naked electric bulb allowed them to see the car.

It was a beautiful Delahaye Grand Tourer, with a laid-back, shield-shaped radiator, headlights faired into the long, sweeping front wings, spatted rear wheels and an elegant sloping tail. The gleaming coachwork, beige for the body, chocolate brown for the roof and wings, was in showroom condition.

'Good God!' Riordan said. 'What a beauty! But you're not . . .? Surely you don't intend driving us through the Vosges in that?'

'Certainly.' Marc was smiling broadly.

'But . . . I mean . . . with all the patrols and spot checks, and such a noticeable machine . . .'

'Exactly. That's why I *can* use it. She's a replica of a special model exhibited at the Paris Motor Show in 1938. And *that* car, with identical colours, belongs to the local *collabo* governor. I only drive her at night, wearing the same uniform as the governor's chauffeur . . . and the buggers simply salute and wave me through!'

'Man, you sure got some nerve,' Frenchie said admiringly. 'What if His Excellency goes visiting the night you're out?'

'He doesn't. I have inside information on his movements. One of the housemaids. An enthusiast in the sack, with a taste for silk stockings and . . . shall we say imported goods? Tonight, for instance, there's a reception for German officers, their ladies and other racially acceptable persons at the governor's mansion. He'll be there until the last guest's gone.'

'And *this* Delahaye?'

'Some of you will have to squash in the boot. If anyone sees those sitting in the back, they'll assume you're guests I've been instructed to drive home.'

'Well,' Riordan said, 'this is certainly one drive I shall enjoy!'

'Let's go then,' Marc said. 'We're too late already for the first flight, and we'll have to give it a bit of boot to make the second.'

He eased himself into the garage, opened the coach-built driver's door and slid behind the wheel. He drove out and parked beside the hut. The engine of the long, low, streamlined coupé was virtually silent.

Riordan directed Zabrisky, Frenchie and Daniels into the luggage space, climbing into the rear seats himself with Van Eyck. In these circumstances, foreign nationality could be an asset rather than a disadvantage.

Marc went into the hut. He came out again two minutes later, wearing a high-buttoned brown tunic and a brown uniform cap with a shiny black peak. García followed him, a dejected expression creasing his face.

'Something wrong?' Riordan asked.

García nodded. 'Very wrong. I just called Dijon. They're on to the trick with the Milice Citroëns. God knows how. But there's a Gestapo priority call out for me and . . . well, I dare not go back.'

Riordan reflected briefly. The man had been an invaluable ally over the past two days, and an efficient, trustworthy organizer. Was there any valid reason why the team shouldn't include *two* members who were experts in the automotive line? Certainly the budget he had been allotted was sufficiently elastic to allow for a supernumerary.

'Why don't you earn yourself some real money and stay with us,' Riordan suggested.

For the first two miles, the Delahaye purred almost at a walking pace along the country lanes, showing no lights at all. 'Whatever happens,' Marc explained, 'I don't want the car associated, even indirectly, with the dump or its immediate area.'

Once on a main road, with the masked headlights on, they were flagged down three times, each time at the exit from a village. And each time, as soon as the car was recognized, they were waved on with a smile and a salute.

The real trouble came when they were skirting the southern fringe of the Forbidden Zone, in the Vosges foothills. No roadblock this time. No smiling sentry with a rifle slung over his shoulder. Just a motorcycle combination parked by the roadside, and two Feldgendarmerie NCOs with Schmeisser machine-pistols held at the ready.

One of the soldiers approached the driver's door. 'Your papers.'

'This is the governor's car,' Marc said loftily.

'I can see that. I must ask to see your papers.'

'These gentlemen – representatives of neutral press agencies – have been guests at a reception. I have been instructed to drive them to their hotel in Montbarrey.'

'Possibly. My instructions are to check the papers of anyone passing this way after curfew. No matter who they are. I repeat: show me . . .'

'Very well, very well,' Riordan interrupted. He leaned across from the white-hide rear seat and switched on the courtesy light. He held up his accreditation in the middle of the car, so that the illumination fell across the photograph and Propaganda Abteilung stamp.

The NCO poked his steel-helmeted head through the open window to peer at the document. He was bringing up his free hand to reach for it when Marc wound up the window with frenzied speed, catching him beneath the chin and effectively trapping him between the upper door frame and the glass.

Riordan had already produced his Walther behind the front seats. Before the German could cry out, he shot him, left-handed, through the eye.

Marc shoved open the door and lowered the window to allow the body to drop into the road.

The second NCO had brought up his machine-pistol at the sound of the shot, firing a burst which shattered the windscreen in front of the passenger seat. But Van Eyck, sitting there a tenth of a second before, had already burst open that door and hurled himself out sideways, firing a single shot from the heavy-calibre revolver as he fell.

Drilled immediately below the brim of his helmet, the man hit the ground at the same time as his dead companion.

'All right,' Riordan snapped. 'First we must hide the . . . evidence. Then, if we get stopped again, we explain the broken windscreen by saying we ran into an ambush – some dastardly partisans were attacking a German patrol.'

The members of the patrol were carried up the road a hundred yards to a narrow bridge spanning a stream, and left on a ledge beneath the bridge's single arch. The men in the boot, glad to stretch their legs after the fraught few minutes terminated by the shots, wheeled the motorcycle combination behind an abandoned cowshed in a field by the stream.

Thirty minutes later the Delahaye arrived at the target farm.

No lights showed from the group of low buildings huddled in a wooded hollow below the road. Between two outhouses, wooden gates hanging crookedly from rusted hinges stood open. Marc drove through and stopped in a cobbled yard. He switched off the engine and remained silently behind the wheel.

Here in the hills the moonlight was bright. They could see the branches of trees behind the farmhouse tossing in the breeze. Farmyard smells filtered into the car. Nearby an owl hooted. The only other sound was the stealthy tick of contracting metal as the engine cooled.

Someone tapped on the coupé's rear window.

Riordan started. Two men stood by the car. Noiselessly, they had materialized from the dense shadow at one side of a barn. Nobody had heard them approach; no fleeting shape had disturbed the bone-white stillness of the moonlit yard.

Marc turned off the headlights and got out of the car. The fugitives heard a short exchange in low voices, then he leaned back in. 'You must come now. We have ten minutes. And, please . . . no questions, no answers.'

They stood in the yard, the men released from the boot gratefully stretching cramped limbs once more. The partisans who were to mark out the landing area remained in the shadow, indistinct figures in nondescript clothes, with peaked caps pulled low over their eyes. 'The plane was on time,' the taller one told Riordan. 'He circled the hillside twice, and then, seeing there were no flares, flew away again towards the east.'

'As planned,' Riordan murmured. 'But he'll be back.'

'Once more, yes. We received radio confirmation that the fall-back flight will proceed as planned. The pilot will . . .'

The Resistance man stiffened, breaking off in mid-sentence.

Over the clucking of chickens, awakened in their roosts by the activity in the yard, they heard the distant, rackety beat of an engine. 'That's a Boche scout car,' the shorter partisan said. 'I'd know that sound anywhere.'

'Right,' García agreed. 'A flat four, air-cooled. Originally designed to power Hitler's planned "People's Car".'

The distinctive exhaust note grew louder. The vehicle was approaching. The men in the yard froze still as statues.

They heard the driver shift down. The noise of the engine and gearbox rose up the scale. The scout car was climbing the hill that led to the farm.

'All into the shadow. Quick!' hissed one of the partisans.

The members of the group melted away, leaving the gleaming Delahaye bold as a showroom model in the moonlight.

With the noise of the engine now came voices, bursts of laughter, two men singing tipsily. Clearly the armoured scout was carrying at least half a dozen passengers.

The road ran along the lip of the hollow sheltering the farm. If any of the soldiers happened to be looking down and saw that coupé . . .

Riordan put the thought from his mind. Headlight beams fanned the lower branches of trees on the far side of the road. Suddenly the scout car burst into view from behind the gable of the farmhouse. Uniformed soldiers crammed the open rear. He held his breath, watching it race across the gap and vanish behind the roof of a barn.

He was releasing a sigh of relief when there was a squeal of brakes. The scout car had stopped a short way beyond the farm. Over the idling engine, German voices argued.

A metallic snick – a hammer cocked? a slide pulled back? a bolt pushed home? – broke the anguished silence of the shadowed yard.

There was a lull in the guttural German. Very faintly, Riordan heard the sound of splashing. And then the voices again.

'Why in God's name does Klaus have to choose this God-forsaken spot to take a leak?'

'Ersatz French beer!'

'He can hold his drink but he can't hold his . . .'

'Klaus! For pity's sake!'

'Hey! That farm back there . . . the old man's got the prettiest daughter! Kid can't be more than sixteen. What say we wake them up and show the girl a length or two of Fatherland cock?'

'Don't even think about it. You know we have to be back in camp by dawn.'

'But we have a *duty* . . . show them the virtues of the New Europe!'

'Shut *up*, Gerhardt. Pack it in.'

'*Klaus!* Man's like a bloody horse!'

And then, drunkenly, more laughter and, predictably: '*Deutschland, Deutschland, über alles . . .*'

A door slammed metallically and the scout car drove away.

In the farmyard, nine pairs of lungs released held breath in a single sigh of relief.

'Come,' the tall partisan said. 'Now we must run.'

He led the way through a gate at the far end of the yard and across a field planted with a low-growing crop. It was only when he heard the soft chirr behind him of the Delahaye's electric starter that Riordan realized that they had neither thanked nor said goodbye to their ingenious and daring angel from the scrapyard.

The partisans ran at a steady jog through two more fields. Beyond, a stretch of grassland, perhaps twenty acres in extent, rose gently to a wooded ridge.

The drone of an approaching aircraft was audible now in the eastern sky.

'Wait here,' the shorter partisan said. He ran off, sprinting this time, with his companion. Every thirty yards or so, each man would crouch down momentarily, and when he straightened up to run on, a wavering flame would be rising from the ground behind him. Oily, petrol-soaked rags stuffed into buried flowerpots were acting as an improvised flare-path – and a come-in-please signal – for the rescue pilot.

The plane skimmed the rolling, conifer-packed crests of

the Vosges and glided down towards the farm. It circled the field twice, flew away for half a mile, then flattened out for an approach.

Watching the gaunt, mosquito-like silhouette coming in at no more than fifty feet above the ground, Riordan grinned in admiration. The choice of transport was shrewd. The machine was a Fieseler Fi-156 Storch, a short-range observation and artillery spotter. Its two immediate advantages were that it had the shortest landing and take-off distances of any plane in the world, and that, being German, with a very distinct shape, it was less likely to get shot at, crossing the Forbidden Zone in bright moonlight.

The Storch touched down, bounced twice on the rough grass, and taxied towards them. The roar of the throttled-back 240hp Argus engine sounded frighteningly loud in the country landscape.

A high-wing monoplane with a glassed-in cabin, the machine stood awkwardly on the tall struts of its spidery fixed undercarriage. As it stopped by the waiting group, the pilot opened a fabric and Perspex door and leaned out to call: 'How many are you?'

'Seven,' Riordan shouted. And then, remembering Marc had gone: 'No, six.'

'Christ! This kite normally carries a crew of two. Four top weight. Why does nobody tell a bod these things?'

'Any chance of your taking four, and coming back for the other two?'

'Not Pygmalion likely, old boy. It'll be light in half an hour, and we're flying with Swiss markings. A shade dicey, if you see what I mean.'

'So what do you suggest?'

The pilot shrugged. 'We'll have to rise above it – in every sense,' he said resignedly. 'Pile in, pile in . . . but I warn you, you'll either be warped back into the old foetal position, or sitting on each other's knees in a highly enforced intimacy. If I can coax the crate off the ground, that is!'

Riordan sat in the spotter's seat next to the pilot. Van Eyck and Frenchie, the two biggest men, took the occasional seats behind, with García and Daniels on their laps. Zabrisky, the smallest, cramped himself into the narrow space among the wires and conduits and controls leading down the fuselage to the tailplane.

No further words were exchanged with the Resistance men. Raising hands in farewell, they melted into the shadows of a birch spinney, as featureless and anonymous as when they came.

The pilot kicked the rudder and swung the plane around. Lumbering over the sloping pastureland, the Storch regained the place where he had originally touched down. He turned into the wind. And then, giving the motor everything it had, lurched back down the grassy runway with the throttle fully open.

The little plane seemed painfully reluctant to gather speed.

Riordan knew a Storch could remain airborne, in neutral wind conditions, at speeds as low as thirty miles per hour. But taking off was something else.

The wooded ridge was agonizingly near when at last the overloaded machine staggered into the air, dipped, and then soared away over the rolling green pinewoods below.

As they banked over the darkly moonlit countryside to turn east, Riordan saw, looking down through the canted Perspex, that the lights of their temporary landing strip had already been extinguished.

Fifteen minutes later, the moonlight paled beneath the dazzling glare of illuminations outlining the street plan of neutral Geneva.

10

In his small operations room in the Citadel, Captain Seamus McPhee O'Kelly frowned heavily as he sifted through the concertinaed rolls of teletype spewed out by the printer during the night. There had been a heavy raid just before midnight, and the docks were still ablaze.

All the news was bad. German and Italian bombers continued to pulverize Malta: most of the Spitfires sent to reinforce the island's tiny Hurricane defence group had been shot down or destroyed on the ground. In North Africa, although violent sandstorms had halted any land activity by Rommel's desert army, the besieged city of Tobruk had again suffered intense bombardment by artillery and air forces. Burma was clearly lost, and the Royal Navy had withdrawn from the Indian Ocean to seek refuge in the Gulf. To counter seductive propaganda by the Japanese, India itself had been promised independence after the war.

In the Philippines, after the murderous attacks decimating Mindanao and Bataan, 76,000 Allied prisoners of war had been ruthlessly forced into the inhuman 'March of Death' to San Fernando, many thousands of whom had already died from privations and dysentery.

The Black Sea port of Sebastopol, southern bastion of the Russian front, was liable to fall into the hands of besieging Germans any day.

O'Kelly shook his head. Murphy's law was really at work here.

Commander Lang sauntered into the operations room. 'Just got back from MoI,' he drawled. 'There's something

118

of a flap on because Roosevelt has sent two high-echelon Yanks to see the Old Man.'

'They come and they go,' O'Kelly said. 'What kind of a flap?'

'The kind that has Admiral Thompson doing his nut. Red Memos and Dead Stops flying about all over the shop.'

O'Kelly raised enquiring eyebrows. 'Why should a top-brass visit by a couple of Allies disturb the head of the Ministry of Information's Press Censorship division? As I said, it happens all the time.'

Lang hitched himself up on to a steel desk and sat swinging one elegant leg. 'This is rather special brass,' he said. 'George Marshall, the US Army Chief of Staff, and the President's personal adviser, Harry Hopkins. They've brought a plan which they want us to evaluate.'

'What kind of plan? What are we talking about?'

'We're talking basically about the fact that Stalin is getting more and more querulous, demanding that we open a second front in Europe, to draw away German forces from Russia and ease the pressure on Moscow. Since he's been getting no change out of Winston, he's turned his guns on Franklin D.'

O'Kelly grinned. 'Divided they fall,' he said. 'And this plan?'

'It's a detailed project for an invasion of the European mainland, maybe some time next year. But not, as might be expected, in the Low Countries or even Norway – in France, the hottest, most heavily defended, most obvious choice of all. Kind of a double-bluff thing. Apparently it's been worked out by a fifty-two-year-old regular army lieutenant-colonel, chap with the odd name of Dwight Eisenhower.'

'Well, there's nothing like starting at the bottom of the ladder,' O'Kelly said. 'So I suppose Thompson's told his censors to slam a Dead Stop on everything?'

'The lot. No British newspaper, no radio programme,

no newsreel, no story cabled out by a foreign press correspondent is to contain any reference to second fronts or invasions; no features on possible strategy is to be linked in any way with the names of Marshall and Hopkins or their visit here. That kind of thing.'

'And the best of luck,' O'Kelly said. 'But the press boys, the foreign ones, will get around it somehow. They always do. But talking of Norway reminds me: there's a couple of Dead Stops I want the Admiral to slap on certain references on *our* behalf.'

'Such as?'

'Other than official figures of ships lost, no references whatsoever to Arctic convoys for at least the next ten days; no speculative articles or 'think pieces' on secret weapons for the same period, and no reminders of Hitler's threats in that direction. And, come to think of it, a stop on any articles on the general situation that focus on the extreme north of Europe.'

'I'll see to it,' Lang said. 'You don't think any of the ace foreign correspondents have actually got on to our . . . conspiracy . . . do you?'

'No I don't, frankly. But any of those references might, quite innocently and coincidentally, give the Germans the idea that *we* had got on to something. I don't want to give their intelligence analysts the faintest hint of our interest in the area. As they have something to hide up there, they'll be specially sensitive, alert to read too much into *any* mention.'

'Right,' said Lang. 'You're off to give this man Riordan a final brief this afternoon, aren't you?'

O'Kelly nodded. 'One of the ATA pilots ferrying a Stirling out to Cairo is giving me a lift to Lisbon,' he said. 'After that it's Switzerland again.'

'You'll have a lot to organize there.'

O'Kelly nodded. 'Logistics are the problem. His men have to have the right clothes, weapons, equipment. Transport in the right direction. Means of communicating with

ACTION IN THE ARCTIC

us without involving London . . . all of it underwritten as far as possible by this department, but with no overt link that anyone could ever unearth. Do you have any final intel I should pass on to Riordan?'

'Just a couple of minor things that came in this morning,' Lang said. 'Both a shade enigmatic, as it happens. But they *might* be relevant.'

'Fire away.'

'One came via SOE; the other's from the Ultra deciphering chaps out at Bletchley. They report continuing very heavy radio traffic between Berlin and Narvik, and Berlin and the North Cape area. Well, we knew that. But now they add that the decoded messages incorporate increasingly frequent references to something or someone referred to only by the initials WVB. Up to the present there's no elaboration or explanation – just the letters and the fact that they're used often.'

'Interesting,' O'Kelly said. 'I'll pass it on. And SOE?'

'One of their agents reports seeing an unusual number of fire engines heading for the region we're interested in.'

'Fire engines?'

'Yes. The big tenders. I think they're referred to professionally as turntables – the ones with the brass bell and the long telescopic ladders lying along the top.'

'How very odd,' O'Kelly said. 'What on earth is there to catch fire up there? It's too far north for forests. I mean, very well, most of the buildings are wooden . . . but an *unusual* number! That's most mysterious!'

'Agreed,' Lang said. 'But like the initials, there's no explanation so far.'

'Also,' O'Kelly said, 'there's the question of those ladders. Such buildings as there are in Lapland, being made of wood, rarely exceed one or two storeys. Again, if there is a base and they are afraid of some possible conflagration that could be caused by a mishap with explosives, that too would presumably be at or near ground level. So what is it that firemen might wish to climb to?'

121

'And why would it require a *number* of fire engines?'
Lang added.

'Perhaps Riordan will be able to tell us,' O'Kelly said.
'But something tells me . . . I don't know. Perhaps because
it is so inexplicable, something tells me that these fire
engines may prove a great deal more important than
we think.'

He slid open the bottom drawer of his desk and produced a bottle of gin. 'Something else tells me – perhaps
more importantly than the news about the fire engines –
that we have just time for a couple of large pinkers before
we tool off to Scotts for that new freshwater crayfish bisque
that Bernard is so proud of . . .'

11

Riordan had recruited the two remaining members of his team before O'Kelly arrived in Switzerland.

Alessandro Aletti, his original choice as engineering expert, had much in common with José Manuel García, the co-opted mechanic from Dijon. Aletti had fled the Mussolini regime in Italy and found refuge in Spain; García had fled the Franco regime in Spain after the civil war and found refuge in France. Each of them was a wizard with any kind of automotive machinery, from aircraft engines to motor cars to powerboats. But whereas García had concentrated on the nuts and bolts of the business, maintaining, repairing and selling run-of-the-mill cars and lorries, Aletti was a specialist in the more highly tuned power units. He had worked as a mechanic for the world-famous racing driver Tazio Nuvolari; he had been part of the team designing the revolutionary Bimotore twin-engined Alfa-Romeo which won the 1937 Tunis Grand Prix, beating the all-conquering Mercedes and Auto-Unions from Germany. As an apprentice, he had worked on Italy's Macchi-Castoldi racing float-plane – intended to win the 1931 Schneider Trophy air race, but withdrawn when Mussolini's industrial spies reported that the Supermarine S-6A, prototype of the Spitfire, was faster.

Perhaps the most striking thing about Aletti, however, was his language. His family was Jewish. He had spent two years as a teenager with immigrant relatives in New York, and he had returned to Italy with an English that was fluent, but as idiosyncratic – and as idiomatic – as anything to be heard in the city's Seventh Avenue garment district, or read in the works of Jerome Weidman.

Beverley Hills, the second gunnery expert, was in his own way as noticeable linguistically. His speech patterns, laced with slang as racy as anything favoured by the fighter pilots of the RAF, delivered in a distinctive 'Oxford' drawl, could have come straight from the pages of P.G. Wodehouse.

Riordan found him in Basle, in a garret overlooking the slow curve of the Rhine, where he was trying to earn his living as a painter. Radical as many upper-class English eccentrics, Hills had renounced country and county life after his stint with the Husqvarna arsenal in Sweden, preferring a vagabond existence in Europe to a social existence conditioned by hunt balls, grouse shooting and the London 'Season'. For some time now he had been telling himself that he really ought to return to Britain and enlist, but had never actually found a valid way to get there. Perhaps next month he would be able to work out a method.

Meanwhile, Riordan's offer, with its raffish, swash-buckling overtones and its promise of danger coupled with daring, was too tempting to refuse. 'Battle, murder and sudden death, old lad,' he enthused. 'Just my jolly old line – especially with a touch of the old oof thrown in!'

He left with Riordan the same day. Meanwhile Aletti had been tracked down in Barcelona, the Catalan capital with the most liberal outlook in Franco's Spain. A brief phone call brought him to Switzerland within forty-eight hours.

The meeting with Huefer took place in a small hotel in Fribourg, capital of one of the larger *cantons* in the south-west, but sufficiently small to be ignored by the coterie of international spies, confidence tricksters and intelligence chiefs intriguing in Geneva, Berne and Lausanne.

There was an additional attraction recommending the

town unreservedly to O'Kelly. The first-class and second-class travel system on Swiss railways extended to the food available to those using it – and the woman who ran the first-class restaurant on the upper floor of Fribourg station offered, in O'Kelly's considered opinion, some of the best cooking in Europe.

Disguised once more in his Swiss persona, he had booked the hotel's largest reception room for a 'conference'. A glance at Riordan and his mercenaries on that first morning, however, convinced him that it would be hard to find a group of men less likely to be taken for European business tycoons.

Apart from the leader himself, whose rangy efficiency would have been acceptable in any company, only two of them would have looked comfortable around a boardroom table. Van Eyck and Hills, each of them a world-class marksman, were curiously alike physically: the Dutchman was tall and fair, with a lock of hair falling over one eye; Hills was tall and dark, also with a lock of hair falling over one eye.

García and Aletti, the mechanical geniuses, shared a visual resemblance too – spare, nut-faced Mediterranean types with a built-in air of total confidence and a certain quiet assurance in the way they used their hands. Frenchie Delorme, the most powerful among them, could have been a champion lumberjack from the Canadian backwoods. Chunky Art Daniels, with his knowing, middle-aged features and bristly ginger hair, was unclassifiable. Zabrisky – there was no getting away from it – looked like a small-time crook.

Seated at the head of the conference table, O'Kelly-Huefer mentally ran the group again: Aletti, Daniels, Delorme, García, Hills, Riordan, Van Eyck and Zabrisky. A Jewish Italian, a stateless gypsy, a French-Canadian, a Spaniard, a renegade Englishman, an Irishman, a Dutchman and a naturalized Frenchman. It would scarcely be possible, O'Kelly thought, to assemble a squad less likely to be associated with any particular belligerent – and even less with the Combined Operations (Security) Executive in Whitehall. Good for Riordan, he thought. Even though his men brought to mind one of those dire smoking-room stories beginning: 'An Englishman, an Irishman and a Jew . . .'

He had a suspicion anyway that the task he was entrusting them to carry out would prove to be fairly unfunny too.

Without preamble, he outlined the mission, detailing the data and deductions which had led to the decision to commission it. He left the table and moved to the wall, pulling down a large-scale map of Scandinavia from a wall-hanger. Using a billiard cue as a pointer, he went over the geographical possibilities a second time. He explained how the interpretation of intelligence reports, radio intercepts and the movements of military traffic on the roads had narrowed down the area in which the base – if there was a base – could be expected to exist. He summarized the activity, constructive and destructive, required by his principals once the base was located.

'Yeah,' someone from the table called out; he thought it was Aletti. 'But what principals? What intelligence reports? What radio? Exactly who are we working for here?'

'You are working for me,' O'Kelly said. 'That is all you need to know. The money has already been deposited, here in Switzerland. Your individual financial arrangements are a matter for yourselves and Colonel Riordan.' He thought somehow that the conferment of an honorary rank on the leader of the expedition lent a certain spurious legitimacy to this most clandestine of operations. Riordan was in fact, according to the dossier, a colonel in the Paraguayan army.

'The most urgent – and in some ways the most difficult – question is the matter of logistics,' O'Kelly said, resuming his place at the table. 'Weapons and supplies can be determined between myself and Colonel Riordan. But how are we going to get you there in the first place?'

'Get one where? In the area of the base?' Van Eyck asked.

'No. It's up to you to pinpoint that area; it's one of the things you are being paid for. Getting you into Finland at all. We have to remember that the country is an Axis satellite: they threw in their lot with the Reich as a way of getting back at the Russians after the armistice imposed on them at the end of the Soviet invasion in 1940. The Allies declared war on Finland at the end of last year.'

'Land us at some deserted spot on the Finnish coastline?' Daniels suggested. 'Not too hard to find: the population density up in the north there is nil.'

O'Kelly laughed. 'Look at the map.' He half-turned in his chair. 'You'd need a German E-boat or an air-sea-rescue launch to give you the speed to avoid the coastal patrols. But look,' he added, pointing, 'even if you got through a hundred miles of Kattegat and another hundred of Skagerrak, even if you squeezed through between the islands of occupied Denmark, you'd still have to pass Kiel, the most heavily defended naval base in Europe. After which you *still* have almost four hundred miles of Baltic before you reach the Gulf of Bothnia . . . and that's blocked by a dense archipelago of Finnish islands. No, don't think *we* haven't thought of it, but the idea's a non-runner.'

'A sub, then?'

'Where can I hire a submarine manoeuvrable enough to escape the German navy?' O'Kelly asked.

'Actually,' Daniels said mildly, 'I was meaning land us from an airplane.'

'Investigated that too. The only machine with both the range and the capacity is a Sunderland flying boat – and that's far too vulnerable to Messerschmitts and Dorniers. Even if it got you there, it would never make the return journey.'

'Just a stray thought, sir and master,' Beverley Hills

put in, 'but would it be on the bally cards to row in Uncle Joe?'

'What do you mean?'

'Well, dash it all, it's stuff he's agog for that's drifting down to Davy Jones every time a ship from an Arctic convoy is lost. It'd be to his advantage if the bloody base was pranged. So why couldn't we put in a chit for a mite of co-operation? What I mean is, let our lot stow away on a merchantman in one of the convoys, and then land with the merchandise at Murmansk.'

'And cross the Russian frontier into Finland?'

'By far the quickest way in. It's less than a hundred miles to Lake Inarf, just across the border. And there we are, practically on the spot.'

O'Kelly was finding it increasingly difficult to disguise the British involvement in the project, and at the same time maintain the credibility of a supposedly civil organization undertaking such an operation. 'Two reasons,' he said. 'In the first place, the insistence of my principals that there must be *no* involvement whatsoever with any of the Allies; and secondly the fact that the Russians, even that far north, are over-sensitive when it comes to the question of their frontiers being crossed. Either way. Even with a *laissez-passer* from Moscow.'

'Yes, old man, but I don't see . . .'

'Surely Sweden's the obvious – the only – choice?' Frenchie interrupted.

'Geographically, yes,' O'Kelly agreed. 'But like our hosts here, the Swedes are very jealous of their neutrality; they don't want to get involved. If a group subsequently shown to be saboteurs was to assemble at the head of the Gulf of Bothnia and cross the frontier into Finland, there'd be hell to pay – especially if anything went wrong. Ditto in the case of a sea crossing: they'd claim that neutrality was violated if a boatload passed through their coastal waters. So far, Sweden has held out against Hitler: No, you cannot lease bases; no, you can't have free passage for troops on the way to northern Norway. But any action that could be interpreted as favouring one belligerent over another might cause the Swedes to change their minds – just to keep the balance even.'

'Apart from which,' Riordan said, 'how the hell are we going to hump weapons and explosives and the rest of our gear secretly up through more than five hundred miles of Swedish forest?'

There was a sudden chorus of suggestions, as everybody tried to talk at the same time.

'All right, all right,' O'Kelly called, quelling the outburst with an uncharacteristic snap of the disciplinarian. 'In fact the decision has already been taken; I just wanted to make sure you were all aware of the problems involved. It saves any grumbling later, with people saying, Oh, but why couldn't we have done it *this* way?' He turned to Beverley Hills. 'In general, lad, your thinking was right. We *are* going to use the convoys, but without the help or knowledge of the Russians ... and not in the way you think.'

12

The weather forecasters in the Met Office had been right
about one thing. There was plenty of cloud on the night
that the Panamanian freighter *Maria Sánchez* detached
herself from the front-runners of convoy PQ-15C and
headed south. Black streamers raced low across the sky
during the two hours of near darkness, blotting out the
stars and hiding the late-rising moon where it hung above
the icy waters of the Barents Sea.

What they omitted to mention was that there would be
a Force Seven gale blowing those clouds in over the pack
ice from the Atlantic.

'Bloody Met men!' Commander Archie Lang said to
Riordan. 'Trust the silly buggers to get it wrong. I mean,
you can actually rely on it!'

The *Maria Sánchez* was loaded with small arms, anti-
aircraft guns, radar equipment and motorcycle combinations for scouts. She had left Iceland along with twenty-six
other merchantmen and an escort of six destroyers, two
submarines, three aerial defence ships and nine smaller
craft. Four cruisers – two American and two British –
and three more destroyers were in close support, and a
task force including cruisers, battleships and the aircraft
carrier *Victorious* covered them fifty miles north-east of
Bear Island.

Nine of the twenty-seven merchantmen in the convoy
had already been lost to enemy action: seven sunk by
submarines and two torpedoed by aircraft.

O'Kelly, left with the entire responsibility of getting
Riordan and his mercenaries into Finland, had stretched

the resources of CO(S)E to the utmost, even rowing in SOE, the Air Transport Auxiliary and various departments of the Royal Navy to overcome difficulties that at first seemed insuperable.

It was O'Kelly who had taken the decision to put them ashore on the wild coast of northern Norway, landing them from the next Arctic convoy heading for Murmansk or Archangel. 'It's hellish rugged, the country you'll have to go through,' he told Riordan. 'But crossing the frontier into Finland should be no big problem, since they're both effectively in Axis hands. It's a hundred miles from the coast to the supposed site of the base . . . but even if we could have got you to the very head of the Gulf of Bothnia, you'd have had twice that distance to cover – the first part of it through more populated areas. Also we can arrange some landfall support from – er – local partisans.'

'As you wish,' Riordan had said. 'You're calling the tune.'

Most of the obstacles following on from O'Kelly's decision related to two priorities: keeping from the mercenaries the fact that they were being ferried and supplied by essentially British personnel; and keeping from the personnel involved the real purpose of the mission and the real identity of those carrying it out.

There was also the inconvenient detail that no ship in any convoy came nearer than 300 miles to the Norwegian coast, so that the concept of 'putting them ashore' itself became a major problem.

Compared with this, the furnishing of supplies and equipment, the transport of Riordan's crew to the convoy, and the explanation of their presence there were minor items.

With the reluctant acquiescence of the RAF, a Polish ATA pilot in plain clothes was detailed to fly them, in a Lockheed Vega with Spanish markings, from Geneva to Lisbon, and then from Lisbon to Shannon. From there, an Irishman who had skippered a Handley Page airliner before the war piloted them in an unmarked Halifax to Reykjavik, where 107 loaded merchantmen waited to be assembled into convoys and sent to Russia.

The choice of a ship registered in Panama was an obvious one, since the crew had no connection with Britain. And for reasons that were equally obvious O'Kelly was denied the collaboration of the Navy escort vessels, which he would much have preferred. Lang, posing as a civilian colleague of Huefer, went on his second Arctic convoy that year – not this time with a watching brief but to supervise the landing of the mercenaries.

They had been instructed to speak to no one during the voyage, and Lang allowed it to be assumed – by them and by anyone aware of their presence – that huge sums in bribes had been dispensed to ensure their passage on the *Maria Sánchez*.

When the ship left the convoy and steamed south, it was not to approach the Norwegian coast, but simply to make sure the next step in the operation was not witnessed by any other vessel. The escort destroyers had been warned that a top-secret cloak-and-dagger operation by combined ops was involved. The *Maria Sánchez* was not to be chased and coaxed back within the protective screen; she would rejoin the convoy later that morning.

On paper the next step was a formality: Riordan and his men would be transferred to a high-powered motor torpedo-boat capable of some forty knots, offloaded a second time a couple of miles from the shore, and allowed to complete the journey in silent, electrically propelled dinghies.

There was no provision, on paper, for a Force Seven gale.

In the grey light of the Arctic morning, Riordan stood with Lang on the starboard wing of the *Maria Sánchez*'s bridge, braced against the dodger as the merchantman pitched and rolled in the steep seas. The convoy was a smudge of smoke teased out along the northern horizon.

'Sorry we couldn't arrange to ship you nearer inshore,' Lang called, raising his voice to make himself heard over the wind moaning around the ship's upper works and shrieking through her aerials. 'We daren't risk separating the vessel from the convoy any longer. She'd be a sitting duck for Fritz's subs if she got left behind.'

If Riordan found it odd that a Swiss businessman – representing, he assumed, a consortium of armaments manufacturers – should choose as his number two the most typical British naval officer imaginable, he had refrained from comment. 'You play the cards you have been dealt,' he replied.

'What's that, old boy?'

'You play the cards . . . I said it's part of the deal.'

'Part of the what?'

'The deal,' Riordan yelled. 'Not to worry.'

'Oh . . . Yes, quite.'

The leader of the expedition screwed up his eyes, squinting out across the waves. 'Any chance . . .' he began, but broke off in mid-sentence as the *Maria Sánchez* buried her bows in a gigantic comber racing crosswise over the swell. The entire hull shuddered as the sea exploded in a burst of white water, swamping the forecastle and swirling over the forward well-deck.

'You were saying?'

'I was wondering if we could hope for an improvement. Any chance of it letting up?'

'It's not as bad as it looks . . . once you're down there,' Lang said.

'It's getting down there that concerns me.'

'How's that again?'

'Can you lower us in this kind of sea?'

'Oh, we'll get you afloat all right,' Lang reassured him. 'No problem there. As for the weather . . .' He staggered to the chartroom, vanished inside, and returned a moment later, shaking his head. 'Freshening to Force Eight,' he reported tersely. 'And there may be rain on the way.'

Riordan smiled wryly. 'Let's hope it's heavy. Less of a reception committee to greet us!'

'What did you say?'

'I said there'd be less people about to spot us arriving,' Riordan shouted over the blustering of the gale.

He hoped he was right. This was the one part of the operation in which his confidence was less than 100 per cent. Until now he had no reason to doubt the efficiency of his employers' arrangements. But – aware as he was of the grave problems involved – he was nevertheless dubious about the outcome of a plan on which he had not been consulted, and over which, at least for the next twenty-four hours, he personally had no control. Success or failure of the entire mission, after all, depended on the smooth running of this initial phase. And smooth – he glanced at the angry sea – was something the landing itself was certainly not going to be!

'Well,' he said to Lang, 'I reckon we ought to get cracking, all right?'

The MTB, which had been battened down amidships, was swung out and lowered from davits. Riordan was certain, watching the deft movements and trained teamwork of the seamen handling the launch, that these were not the normal, regular members of the *Maria Sánchez*'s crew. The expertise with which the powerboat was settled into the raging sea, the accuracy with which the varying freeboard of the hove-to freighter was judged as she rolled, the skill of the men fending off the hull of the launch while it was in mid-air, would have been far beyond the talents of ordinary sailors – even those customarily crewing ocean-going merchantmen.

'We're putting you over with the nets,' Lang told the mercenaries, 'since there's a bit of a breeze blown up. The chaps here will fend off until you're all aboard. After which there's nothing more I can do except wish you the best – the very best – of luck.'

Through an open hatchway in the ship's rusty hull, Riordan saw the white-capped crests sweeping past towards the far-distant land. The MTB, painted battleship grey overall, with no identification marks, looked curiously frail, rising and falling in that wilderness of water. Oh, well . . . his not to reason . . .

Stepping out into the void, he clung, fly-like, to the net draped over the hull while seamen stationed at an open hatch on a lower deck and at the foot of a companion ladder manoeuvred the MTB for the embarkation. The leap from netting to launch was difficult: the relative rise and fall was hard to judge, the space in the MTB's cockpit was limited, and there was a constant drifting apart laterally, due to variations in the size of the waves. A plunge into the grey water hissing between the two hulls was always a scary possibility.

Riordan himself made the jump first, while the members of his team flattened themselves to the netting above. One by one they clambered down, poised for agonizing seconds, minutes in some cases, over the boiling sea, waiting for the leader's shouted command as he steadied himself to help them aboard at precisely the right moment. He had been joined by Van Eyck, Daniels, Frenchie and García when the accident happened.

Zabrisky was next in line, with Aletti and Beverley Hills waiting above. The safe-breaker hesitated, took his eyes off Riordan, and then – missing an opportunity when the leader called – decided to jump in his own time and misjudged the speed with which the ship was rising. He landed clumsily, on the gunwale instead of the launch's cockpit thwart, twisted his ankle, teetered for a horrifying instant off balance, and then plunged backwards into the sea.

Riordan shouted. The rating assisting the mercenaries from the open hatchway, and another clinging to the net, were carried up out of reach. An arm, a hand with clutching fingers, rose despairingly from the water, was swept towards the freighter's stern . . . and suddenly it was Van Eyck, with his marksman's eye and his split-second reflexes, who had hurled his long body over the launch's stern and grabbed Zabrisky's receding wrist. Frenchie threw himself across the Dutchman's legs as the weight of the body and the pull of the current almost dragged him overboard. By then Riordan too was at the stern, and together they hauled the half-drowned man back to safety.

Minutes later, as Daniels attended to Zabrisky, Hills and Aletti jumped with no trouble. Then Riordan started the engines and waved, and the seamen pushed the MTB away for the last time. Riordan opened the throttles wide, steering the vessel away from the *Maria Sánchez*.

Once they were clear of the shelter afforded by the towering flank of the freighter, the full force of the gale hit them.

The Arctic rollers were breaking up into short, steep waves crossing and recrossing the surface as the wind whipped foam from their crests. Although small compared with an Atlantic swell, many of these waves were fifteen or twenty feet from trough to crest – enough to dwarf the high-speed motor boat and threaten to engulf it at any minute. The craft, although officially categorized as a motor torpedo-boat, was not one of the 268 seventy-foot models built for the Royal Navy with three Packard engines developing 4050hp. It was a twin-screw, forty-foot prototype, powered by two Rolls-Royce marine engines, which had never been put into series production because it was considered too small. It was only because it was lying unused in a Portsmouth dockyard, looking like an outsize air-sea-rescue launch, that O'Kelly had been able to persuade the Admiralty to release it for his mercenaries.

Within seconds of leaving the *Maria Sánchez*, the wallowing merchantman was lost from view and the twenty-ton MTB was alone in a maelstrom of howling wind and water. Time and again a huge comber would rear up behind the stern, its towering crest dissolving into foam, lifting the launch inexorably onwards. And then, as Riordan wrestled with the wheel, it would go hissing past, allowing the craft to drop sickeningly into the trough before the next one surged up.

'Running before a sea like this,' he yelled to Daniels and Van Eyck, who stood beside him behind the armoured windscreen, 'we risk being carried ashore long before our ETA.'

'The sooner the better,' Daniels shouted, grabbing for a rail as the bows smashed down between two waves.

'Don't be too sure. We have 300 miles to cover: the whole of today and the evening until the northern dusk. Arriving in full daylight means that we'll be at the mercy of any telescope or spyglass turned our way. Which could mean a pretty dodgy start to the mission.'

Soon, the rain came, sweeping across the wild seascape in hissing bursts.

Van Eyck stayed with Riordan, relieving him occasionally at the wheel, while Daniels exercised for the first time his function as forage master, contriving hot coffee, glucose tablets and condensed chocolate bars from the supplies packed forward with their weapons and equipment. The others, although they were already soaked to the skin, took refuge in the cabin beneath the foredeck – all except Zabrisky, who huddled morosely in the cockpit stern, wrapped in a blanket, his teeth chattering, apparently cowed by his narrow escape from death. 'He refuses to go below, won't eat, won't drink, and answers in monosyllables,' Daniels reported.

Riordan nodded, staggering to keep some coffee in the waxed carton as the bows smashed down into an extra-large wave, sending sheets of spray over the stern. 'Shock,' he said. 'He'll come out of it. Best to leave him for now. But try him again with a hot drink in half an hour.'

Battered by the furious seas, the MTB surged on southwards. Frenchie emerged and took over the wheel. After two hours the rain stopped and the cloud cover lifted slightly. Zabrisky had recovered a little and managed to swallow some coffee, but remained on his own, a solitary figure near the stern. In the cabin, Hills was playing cards with the two engineers.

Once, far away to the east, they saw a Dornier float-plane flying low above the sea. Later, a twin-engined Heinkel circled above them at a thousand feet, but no guns were fired and no bombs dropped. Perhaps the crew were unable to believe that anything but a locally based S-boat could conceivably be in this position, at this time . . . in this weather.

Altogether, it was a long day.

Late in the evening, not long before the brief Arctic night fell, heavy squalls of rain reduced visibility to less than a hundred yards, blotting out the distant, jagged outline of coast which for some time now had been visible each time the powerboat lifted to the crest of a wave.

'And blotting *us* out from any watchers on shore,' Riordan said, 'if we're lucky. We'll go in to within about a mile . . . and then cast off.'

A mile offshore, sheltered by the steep cliffs on either side of the fiords surrounding the North Cape, the turbulent sea calmed slightly and the wind dropped. However, the rain continued to pelt down relentlessly, slanting in almost horizontally from the west, stinging their faces with icy drops. 'I reckon this is about as easy as we'll get it,' Riordan said. 'Frenchie, take Pieter, Daniels and García, and ready the dinghies.'

The inflated rubber boats were similar to those used on air-sea rescue missions, with the addition of electric outboard motors. These, powered by accumulators with a life of two hours at full bore, drove screws sunk eighteen inches below the surface, producing no wash or turbulence behind the bulky craft. In calm water, the dinghies could proceed at a speed of four or five knots in perfect silence.

'Kind of a shame, quitting this launch,' Frenchie said, starting to stow the supplies. 'Seems like a wild coast. If we could have hidden her someplace, she could have been useful for a fast getaway.'

'The orders are specific,' Riordan said. 'The getaway is through Sweden. The MTB is to be sunk in deep water.'

'Yeah, but if we could have run her ashore, it would save . . .'

'Face it, Frenchie, if the Germans found an empty, undamaged ship beached, it would be a dead give-away, wouldn't it, that hostile elements had come ashore. The operation hinges on the supposition that they have no idea anyone's within hundreds of miles.'

'It would have been better in that case,' Beverley Hills said, 'if your Mr Lang had organized someone else to drive the bally cockle-shell, ferry us to the coast, then about face and scurry back to the jolly old convoy. On the face of it, I should have thought that would've been well within the powers of the gent – who normally wears, I strongly suspect, at least three gold rings on his sleeve.'

'No questions about Lang, Huefer and their principals,' Riordan said. 'The range of this craft is four hundred miles. We'll have used up three hundred – probably more in this weather – getting here. The idea was considered, including the fitting of extra fuel tanks, but a return to the convoy is definitely not on. That's why we were given no crew to ferry us.'

The supplies – weapons, explosives, iron rations and equipment – had been divided into eight separate packs of roughly the same weight, one for each man in the team. Strapping these on, they prepared for the difficult embarkation.

'We have to be bloody quick about it,' Riordan told them. 'With seas like this still running, it'll be hell's own tough to keep the dinghies alongside. We'll block the steering and leave the engines at half speed ahead, but the moment she yaws or swings broadside on, we push away like fuck. Or risk being capsized.'

He prepared to scuttle the MTB.

Extra cocks had been fitted, and soon, as the water level inside rose, the launch was moving more sluggishly up the steep slopes, dropping with a heavier flop into the troughs. Riordan directed Zabrisky, Frenchie and Aletti into the first dinghy, with Van Eyck at the tiller.

'You know the drill,' he yelled as the other four fought to keep the craft close to the MTB's heaving hull. 'You're familiar with the coastline from the sand-table model. We should be within two miles of the target fiord. Get your bearings once the moon's up; RDV at dawn as planned.'

With a final good-luck wave, he signalled his three companions to release the dinghy.

Freed from their grasp, it was whisked away, the four men paddling furiously, swirled to the foaming crest of a wave, silhouetted there for a heart-stopping instant before it plunged into the trough beyond.

The waterlogged MTB had settled low in the racing combers now, wallowing between crests, no longer lifting to the swell, riding the waves, but ploughing heavily through with big seas washing over her stern. 'No time to bring the second one alongside now,' Riordan shouted. 'We'd run the risk of being sucked down with her when she founders. Put the dinghy on the transom and climb aboard.'

The doomed craft was indeed starting to behave erratically. It shuddered under the onslaught of a breaking roller, rode halfway up a receding slope and then fell back. Buffeted in the following trough, it turned suddenly broadside-on to the creaming tide, the starboard rails of the foredeck already submerged.

Riordan scrambled into the second dinghy with his men. A menacing wave reared up, washed over the length of the boat, soaking then with freezing spume, and sped away. A second passed, a third. The fourth, bigger than the others, shifted the dinghy, lifted it . . . and finally floated them free.

From one of the succeeding crests, they saw the MTB roll over. For an instant they saw the keel, pale as a whale's belly among the tumbling breakers, and then the stern sank away . . . the bow lifted to point an accusing finger at the sky . . . and the whole ship slid smoothly into the deep.

They were alone with the howling wind in the almost-dark.

If the waves seemed to have become smaller from the MTB, from the floor of a rubber dinghy they were mountainous.

How near or how far they were from the land became academic: they lived only in the now of each succeeding roller, all their energies, mental and physical, devoted to the back-breaking task of paddling while Riordan fought with the rudder to keep the unwieldy craft from falling beam-on to the huge seas. Once caught like that, it would be all over: a breaking crest could overturn them in an instant.

Mercifully, low, black clouds and the rain hastened nightfall. Already the coast was no more than a darker blur against the darkening sky.

But soon the roar and hiss of the waves, the shriek of the wind, were drowned by another, more sinister sound. Over the fury of the gale, they could hear the pounding of surf on the reefs beyond a headland at the entrance to a fiord.

From time to time now, as they lifted to the swell of some extra-large wave, they could make out, far off to the right, an irregular line of white creaming against the sombre bulk of the land.

Battered by the relentless combers, stung by icy spray, feet submerged in the freezing water swilling between the dinghy's inflated gunwales, they surged shorewards, straining to keep the bows heading to port. When the thunder of the surf had become deafening, the waning moon swam unexpectedly out from behind a barrier of cloud.

Minutes later, there was a sudden, unexpected acceleration, the whitecaps fell away behind them, and they glided
out on to a stretch of water that was relatively calm. A big
swell rose and fell, and a strong current seized the small
craft, carrying it shorewards, but now the dark surface
was broken only by a lacework of eddies and swirls; the
seas no longer piled themselves up and tumbled into foam.
Sheer cliffs rose massively ahead.

After the buffeting they had suffered, the lack of noise
was uncanny. They could still hear the booming of breakers off to the right, and the wind moaned over their heads,
flattening the surface of the swell in trembling streaks, but
the sea itself made scarcely any sound now. Apart from
the splash of paddles, an occasional gurgle to one side or
the other, and the chuckling of water beneath their stern,
it was ominously quiet.

'We must have hit a deep-water channel leading to the
fiord,' Riordan murmured, nodding towards a gash in the
land mass ahead. 'Let's hope it's not too far from the fiord
we're aiming for.'

Starboard, on the far side of the promontory shielding
the inlet, the moon silvered the swell, gleaming on the
rows of breakers dashed into a welter of foam on the reefs
stretching seawards below the cliff. Once again they heard
the snarling of surf over the stealthy swirl of current.

Riordan had altered course to approach the fiord, and
the rough water looked dangerously close. He watched the
combers crumble over the reefs, to explode in showers of
spray against the larger rock outcrops. He was glad they
hadn't come in a few hundred yards further west.

'Oh, Christ – look at that!'

The shocked cry – it was from Beverley Hills – startled
Riordan into alertness. Before he could shush the Englishman into silence, he saw what it was that had caused the
outburst. In the nearest stretch of broken water, hurled
from side to side like a fountain-ball at a shooting gallery,
was the unmistakable outline of the other dinghy.

Riordan could see the shapes of Van Eyck and his three companions desperately wielding their paddles; he watched the craft's inexorable progress towards a mill-race of breaking waves where the tide swept over a shelf of cruel rocks; he stared, powerless to help, as the frail dinghy grounded, spun round, was spilled on to its side, and rolled into deeper water. A huge breaker at once lifted it and smashed it high up against the side of a granite outlier as big as a cathedral. The wave fell away, leaving the stricken craft perched for an instant on a pointed crag, and then dinghy and crew dropped back into the seething surf.

The rubber underside glistened momentarily in the wan moonlight as the dinghy, upside down now, was dashed against a reef. Deflated, it vanished into the foam. Riordan and his men saw what might have been human figures struggling in the welter of surf. And then there was nothing to see but the spray bursting over the rocks, and nothing to hear but the pounding of the waves.

13

The northern third of Finland is shaped roughly like a right hand, palm down, fingers together and thumb slightly spread. Sweden is to the west, Russia to the east, and draped around the fingertips, from the first knuckle of the little finger to the tip of the thumb and beyond, is the extraordinarily indented fretwork of the Norwegian coastal fringe. The Finnish hand, reaching northwards for the open sea, comes nearest to it at Polmak, less than twenty miles from the Varangerfjord (tip of the middle finger), and again at the thumb tip, which is fifty miles from Tromsö. In between lies the desolate, glaciated Palaeozoic landscape known as Finnmark. Many of the fiords gashing this ancient mass penetrate far into the hinterland; the Porsangen stretches seventy miles south-west of Nordkapp, the North Cape.

Riordan's landfall had been planned east of this, at the mouth of the Kjöllefjord. The tempest had of course rendered navigation at best imprecise, but the fact that the dinghies had been carried more than ten miles off course proved less of a disaster for the expedition timetable than it might have been: the cliffs against which the dinghy had been lost were midway between the Sletness lighthouse and the Nordkinn promontory, both easily identifiable from the map and the sand-table relief the mercenaries had studied.

If they went ashore here and headed south-west across the bleak uplands, they should intersect the target fiord at a distance not much greater than the ten lost miles. But the first priority was the search for survivors.

After the initial shock – to have come so far, to have overcome such climatic obstacles, yet to have succumbed at the very last minute – Riordan allowed the remaining dinghy to be carried into the inlet east of the treacherous reefs. This was no fiord proper, no rift between two land masses flooded by an encroaching sea, but a simple fault in the metamorphosed strata which had been attacked, widened, hollowed out and finally smoothed over by thousands of centuries of raging breakers. No stream ran into the head of the inlet; no gully split the rock-face rising sheer from the deep water surging and sucking at the base of the cliff. But there was a small beach beneath a massive overhang on the western side of the cove, and it was here that Riordan ran the dinghy ashore.

They pulled it up into the shelter provided by the huge rock slab and shrugged gratefully out of their heavy packs. 'I wouldn't think there's a chance in hell,' Riordan said, 'but before we change out of our waterproof gear and into the cold-weather stuff we've been given, I'm going to see if I can make it to the mouth of the inlet and then round behind the reefs. That's where they'll have been washed up, if any of them are still alive.' A moment later, his tall, lean figure had been swallowed up in the dark.

Daniels, García and Beverley Hills, exhausted, remained silent for a while after he had gone, slumped on the grey sand, leaning their backs against the cold rock wall at the inner end of the cave. Over the swash of the deep swell at the head of the inlet, they could hear water dripping from some crevice overhead, and the distant roar of surf. Out beyond the vertical cliffs cradling the cove, three lines of whitecaps tumbled shorewards.

'Hey, chef,' Hills said finally to Art Daniels. 'How about a touch of the cup that cheers, eh?'

'How's that again?' the Romany said sleepily.

'Something to warm the old tum. You've got those solidified meths tablets: won't take a minute; you could brew up a gastronomic feast in a jiffy. Tea, coffee, hot chocolate – it's all the same to me.'

'You must be joking,' Daniels said. 'The emergency provisions pack stays closed until the boss says otherwise.'

'Oh, come on, mate . . . do the lad a power of good if there was a cuppa all ready and steaming for him on his return.'

'Not on your bloody life! You shouldn't come on this kind of caper unless you're going to follow the rules.' Daniels's voice had risen. 'Now pack it in and stop moaning.'

'Too much noise!' Riordan said curtly, dropping to the beach from a ledge higher up the cliff face. 'What's the trouble here?'

'Nothing. I was just trying to twist his arm and get a hot drink,' the Englishman said. 'He wouldn't jolly well play, that's all.'

'Let us get one thing clear.' Riordan's voice was pitched low but there was a whipcrack quality to it that commanded obedience. 'If you want to stick up two fingers at the establishment and your family and the country you come from, that's your business and that's your right. You want to break the rules, OK. But here the rules are laid down by me – and they must not, shall not, be broken *under any circumstances whatsoever*. Do I make myself . . .?'

'All right, old boy,' Hills interrupted. 'All *right*. I was only asking. It's a long time since the last sip in the MTB.'

'It may be a long time to the next,' Riordan said sharply. 'You'll get your hot drink, like everyone else, for breakfast. If we have breakfast.'

'You didn't find anything? By the reef?' García said.

'I couldn't get to the reef. A hundred yards from here there's a dyke, probably a basalt intrusion, standing out at right angles to the cliff, like a buttress, completely blocking the way. This is not water for swimming in, not at this latitude. Either we'll have to find better rocks and ledges than I did and go over the top. Or, if that's not possible, paddle around the dyke in the dinghy. In either case, we'll have to wait for daylight.'

'You want to bivouac?' Daniels asked, reaching for one of the packs.

Riordan grinned. 'You're forgetting where you are. It'll be dawn in just over an hour.'

The sky paled, and then flared to life in the east. Frowning cliffs, four or five hundred feet high, assembled themselves out of the darkness to frame the inlet. The rain had stopped. Apart from a very high shield of altocumulus, the clouds had blown away. Soon a bar of cold sunlight outlined the western cliff top above them.

In the bright daylight, they could see that the smooth, black dyke emerged from the rock-face at an angle about halfway up. And, yes, it would be a tough climb but there were boulders and ledges and traverses enough to get them over it and – hopefully – down the far side.

The far side in fact was easier, a chaos of jagged outcrops slanting down to the point sheltering the inlet – and off the point the canted, near-horizontal ledges of the treacherous reefs.

If there was a tide, it was out. The waves, less menacing than the night before, broke over the sharp outliers at the extremity of the nearest reef, only reaching the cliff face in powerful, foamless swirls.

They found the body of Zabrisky wedged into a crevice between two layers of rock, deposited there by the receding tide with features so battered as to be virtually unrecognizable. 'Poor Ziggy,' Riordan said softly, shaking his head. 'He was a treasure at the beginning; I'd never have got the team together in such a short time without him. He was thrilled at the idea that he was at last getting into the big time – legally. He was planning to set up a locksmith's business. Let's hope he died quickly, with that thought still bright in his mind.'

'Do we share out his cut among the rest of us?' Beverley Hills asked.

Riordan stared at him. 'Certainly not. This is not a fucking bank robbery,' he said harshly, 'with spoils to be divided equally when the heat's off. You are hired men; you agreed to do a job at a certain rate. A pretty generous rate, given the wartime conditions. Zabrisky's pay goes to his next of kin.'

The peterman's pack had been torn from his back; his oilskins and waterproofed inner garments were shredded, the livid flesh visible through the rents cruelly lacerated. 'I reckon he drowned,' García said, 'despite the injuries. He told me he couldn't swim. And look: there's no bruising.'

They extricated Zabrisky's remains from the crevice and lodged him on a rock shelf above the high-water mark. 'We'll have to find a beach with sand deep enough to bury him,' Riordan said. 'If the Nazi coast patrols found the body of a drowned foreigner washed ashore, it could focus . . . unwelcome military attention . . . on the area.'

There was no sign of any human activity at present. The cliffs towered above them, rising sheer into the cold sky; grey streaked with tumbling white, the empty sea stretched to the horizon. Riordan led the way, wading through the freezing water at the inner end of the reef, around the point.

They found no more bodies. 'In last night's weather,' Daniels said, 'they could be anywhere within ten miles. Or dragged out to sea by an undertow.'

Any icy wind numbed their faces on the far side of the headland, where the cliffs were a little lower and the rugged coastline was gashed once more by a narrow inlet. At the head of this one, a steeply piled crescent of grey sand lay below a precipitous zigzag path climbing the wall of a ravine.

Between the sand and the cliff, a bivouac of camouflage-marked tarpaulin had been erected.

'Good Christ!' Riordan exclaimed. 'Could that possibly . . .?'

A whistle hung from a cord around his neck. He blew four shrill blasts: three short and one long: the first notes of Beethoven's Fifth Symphony, used as a V-for-Victory call by anti-Nazi resistants all over Europe.

No movement stirred the taut sheet of tarpaulin slanting from cliff to shore.

He frowned . . . and then whistled again: this time, three long, followed twice by three short blasts. OSS – the initials of America's Office of Strategic Services, the cloak-and-dagger organization seeding undercover agents throughout occupied Europe. It was all he could think of on the spur of the moment.

There was movement. At each end of the bivouac, sunlight glinted on metal. A rifle on the left, Riordan thought, and a machine-pistol. Held by men dug into the sand beneath the shelter.

The message, he was sure, would have registered: someone connected with anti-Nazi undercover work wished to attract the attention of the bivouackers. But they would be suspicious; it could be a trap.

From the knee-deep tidal swirls, he climbed on to a seaweed-covered boulder and stood silhouetted against the pale northern sky.

Light flashed again – this time from a pair of binoculars.

Van Eyck and Frenchie crawled out from the bivouac and stood upright, waving their arms.

'Thank God,' Riordan breathed.

'One was favoured by luck, just nothing but good old luck,' Van Eyck told them when they had scrambled over rocks and ledges to reach the head of the inlet. 'One grabbed the dinghy and held on, letting the sea decide where one was to be beached. And Frenchie too.'

'But I thought . . . I mean I *saw* the dinghy ripped open and deflated,' Riordan objected.

'It was wrecked *as a dinghy*,' Frenchie said. 'But the gunwales are in separate compartments. Three-quarters of the thing was destroyed, but a couple of sections — something like a large bolster — remained full of air. We clung to that. And hoped!'

'What about the packs?'

'I'd already lost mine. Jesus knows how, but Van Eyck hung on to his.'

'Happily, because much of the weapons is there,' the Dutchman said.

'And no news of Aletti?'

The survivors shook their heads.

'Right. Well,' the leader said briskly, 'we'll press on with what — and who — we have. We'll redistribute the remaining supplies six ways, and check out what we actually have later. Right now, we have to hustle. It may be daylight, but it isn't daytime yet: it's only just after four. We can get a lot done — and get away from this coast — before anyone crazy enough to live or work or be stationed around here is properly astir.'

He looked briefly around the group. 'Daniels, take Piet with you and go back to the other inlet. Paddle the dinghy and supplies round here PDQ, while the water's still slack. García, show Frenchie where we left Zabrisky's body and bring him back here between you. Hills, go and recce the path climbing that ravine. Find out where it leads to, and what the country beyond is like. I'll stay here, dismantle the bivouac, bury what remains of the wrecked dinghy, and dig a hole for Ziggy.'

At twenty to six they left the beach. Zabrisky was buried. The distribution of supplies had been reorganized because of the unexpected problem provided by the surviving dinghy.

It had never been anticipated that the craft would have to be carried overland to the Kjöllefjord: the original plan had been that both dinghies should float there from the open sea. For the six remaining members of the team, the added weight and bulk made a big difference.

Frenchie, as the strongest member of the squad, was entrusted with the outboard engine. The dinghy, deflated and rolled into an unwieldy cylinder, was slung between Van Eyck and García. Each one of these three carried in compensation a much lightened backpack, the extra material being added equally to the packs of Daniels and Riordan himself. Beverley Hills, the only one with the same load as before, was supplied with a Garand carbine and sent ahead as a scout.

The ravine snaked inland for half a mile. In that distance, the uneven, rocky path, strewn with sharp, frost-fissured fragments, climbed more than four hundred and fifty feet. It took them almost half an hour to reach the top.

Breasting the final rise, they stared at a barren, near-lunar landscape scoured by the chilling Arctic wind. The skyline, several miles away, was naked rock. No grass, no bushes and no trees relieved the bleak monotony of the smoothly undulating, glaciated country in between. Far away to the east, a thin column of smoke was teased out above the uniform grey-green moss and lichen of the tundra, but no road or track was visible and there was not a single man-made structure to be seen in all that empty countryside.

Beverley Hills appeared from a depression two hundred yards away along the cliff top. 'There's a cabin, a hut, down there,' he reported. 'Built on a shelf just below the edge and looking out to sea. I suppose it may have been a coastguard lookout or something once. But it's all shuttered up, looks as if no one's been near it for years.'

Riordan glanced at his watch. 'We'll take a shufti,' he decided. 'It's too late in the day to push on any further now. There's no shelter for at least five miles anyway. If we could hole up there and get organized, snatch a few hours' sleep and leave again around 2100 hours, we should hit the fiord at dusk. We relaunch the dinghy then, sail through into the

Laksefjord . . . and after that it's a silent cruise of more than thirty miles into the interior.'

'And a meet with the Norwegian contact?' Daniels said.

'With luck! He'll have been there last night, but there's a treble fall-back: he makes the RDV on three successive nights, one hour later each time.'

'And we finally get shot of this fucking dinghy?' Van Eyck asked, blowing on his chafed hands.

Riordan smiled. 'We finally get rid of our life-saving fucking dinghy!' he agreed.

The lookout hut was made of rough-hewn timber beams dovetailed at each corner. Wooden slats weighed down with stones formed the roof. A barred and shuttered window was only two yards back from the dizzying drop to the sea. The place certainly had an unused, abandoned look, as if the bleached and fissured timber was becoming one with the cold grey rock surrounding it. The door, in the west wall of the cabin, was barred and secured with a rusty padlock. Frenchie reached out and wrenched the padlock and both hasps from the weathered wood with a single twist of his powerful hand. He lifted the bar from its supports and kicked open the door. It went only a few inches and then jammed on the warped floorboards. Frenchie had to lean all his weight against it before he could coax it further. Riordan went inside.

The hut was no more than fifteen feet square. It was completely empty and penetratingly cold. Wind whistling in through cracks between the deformed timbers stirred the stale air to agitate dust motes visible in the rays of intrusive sunlight. Riordan returned to the open door. 'All right, we'll take it!' he announced. 'Art, it's time we ate and drank.'

Daniels nodded, reaching up to ease the heavy pack from his shoulders.

He brewed hot chocolate on a compact Primus. For the first two days each man had a supply of American army

ACTION IN THE ARCTIC

K-rations: small cartons packed with miniature tins of processed ham, cheese and tomato juice, along with hard biscuit, a Hershey bar and chewing-gum. Cigarettes too were included.

For thirty minutes, Riordan allowed the exhausted men to relax, basking in the relief from tension, easing strained muscles. During this period nobody spoke. Then it was time to change clothes.

The insulated waterproofed garments were stripped off and replaced by specially designed thermal clothing developed for Arctic wear and supplied by O'Kelly. This included layered inner garments worn loosely to trap air, ventilate and provide heat insulation; windproof – although not waterproof – outer layers thermally balanced to retain heat but allow moisture out and not in; Mukluk boots of waterproof canvas with rubber soles and three pairs of graded socks; and hooded, fur-trimmed parkas, kapok-filled and camouflaged to resemble the colours of tundra vegetation.

'What do we do with the waterproofed stuff?' Hills asked. 'Chuck it over the cliff into the briny?'

Riordan shook his head. 'Aletti may be washed up and found. It's not exactly a pleasure beach below, but even one set of clothes similar to his discovered down there could stir up a hornet's nest, let alone half a dozen. No: leave the discarded clobber right here. We'll lock up again when we go. The stuff could stay here for years. It could have *been* here for years if anyone ever comes in.'

'Unless they come soon and it is connected with Aletti?' García suggested.

'Well, yes.' Riordan smiled ruefully. 'Then we could be in deep shit. But I'd say the circumstances warrant the risk. I wouldn't want to waste time digging a hole big enough to bury it all in the bedrock outside!'

Art Daniels prised open the shutters and prepared to check the remaining packs and find out how much they had lost in the storm. In the cold glare of northern daylight

153

they could see the sleek shape of an E-boat from the Kriegsmarine forging westward through heavy seas about three miles offshore. The two torpedoes normally mounted on deck on either side of the narrow central bridge had been fired.

Van Eyck lowered his binoculars. 'That means maybe a couple more ships in our convoy have gone to the bottom,' he said. 'Maybe we better can leave here right away and start our own work more quickly?'

'No, Piet. We'll go when I give the word,' Riordan said.

Explosives, timed fuses and tools were the most important items lost with the missing packs. There had been weapons and ammunition too, but this was less important since two of the three men who would have used them were missing too.

Riordan had demanded a standardization of ammunition in the non-British weaponry supplied to his men. All the handguns accepted 9mm Parabellum rounds, and the machine-pistols were chambered for cartridges of that calibre. The rifles dismantled in the packs all fired standard 7.62mm stock.

There were four of these: two Garand M-1 semi-automatics, and two specialized snipers' guns for Van Eyck and Hills. O'Kelly had been unable to obtain the Husqvarna Hills would have preferred, but supplied instead an Austrian Steyr SSG with a Mannlicher five-round magazine and a Smith & Wesson image intensifier. The Dutch marksman was equipped with a Russian Mosin-Nagant Dragunov M1891/30 incorporating a PSO-1 telescopic sight.

Two Bergmann-Schmeisser MP-38 machine-pistols, plus a Steyr-Solothurn and a Suomi, had completed the longer-range firearm supply. All the mercenaries except Riordan carried Sig-Sauer P-220 automatic pistols, the leader retaining the Walther P-38 he had picked up in Amsterdam. From this original arsenal, three automatics

– the Suomi and the Steyr-Solothurn and a Garand rifle – were now missing.

'From now on,' Riordan said after Daniels had delivered his report, 'we march with anything that can be slung, assembled and ready to fire: that is, the M-1, the snipers' rifles and the two MP-38s.'

When the weapons were ready and packs closed up again, he ordered: 'Time now to sleep. We'll take two-hour' watches, two men on each watch, running through the whole squad twice. That will allow each of us eight hours rest, in two stints of four hours, and require four hours' guard duty. By that time it will be late afternoon, and we'll run over the entire raid in as much detail as we can before we head for the fiord.'

He looked around the seated group of unshaven, travel-weary men. 'Right. Hills and I will take the first watch, García and Van Eyck the second, Daniels and Delorme the third. Close the shutters, Art – and the rest of you get your heads down while you can.'

It was not until halfway through Frenchie and Daniels's second watch that the stranger came within sight of the cabin.

Refreshed after their full quota of sleep, the two men spent most of their time tramping up and down the rock shelf between the shuttered window and the precipice, stamping their feet and swinging arms in an attempt to defeat the numbing cold. They were under strict orders not to speak.

The day passed slowly. The sun dawdled between apparently motionless strips of altocumulus, and the bellow of surf from below diminished as the sea quietened after the storm, but the whitecaps still stretched emptily away to infinity. In all that time, the sole sign of life was the appearance far to the west of half a dozen distant specks, probably fishing boats, but they soon vanished behind the bulk of the North Cape. Even the birds nesting on the perpendicular cliffs seemed reluctant to soar, screaming, into sight.

The guards had been instructed to remain on the seaward side of the cabin, one of them only circling behind it every ten minutes to peer out over the featureless landscape from the rim of the depression.

It was Frenchie's turn to make the circuit. Daniels started when he felt the touch on his arm some time before he expected the French-Canadian to return. He swung around. 'What is it?'

'There's a guy,' Frenchie whispered. 'Out there.'

'Where? Who? How many?'

'I only saw one. Over there.' Frenchie swung an arm to indicate the whole country behind the hut. 'I think he's heading this way.'

Daniels unslung the Garand. 'We'll go and check.'

'Shouldn't we wake the boss first?'

'Not before we check,' Daniels said.

One each side of the wooden shack, they stole up the depression, lowering themselves to the slope at the top, so that only their heads appeared over the rim.

'Where?' Daniels asked.

'Ten degrees south of that smoke. About two hundred metres. Heading west.'

Daniels strained his eyes. The undulating moonscape of the tundra at first appeared monotonously smooth, but a closer look revealed depressions, hollows, small moss-covered hillocks punctuating the Arctic floor. Enough to provide cover for an experienced man.

'Look!' Frenchie grabbed Daniels's arm. '*There!*' He pointed. 'Yes, now . . .!'

And indeed there was movement. A blur. A whisk of darker colour. A quick shape flitting from hollow to hollow. A man crawling fast? Bent double? Hidden by a ditch or trench? Whoever he was, he was certainly experienced.

'Is he armed?'

'I didn't see no weapon,' Frenchie said.

'Why is he hiding? What is he doing?'

'Maybe *he* saw *me* – or you, last time around – before I spotted him.'

'We'll take him,' Daniels decided.

'You mean knock him off?'

'No. The sound of a shot here would carry a long way. Take him alive. Riordan will want to know who he is and what the hell he's doing out here. Creep up on the bastard.'

'He's changed direction; he's definitely heading this way now.'

'Right. There's a dip just ahead. See? You crawl out and hide there, a mite to his left. I'll circle around behind and flush him when he's within your reach. OK?'

Frenchie nodded. He slid slowly up over the lip. Daniels unslung the Garand, laid it on the ground and checked the slide of his P-220 pistol. Very carefully, he crawled out into the open, flattening himself between clumps of reindeer moss, bearberries and mats of rock tripe, moving as fast as he dared because he would have to cover twice as much ground as his quarry if he was to come up behind the man before he was level with Frenchie.

The hard ground distilled a cold as intense as the wind whistling through the spiny, twelve-inch-high vegetation; even wearing Arctic mittens, Daniels found it numbing to rest his hand there. Snakelike, he wriggled out wide, hoping the noise of the wind would hide the scrape of his boots, the stealthy rustle of his parka against the stalks.

Now he should be level with the man . . . now turning, circling, coming in behind. Now he dared raise his head, glance left, right, towards the depression – and, yes, nearer than he thought: in a hollow between two patches of dwarf salix, the waterproof cape of a man lying flat on his face, parting the leaves to stare ahead.

Daniels risked another hasty advance, rose to his feet . . . and leapt as the quarry, alerted, turned to flee. At the same time Frenchie rose massively from the tundra in front and hurled himself into the hollow. Together, they knocked the man to the ground, pinned him there, and pinioned his wrists behind his back.

'A fine thing!' the unmistakable Brooklyn accents of Alessandro Aletti protested. 'A man risks his life he should rejoin his brothers-in-arms, dropping dead every six minutes all the way, and the earth rises up to hit him just as he arrives . . .'

14

'I was washed ashore further east, don't ask me how,' Aletti said. 'I mean don't ask. But I knew we were way out on the original plan, that we'd have to make the high ground and hike overland to join this fiord or whatever lower down. So I climbed, is all. I am heading across these heights, like the man said, when what should I see but a French-Canadian *goy* he has the word 'mission' spelled out in neon above his head. Naturally, I investigate – why go on if the rest of the cast is behind you already? – and naturally the schmuck clobbers me before I can drag out my ID and say: Look, I'm on your side.'

'Equally naturally,' Daniels said, 'you lost your pack and all the useful items it contained floating someplace over the Davy deep?'

'Of course I lost it,' Aletti said. 'I should hump sixty pounds of excess baggage all the way from the North Cape to Sachsenhausen extermination camp, not knowing if I was the only one left alive or not? Now be your fucking age, my nomad friend.'

'OK, Ok,' Riordan said, smiling. 'It's good to have you back with us, Alex, pack or no pack. As a reward for devotion to duty, from now on you carry not an ounce over fifty pounds. Plus a nine-and-a-half-pound Garand.'

'Now he tells me!' Aletti said.

They were about to launch the reinflated dinghy into the dark waters of the Kjöllefjord, after a twelve-mile tundra traverse of unimaginable tedium. Apart from an occasional sea bird, they had seen no living thing throughout the four-hour journey. Once, a flight of three Dorniers had passed several miles to the west, heading out to sea over the North Cape; once they heard the rumble of a distant explosion. For the rest, it was a relentless, back-breaking slog across a landscape so monotonous, so dead, that before long it seemed like insanity to skirt the rises, crouch in the hollows, take such elaborate care never to appear on the skyline. Who was there to see? Who was there to hear if they lined up on a crest and sang 'Onward Christian Soldiers'?

Now they were at the foot of a gully carved into the bedrock by a stream running into the fiord. There was a small settlement here – half a dozen log cabins, a frost-rotted jetty – but Beverley Hills, sent ahead once more as a scout, reported that the place was deserted, the shacks all shuttered and silent. Perhaps the hamlet was used by fisherfolk in the permanent-daylight summer? 'Maybe the Nazis they change their minds and start building a *holiday* camp?' Aletti suggested.

At dusk, the inflated dinghy was lowered from the jetty and the party embarked. Crammed with seven bulky men and their equipment, the craft was grossly overloaded. Hills and Van Eyck, the two marksmen, were stationed in the stubby nose; Riordan sat in the stern and steered; the others wedged themselves in as best they could.

Riordan switched on the batteries and started the motor. The single screw, turning at the end of a shaft eighteen inches below the surface, created no ripples, no distinctive burble, pushing the dinghy silently through the water at five knots.

Very soon the steep cliffs framing the fiord opened out and the dinghy cruised into the Laksefjord – a much more important arm of the sea which was almost ten miles wide at that point. This was Riordan's original target, for it penetrated over twenty miles of Norway, carrying them south far more rapidly than they could have travelled overland. Perhaps, after all, he reflected, the forced march over the heights from the inlet had been no bad thing: if they had entered the Laksefjord from the open sea, as planned, there would certainly have been coastguards, lookout posts, a military presence of some kind. Now, according to his briefing, there was no German garrison until Lebesby, near the southern end of the fiord, although each village would probably have a few occupiers – a corporal and two men, perhaps – stationed there.

They were passing a village now, two miles away on the port side. This one was inhabited. They saw lights, heard a lorry in low gear, the barking of dogs. A hint of woodsmoke drifted over the water.

Now they were in total darkness. The moon had not risen. The tall cliffs on either side of the fiord were no more than sombre blurs to left and right. Despite their specialized clothing, the north wind whispering down the channel was chilling them to the bone.

'We've twenty miles to go,' Riordan murmured. 'The batteries last for two hours. At five knots that's half the distance. After that we paddle. But paddling makes a noise, the electric motor doesn't. So we paddle now . . . where there's nobody to hear, leaving the power until later, when there may be someone.'

'And when it'll be light again anyway?' Daniels queried.

'Yeah. But still between two o'clock and four o'clock in the morning. It's a risk we have to take. We must hope Norsemen sleep in!'

They paddled, grateful for exertion that stirred the circulation in their frozen arteries and veins.

Riordan kept them relatively close inshore, about a mile and a half from the western wall of the wide fiord. The map showed only a single village, Veidnesklubben, on that side; there were several on the other.

The moon rose on their left. It was soon swallowed by a dense cloudbank blowing up fast from the north. Drops of rain began to fall. The mercenaries continued paddling.

They were approaching the village when they heard the steady beat of a powerful marine engine approaching from

the south. 'Ship the paddles!' Riordan hissed. He restarted
the electric motor and turned the dinghy through ninety
degrees, heading straight for the cliffs.

The drumming grew louder. And louder. Before long
riding lights were visible: the greenish glow of chartroom
illumination through a raked-back screen. 'Keep as low as
you can,' Riordan ordered. 'Cover your faces.'

Huddled below the rubber gunwales, the invaders
waited breathlessly as the advancing craft drew level and
passed about a thousand yards away – a lean greyhound
shape throbbing northwards, leaving the cold air tainted
with diesel fumes. Probably a naval cutter, Riordan
thought, on coastal patrol. He swung the dinghy back
parallel with the shore.

Veidnesklubben – virtually the halfway mark – was
located on a point where a tributary valley ran into the
fiord. The dinghy was still close in after the manoeuvre
to avoid the cutter when they drew near the village.
Unfortunately, the maps did not show the long spit of
half-submerged rocks that ran out from the point. The
first Riordan knew of it was the voice. It came from a
loud-hailer two hundred yards ahead:

'*Achtung! Wer ist da?*'

'Shit!' somebody muttered. 'A sentry out in the middle
of the fucking fiord! Who'd have thought . . .?'

The challenge was repeated. Clearly across the water
they heard the snick of a rifle bolt.

The dinghy nudged a seaweed-covered rock projecting
above the surface. 'Alex!' Riordan whispered urgently.
'Get out there and decoy – then duck. Piet, Hills, you
know what to do.'

Aletti scrambled over the side of the dinghy as the sentry
called out warning. He climbed on to the rock, stood
up, and shouted in English: 'Excuse me. Am I right for
Finland?'

Guns blazed.

The whiplash crack of the rifle two hundred yards away

was drowned by the deeper, overlapping reports of the snipers' weapons held by Hills and the Dutchman. Aiming in each case for the muzzle flash, they scored straight away. Riordan heard a gasping cry and then a heavy splash as something fell into the water. Fired blind, the German's own shot went wide, but Aletti had in any case already dropped to his hands and knees.

'There may be a second man,' Riordan warned. 'One with the loud-hailer, one with the gun. Be ready . . .'

He bit off the words as a distant gun flamed again. A second man had picked up the fallen sentry's rifle and fired a three-shot burst, following it for good measure with six shots from an automatic handgun. But once again the flashes were fatal: the snipers between them shot him down. The mercenaries heard a scrabbling of boots on rock, but no more shots.

Riordan dragged Aletti back on board and turned the dinghy east, heading for the far shore with the throttle open as wide as it would go.

There was agitation amidships. García was slumped over the gunwale. 'Christ, man,' Daniels exclaimed. 'Are you hit?'

'No,' García panted, struggling to get back upright. 'It was a near thing, though: two of those slugs drilled into my backpack and knocked me sideways. For a moment there I thought I was dead!'

They could hear shouting now from the village. A siren wailed. A spotlight beam probed the dark, settled for a moment on a figure sprawled across a rock at the end of the spit, and then swept across the water.

'Thank God they don't appear to have a regular search-light,' Riordan said. 'So far as the spot's concerned, we're out of range. But there'll be a boat launched at any minute.'

'Are we going to make it?' Beverley Hills asked.

'To the other side? Maybe. It's around five miles. An hour with the engine; perhaps half that if we all paddle like hell as well. I'm hoping they may read it as an attempt by Norwegian partisans . . . and concentrate the search on their side of the fiord. At first anyway. If they do, we should make it – unless there's a reception committee already in place over there.'

'We'll paddle like hell,' Van Eyck said.

Twenty minutes later – a motor boat, as Riordan had hoped, had for some time been checking the opposite shore – Daniels said soberly: 'We're losing air, fast, on the starboard side. One of those shot must have punctured the forward compartment.'

'I thought she was handling sluggishly,' Riordan said. 'We'll beach at the nearest possible point, scuttle her . . . and hope for the best.'

It was another ten minutes before, still paddling, they ran the dinghy in behind an outcrop, waded ashore, and sank her. A high-speed launch with a proper searchlight, probably called up from Lebesby, towards the head of the fiord, was now racing up and down on the far side of the water, sweeping left and right with its dazzling beam.

'Let's hope they stay there,' Hills said.

'They may,' Riordan said. 'That's the side we were, after all – and remember: they are looking for a boat. Nobody alive saw us; nobody knows it was a rubber raft, which could be sunk without trace, that alerted the sentries. My guess is that they'll continue looking for a beached boat before they turn their attention inland. And there isn't one.'

'And if they've warned the Krauts this side to keep an eyes open?'

'They'll be looking, again, for someone landing from a boat; not someone who's already here.'

'Well, lord and master, I jolly well hope you're right!' Hills said.

'Meanwhile,' Riordan said, 'we're still not far short of ten miles from tonight's target, with all this gear to carry.'

'Maybe,' Van Eyck said, 'we better can look for some kind of transport that can – how do the British say? – that can be "liberated".'

A hundred yards from the creek, a gravelled road – the first they had seen since landing – followed the course of the fiord. It was built on a shelf below sheer cliffs, and clearly it led to civilization either side. By a track zigzagging up the cliff they saw a signpost pointing north to somewhere called Hopseidet and indicating that it was eighteen kilometres south to Lebesby. Walking in single file, constantly on the alert for approaching headlights, they turned south.

Half an hour later the moon rode out from behind a bank of cloud, revealing a couple of hundred yards ahead a group of timber-built houses. The rain, which had been falling sporadically since the clouds appeared, ceased. By the wan light of the moon, they saw beside the nearest dwelling, which was built out on stilts over the water, a vehicle parked in an open barn.

It was a tall, square, antique-looking saloon with a projecting luggage boot. The lower part of the body was mustard-coloured, the mudguards and top black. Riordan halted the file. 'Could you hot-wire that jalopy?' he whispered to García.

The Spaniard exchanged glances with Aletti. 'That's an old Chenard & Walcker. French,' he replied. 'It's at least ten years old. You don't need to hot-wire them, just press a button.'

'No key?'

'Uh-uh. That bus was made when people were still relatively honest.'

'Let's go then,' Riordan decided.

Walking wide of the gravelled road, they stole up to the barn. No lights showed behind the shuttered windows of the house.

A circular sticker on the windscreen, stamped and signed, announced that the proprietor of the car was a doctor, with official permission for a weekly petrol ration. 'Just so long as there's still some of it in the tank,' García murmured.

Cautiously, he unscrewed the heavy cap at one side of the boot. The thin, aromatic stink of petrol was at once apparent. He leaned on a rear mudguard, pushing forcefully up and down several times. Liquid swashed somewhere below. 'At least ten litres, I should say,' he reported.

'We're in business, then,' Riordan said. 'Providing the battery's OK.'

'It should be. He's a medic, on call any time. There is one other thing, though . . .' García moved to the front of the saloon. With infinite care, he pulled up the chromed, spring-loaded latches securing the bonnet. The others tensed, expecting a squeak of metal as he folded the louvred panels and jacked them upright. None came. The engine gleamed in the moonlight.

'God, he's kept this in showroom condition!' Aletti enthused.

García was following a group of insulated leads past the engine block. 'What I was afraid of,' he said. 'The distributor head has been removed. Wartime regs.' He reached inside his parka and brought out, one after the other, four circular plugs with knurled edges. 'Six-cylinder, between one and a half and two litres, about sixteen horsepower on the British scale, *neuf chevaux* for the French.' He reached beneath the bonnet with one of the spare heads, manipulated it, and then tried another. 'If the ignition is Bosch, we should be all right . . . *ah*!' The third head had snapped into place.

'She'll start now?' Riordan asked.

'If the firing order's the same. Even if it isn't, she might – but it could be noisy.'

'Stow the gear,' Riordan ordered. 'We'll push her down the road a bit and try there. We don't want a sawbones with a shotgun running out of the house before we leave!'

They opened the saloon's four doors, releasing the rich odour of well-cared-for leather, and loaded backpacks and weapons. 'Push her out, and about a hundred yards towards the village,' Riordan said. 'Alex, take the wheel.'

Three men a side, they trundled the heavy car out from under the barn roof and into the road. Unavoidably, between them, the six pairs of feet and four fat, low-pressure tyres created a loud, crunching chorus on the gravel surface. By the time Riordan called a halt, lights had sprung up in the doctor's house. Somewhere, a man was shouting.

Aletti pressed the starter button. There was a metallic clunk as the pinion engaged with the flywheel. The starter motor whirred. The engine wheezed, coughed, choked into silence. Behind them, boots clattered down an iron stairway. The shouting grew louder.

Aletti cursed. He reset levers on the steering wheel quadrant, advancing the ignition, making the mixture leaner. He pressed the button again. The Chenard & Walcker engine spun, almost caught, then spluttered into silence. There was a loud explosion from the silencer.

The footsteps were now out in the road, hurrying towards the stalled car. 'Christ!' Riordan said. 'He has got a bloody shotgun! Watch out there, men.'

'You want me to knock him down?' Hills asked, reaching through the open rear door for his rifle.

'No. He's a civilian, probably the good doctor himself, certainly a Norwegian. Fire a shot over his head.'

The man was seventy yards away. Too soon, the shotgun blasted. Not a twelve-bore, Riordan judged; probably a .410. A few expended pellets rattled against the boot of the car.

Two shots cracked out from Hills's Steyr. The doctor hurled himself to one side and dropped into a ditch. He fired again.

By now lights had appeared in the houses ahead of them. They could hear shouting from several directions

. . . and suddenly the engine of the big saloon roared to life, shuddering the body on its springs as Aletti fiddled with the hand controls, fighting to keep the motor running.

Riordan and his mercenaries piled on board. Doors slammed. Aletti slid the heavy gear lever into the gate between his seat and the door, and trod on the accelerator. The saloon careered away down the village's one street, past the lights and the shouts, past a volley of shots from a heavy-calibre revolver fired from an upstairs window. One of the car's side windows shattered, showering the men on the back seat with splinters of glass.

Riordan sat in front between Aletti and García. 'OK,' he panted. 'We've got transport – thanks to García. But I don't want to make a big thing of this. So no shooting our way through roadblocks – just getting as far south as we can before the juice runs out. I want the car just for an express getaway, through Lebesby, past the creek at the extreme head of the fiord, and on to the main road running east–west from Tanakirke to Börselv. That's where we find our fall-back rendezvous.'

'How far?' Aletti asked.

'About seven miles. And we'll be lucky to make that. There'll certainly be a phone at the doctor's house, and maybe a resident cop in that village. And there are German naval personnel on a small headland there, looking after a refuelling dump for patrol boats like that cutter we saw. The alarm will have been given by now: I aim to stay with this car only for the short time it will take for the occupiers to get organized.'

They were driving with no lights. Already, above the eastern cliffs, the sky was visibly paling. Ahead of them, the fiord narrowed and the rock walls drew closer together. The road, frost-damaged, had not yet been repaired. The saloon bucketed south, slewing on the corners, spraying small stones, at its top speed of fifty miles per hour.

Despite Riordan's wishes, however, there was a road-block. They had been climbing, with the dull gleam of the fiord dropping away to their right, when the road swung left in a wide curve to cross a tributary valley on a three-arch viaduct. On the far side of the viaduct, a group of soldiers in field-grey stood by a sandbagged wooden hut. Behind the sandbags was a machine-gun. In the dawn gloom they saw a man swinging a lantern in front of a striped barrier pole.

'A lamp?' Aletti exploded. 'A pole! Who do they think we are? Car thieves? *Poachers?*'

'It may just be routine,' Riordan said. 'Maybe they have standing orders to stop everybody. Perhaps they haven't been told yet about us. If they have, it may be that they have instructions to make a routine check. They can't conceivably know that the armed men who stole the doctor's car have evil designs on a military base in Finland!'

'You mean we could simply be Norwegian dissidents, anti-quislings?'

'It's a thought,' Riordan said, with a confidence he was far from feeling.

They were on the viaduct. Far below, the early-morning light silvered a trickle of water frothing between steep, rocky banks. 'I go through?' Aletti asked.

'I can't see any alternative,' Riordan said.

The Italian shifted down, from top to third, to second. The car rumbled over the wooden boards flooring the bridge.

There were six Germans. One behind the sandbagged machine-gun, one with the lamp, the rest on either side of the road with rifles at the ready. Van Eyck and Hills had wound down the windows in the rear doors, sitting tense with their machine-pistols out of sight below the saloon's waistline. Beside Riordan, a white-faced García gripped one of the automatics. Daniels and Frenchie crouched on the floor in the back, and Riordan himself held up the Finnish passport with which he had been provided, so that it was visible behind the vertical windscreen.

Aletti coasted almost to a halt as the soldiers moved into the road, surrounding the car . . . and then, slamming the lever into first, trod viciously on the pedal.

The big saloon surged forward with the engine screaming. Two men on the nearside, struck full on by the iron bumper and heavy mudguard, were flung aside like broken dolls. Blood splashed the screen and a rifle, tossed into the air, crashed down on the roof and slid to the ground. Behind, the machine-pistols roared, pumping out their short, lethal bursts. Other men fell. Rifle shots rang out. The machine-gun flamed, lashing the back of the car with a leaden whip, and then abruptly stopped, the perforated snout pointing at the sky. Aletti steered the nearside wheels up on to a grassy bank, aiming the left mudguard and solid headlamp at the tip of the striped pole. There wasn't room for the whole width of the car to squeeze past, but he reckoned, at almost thirty miles per hour, that the leverage would snap the wooden pole off at the base.

The pole was not made of wood but steel.

The saloon staggered, skidding sideways half up the bank. Glass fountained into the air. There was a shriek of tortured metal . . . and then the pole did snap, spinning away like a broken matchstick, and they were through, lurching away, the wheels spinning gravel as Aletti howled up through the gears.

Turning in his seat, Riordan saw through the rear window the figures slumped on the road, a man sprinting for the hut, obviously to telephone, a second soldier racing behind the wooden structure. It was only then that he saw the second machine-gun. It was mounted on the sidecar of a motorcycle combination and the German was kick-starting the machine to life.

As he watched, the second man came back out of the hut and clambered into the sidecar. The saloon rounded a bend. 'We're going to have company,' Riordan said. 'Keep those guns at the ready.' He drew his own Walther.

'I saw,' Van Eyck said.

'We can't outrun him,' Aletti said. 'That machine-gun almost certainly punctured the tank. And, yes' – he glanced in the rear-view mirror – 'we are leaving a trail of gas on the road. Don't nobody light a cigarette!'

'Something's burning, and it's not cigarettes,' García said, sniffing. The interior of the saloon was filled with the smell of burning rubber.

'That fucking pole,' Aletti told him. 'Front wing's crumpled inwards against the wheel. There's metal sawing into the tyre; it could burst at any moment.' He sighed. 'A fine thing! A man who crewed for Nuvolari should die shot in the back by a *motorcyclist*!'

The car limped around another bend. They were high above the waters of the fiord now. At the side of the road, a flat shelf overhanging the cliff had been used as a dump for lorry loads of granite chippings destined for road repairs.

Riordan snapped out a series of rapid-fire orders.

A minute or so later, the combination skidded into sight around the corner, leaving a cloud of dust behind it.

The car was parked on the shelf, its front wheels perilously near the cliff edge.

The machine-gunner in the sidecar was firing almost before the rider was aware their quarry had stopped. Sparks flew, glass erupted. First one rear tyre and then the other expired with a hiss as a stream of bullets thwacked into the saloon, raking it from front to back.

It was then that the soldiers realized the car was empty.

For an instant they stared suspiciously around. The rider drew a revolver and prepared to dismount. He never got out of the saddle. He and his gunner were each downed with a single shot, the two reports overlapping from a clump of dwarf salix twenty yards up a bank above the road.

Hills and Van Eyck appeared from beneath the leaves, dropped to the road and walked towards the car. Riordan and the others emerged from behind the heaps of gravel on the shelf.

'Sad thing, but this bus has got to vanish,' Riordan said. 'It's a dead give-away, wherever and however it's seen. If it's found, they'll know we must be within a certain radius of that place. If it isn't . . . well, they won't know how far we took it. Not at first anyway.'

They removed the weapons and supplies from the stricken saloon, released the handbrake, and began to shove. The front wheels dropped over the edge; the chassis grounded on rock. Together, the seven of them heaved up the rear, higher, higher, see-sawing the chassis on the lip . . . and then suddenly it was gone, falling away in a burst of earth and rock and small stones, the four panels of the bonnet breaking open to flap away like a wounded bird as it somersaulted down beside the sheer cliff.

It seemed a long time before they heard the splash as the saloon hit the water.

'There's nothing for it now,' Riordan said, 'but for you guys to lie up with the supplies and wait again for the dark. The most important thing for me is to make the RDV with our contact. It's the last chance, and it can't be more than a couple of miles. I'm going to take these guys' helmets and greatcoats, equip myself and Daniels, and ride there in style!'

He issued more instructions, supervised the disposal of the bodies, and left Van Eyck in charge of the remaining mercenaries. Then, donning the German uniforms, he and the Romany mounted the BMW combination and rode away into the brightening daylight.

15

From its highest point several hundred feet above the water, the fiord road looped down a steep hillside to Lebesby and the creek. Riordan stopped the combination and took a pair of Zeiss binoculars from a shelf in the sidecar. He adjusted the focus wheel.

Lebesby was a small town, basically in the form of a cross, the easterly street petering out at the foot of a cliff, the westerly running down to a jetty and a rudimentary harbour. The wooden houses were huddled around the crossroads, beyond which were a church with an onion dome, a garage surrounded by decrepit vehicles, and – beside the road a little further on – a hutted camp with sentries at the gate.

The Lebesby garrison was small, Riordan had been told, a single company of inexperienced recruits fresh from the Fatherland, whose main task was to protect the harbour. Two naval launches were tied up at the jetty.

Beyond the town, the land flattened out and there was a single, larger building where the road joined a wider highway running east–west. And then came the bleak, rolling undulations of the tundra, sweeping south in a tide of cold grey-green.

Riordan's RDV was the building at the intersection.

He released the brake and let the combination coast downhill.

Half a mile further on – the road was rounding a spur – they were passed by a convoy of three Hanomag half-track personnel carriers, led by a scout car carrying an officer, racing uphill towards the viaduct.

The officer shouted something, turning in his seat as they swept past. Without slackening speed, Riordan lifted a hand from the handlebars and gestured wildly back in the direction of the heights, terminating the movement by holding up four gloved fingers, spread. Let the man make what he could of that!

They continued downhill through the dust cloud raised by the convoy. 'Fine, fine!' Riordan shouted to Daniels over the racket of the four-stroke engine. 'There were at least a dozen Wehrmacht men in each of those carriers. So many less to bother us when we hit town.'

The road straightened out and the gradient flattened half a mile before the first wooden houses. The combination was nearing forty miles an hour when it approached the crossroads.

It was still too early for the townspeople to be about. A single man in a fur hat was unbarring the shutters of a store. Dirty snow, frozen into muddy corrugations, lay thickly on either side of the street.

As they rattled through the town, Riordan and Daniels saw blue smoke hazing the cold air outside the garage, where someone was warming up a decrepit lorry loaded with sacks. Riordan swung smartly into the camp entrance and jerked to a stop by the sentry-box. 'The headquarters block? Quick!' Riordan snapped out in German to the young soldier who stepped from the box. He revved the engine with the twist-grip as he spoke. 'It's murder up there by the viaduct. We've got to have help.'

Startled by the urgency in the stranger's voice, the boy forgot his orders and waved them through. There were three lines of huts. 'Up there,' he stammered, indicating the left-hand lane. 'Last b-b-building on the left.' Riordan nodded, lowered himself to the saddle again, and accelerated away.

He passed an open guardhouse with smoke spiralling from an iron chimney cowl, turned into a small motor pool behind the HQ hut, and parked between two Büssing-NAG troop transporters and an armoured personnel carrier. He switched off the engine.

Shielded by the canvas sides of the transporters, the two mercenaries dismounted, stripped off their German greatcoats and helmets, and stuffed them into the nose of the sidecar, from which they had already removed their own parkas. Instead of circling around to the HQ entrance, they ran behind the nearest hut, climbed a wire fence, and dropped into a sunken track outside the camp. They were two hundred yards away, nearing the banks of the creek, when they heard a torrent of angry German from inside the perimeter.

The building at the intersection was larger than the town houses of Lebesby. It was a Swiss-chalet-type structure with two steep slants of roof covering the upper floors on either side. Projecting eaves shielded the front and rear façades from snow and kept the woodpiles dry in winter.

In view of the German naval and military presence in Lebesby, the ground floor, which was the local restaurant and *baari*, had been permitted to remain open throughout the year. It was here that SOE's Norwegian agent was to rendezvous with the expedition leader.

Ten minutes before the final fall-back RDV time, Riordan and Daniels pushed their way through blanketed double doors into a smoke-filled atmosphere loud with conversation and laughter, foetid with sweat and black cigarettes and the fumes of beer. There were perhaps two dozen people in the bar – a handful of Wehrmacht soldiers, two naval ratings, a Norwegian policeman and the rest locals – fishermen? trappers? – dressed almost identically to Daniels and his leader. The only woman was a pink-cheeked barmaid serving raw fish.

Riordan felt himself almost cowed by the noise and the jollity. So long had he been away from company – other than that of his own specialized, frequently taciturn group – that he felt for an instant ill at ease, a schoolboy on his first day in a new class. In such a brawling atmosphere, however, it was easy to pass unnoticed, especially with the anonymity conferred by winter gear. He shouldered his way to one end of the bar, standing beside a large, log-burning stove covered in blue-and-white tiles.

The barman was a tall, dark man with shaggy eyebrows, a bald patch, and a bushy moustache sprouting from his upper lip. He was wearing a white apron over a thick-knit, figured fisherman's sweater. As Riordan approached, the barman snapped out the Norwegian equivalent of 'What'll it be, mate?'

Riordan leaned across the counter, his face hidden by the furred parka hood, and said quietly and very clearly in English: 'A large brandy and soda, if you have such a thing.'

This was the agreed introduction code. The barman's face remained expressionless as he replied, quite loud, with the correct response: 'Doornkaat? I'm afraid we're fresh out of schnapps. Best I can do is Akvavit.'

'Two,' Riordan ordered. And then, when the drinks were brought: 'Where can we talk?'

'Leave it to me.'

A few minutes later, a shorter, red-faced man, also wearing an apron, appeared through a door leading to the kitchen quarters. 'The men from Tanakirke,' the tall man told him, indicating Riordan and Daniels, 'about the water heater. Will you take over while I show them the bastard?' He turned to the mercenaries and jerked his head. 'Follow me. It's out the back.'

He led the way through kitchens that were sparkling clean, past storerooms and out into a yard where the cold burned fingers and ears after the smoky heat of the bar. In an outhouse on the far side of the yard, among creaking copper pipes and the stealthy hiss of water moving through a big immersion heater, he turned to them and said: 'So you finally made it! I was worried: it seems there's been all hell to pay on the east bank of the fiord. Something on the other side too, I was told. At Veidnesklubben. Was that you – or the anti-quisling boys?'

'Guilty,' Riordan said. 'Almost everything went wrong, and we lost a man. I'm sorry if we're bringing trouble to your people. It was, after all, meant to be a *secret* operation.'

'All part of the game,' the barman said. 'Just so long as it puts one more nail in a certain coffin.' He crouched down as though he was busy with the electrical equipment at the base of the installation, and Riordan squatted with him. Daniels appeared to be examining pipes on one side of the cylindrical white tank. 'Do you have any further news for us?' Riordan asked.

'Three things,' the barman said. 'First, the explosions. Since we were alerted, members of the network have reported several more. Something like one every two days, anything between eighty and five hundred kilometres offshore. Nobody's actually witnessed one. But the skipper of a deep-water fishing boat – one of us – says he's convinced that the missiles, whatever they are, stain the sea as they detonate with some kind of brilliant dye. He himself has come across two of these patches, one scarlet, one livid green. And on one of those occasions – the green one – he saw from a distance that a plane was circling the area. After a while, it flew in low and dropped a buoy. Our man said that buoy was emitting a UHF radio signal.'

'"I shot an arrow in the air, it fell to earth I now know where",' Riordan misquoted with a wry smile. 'Well, that certainly confirms the firing-range theory. The dye marks the hit, identifying the area for the pilot; then the signal from the buoy allows the gunnery experts back at base to plot that particular shot accurately on a map or chart. Looks to me as if, for the moment, they're working out time-and-distance tables rather than concentrating on target accuracy.'

'Both the dye and the buoy are subject to tidal drift, of course,' Daniels said. 'But any competent met man could allow for that. Even so, I'd say that 'roughly where they land' – rather than 'precisely where they hit' – is the info they're looking for. Otherwise, why choose the open sea?'

'If that's so,' Riordan observed, 'it suggests the weapon is being developed not for military purposes and specific targets, but for random, anti-civilian use. A terror weapon, in fact.'

'Second point,' the SOE agent said. 'A number of forty-ton tankers have been observed heading for the Finnish border, roughly in the direction of the supposed base. They're in two separate categories, each with a very heavy military escort. Neither is concerned with petrol. There's one we have failed to identify at all; the other is alcohol.'

'Alcohol!'

'Not the kind you drink. Industrial alcohol. To be used, we assume, in some chemical or factory process. Whichever, they are using a great deal.'

Riordan shook his head. 'Search me! Noted anyway.'

'Number three is derived from number two. You've been told that the base lies somewhere between Lake Petsikko, in Finland, and Lake Mollišjok, in this country, right?'

Riordan nodded.

'Well, the tankers can narrow that down even further. There's a highway – if you can call it that – running south and then east from Lakselv, at the head of the Porsangen fiord, where the alcohol and whatever is offloaded from German freighters. We cannot find out any more because there is a Luftwaffe field at Lakselv and the place is very heavily guarded. Anyway, the tankers take this road, which passes through Skoganvarre and Karasjok before it crosses the Finnish frontier at Karigasniemi. In Finland, of course we cannot follow, but we know the road goes to Inari and the biggest lake in that part of the country.'

The agent looked over his shoulder. A woman carrying a basket of laundry was crossing the yard. Soon afterwards, piped water began rumbling out of the cumulus. He straightened up, yawning and stretching his arms above his head. From an inner pocket, he drew a folded sheet of tracing paper, which he opened and smoothed out on the curved tank top. The design on it had been traced from a 1:2,250,000 map of Scandinavia. Riordan and Daniels crowded around as he explained.

'Now, your Lake Mollišjok is some way west of this highway.' A stubby forefinger tapped the road, which had been outlined in red. 'So the base must be east of it. Equally, it cannot be between the highway and the Finnish border, or the tankers would not have to continue and cross over at Karigasniemi.'

'We *are* certain,' Riordan queried, 'that the tankers are going to the base – and not somewhere quite different, further south in Finland?'

'Certain. We have . . . friends . . . at Inari. The tanker convoys never reach there. And, according to the range parameters supplied by London, the lake itself is too far south. What we are looking at, then' – the forefinger made circles on the tracing paper – 'is an area of northern Lapland between Lake Petsikko and the Norwegian border, and not as far south as the tip of Lake Inari – say nine hundred to twelve hundred square kilometres.'

'No problem,' Daniels said. 'We just put an ear to the ground and listen.'

'Not as bad as it sounds,' Riordan said. 'If it's a firing range, the weapons, whatever they are, will make a noise when they shoot. So we can rule out anything too near the frontier – a strip, say, twenty miles wide. None of your people have reported thundery sounds in the night, have they?'

The Norwegian shook his head. 'None. But you have to remember, except for the few towns, this far north the frontier is customarily two men with a dog and a field telephone. I reckon it's a fair risk to take, though, your strip of land.'

'If we take a diagonal across the area that remains,' Riordan said, 'sooner or later we're bound to be within earshot of the range. After that it's just a matter of time.'

'It's wild country just the same,' the agent said. 'Really wild. I mean, population less than one per 2500 square kilometres. What you really need is an aeroplane. Then you could follow the tracks across the tundra made by the tankers once they turn off the highway.'

'It's an idea,' Riordan said with a crooked smile. 'Anything else?'

'Couple of things only. We discovered what the initials mean.'

'Initials?'

'The ones that kept cropping up in the radio traffic intercepts. WVB. It seems it's the name of a person. Werner von Braun, a Kraut scientist. We looked him up. Specializes in powered projectiles, some English invention called a ram jet, and rocketry – whatever that is.'

'Now that,' Riordan said, 'is interesting.'

'The other thing: it seems your expedition is kind of expected.'

'*What?*'

'Is your name Reedon? Ridden?'

'Riordan.'

'Near enough. My brother-in-law works as a cook at a Feldgendarmerie officers' mess in Tanakirke. He overheard this conversation. All security units were warned to look out for a neutral with this name, posing as a war correspondent, possibly with other neutral companions. Enemies of the Reich, the message said – double priority from Berlin. Arrest and imprison at once. Be particularly watchful in the zone under control of 155th Flakregiment. That's right here.'

'But . . . but that's impossible!' Riordan was staggered. '*Impossible.*'

'That's what the colonel said.' The agent stole a glance

at his watch. 'Now, we have orders to help all we can. What else can we do for you?'

'You and your friends have already, with the information you supply, done more than we have any right to expect,' Riordan said. 'I am most grateful. I know very well that you cannot displace yourselves, or alter your normal life patterns. It is too dangerous. You certainly cannot venture up into the tundra with us. All I can say is . . . well, my friends and I would be even more grateful for anything, anything at all, you could do to speed up our arrival at the nearest point on the Finnish frontier.'

'Just over thirty kilometres,' the Norwegian said. 'How did you get here?'

'From Lebesby? We found a lane leading to the creek, below the army camp. After that it was reeds and the river-bank until we could cross the road and make our way to your bar.'

'You came, more or less, by water. So.' The agent thought for a moment. 'And by water is the best way for you to go. After dark, of course. What we will do is this: in the afternoon, we take you east, to Tanakirke – if you do not mind travelling beneath a load of sugar beet. This is not a waste of time because at Tanakirke is the River Tana, running into the Tanafjord. And upstream, after maybe thirty kilometres, the river *is* the Finnish frontier. We can find perhaps a boat. And after dark this will be a much quicker way for you to reach that frontier than walking south overland from here, where there are no roads but perhaps patrols and even aeroplanes after the message from Berlin.'

Riordan smiled. '155th Flakregiment,' he said, 'here we come!'

16

Riordan lay flat between a clump of knee-high Arctic willow and a mat of reindeer moss carpeting the frozen ground with fragile brownish stems that resembled tiny antlers but were never more than four inches high. Through powerful binoculars, he was scanning the base perimeter fence and the motorized patrols monitoring it every few minutes. Cleverly, the four or five half-track carriers involved, patrolling in opposite directions, were driven at varying speeds, so that it was impossible to say with precision: 'That one has passed; we have so many minutes before the next one is due.'

He had made pages of notes but could find no overall pattern in the movements. He wasn't even certain exactly how many of the identical vehicles were involved, because the base itself was invisible. And the far side of the perimeter – perhaps two or three miles of it – was hidden by a gigantic swell of land, a rounded mountain almost two thousand feet high, with snow still lying thickly in the upper hollows. Because no firing of any kind had taken place since they came within hearing range, they could have missed the place altogether if it had not been for the parallel tracks scarring the tundra where the forty-ton tankers supplying alcohol and other things to the base turned off the road to Inari.

Riordan had sent his men – two groups of three, one eastwards, one to the west – to enfilade the base and find out what lay on the far side of the mountain. Before the picture was complete, he could make no plans.

He lay chilled to the marrow, the Arctic cold not only seeping up into his bones from the frozen ground but driven into him by the icy north wind keening through the sparse tundra vegetation. Even the insulated thermal garments perfected by O'Kelly's backroom boys were not proof against that. The rubber eyepieces of the binoculars pressed into his face like iron rings, his breath fogged the lenses and inside the mittens his fingers felt thick, bloated, clumsy.

He was too near the perimeter – perhaps a quarter of a mile away, on an exposed slope where even the movement of a bird would attract the attention of the watchful patrols – too near to employ any of the economical muscular exertions recommended by the cold weather analysts, certainly far too near to stomp up and down and swing his arms, the way he wanted to. The bivouac was on the far side of the rise, well hidden beneath an overhang of cloudberries and Iceland moss. And he couldn't crawl back there until his own patrols returned to him here.

Riordan was a man of action, not an individual prone to abstract speculation. His preferred approach was to be presented with a problem, to evaluate the difficulties, and then to overcome them; in active terms, his pleasure lay in the elimination of obstacles barring his progress to a given target. But in conditions of enforced idleness, when even movement was prohibited and only the eyes could be allowed to work, when the scene they registered was relentlessly monotonous, he was as liable as anyone else to fall into a dreamlike – almost trancelike – state. This near-hallucinatory condition was exacerbated by the conflict between a stressful situation and physical conditions demanding inaction.

Watching now for the nth time the third – fourth? fifth? – carrier patrol the chain-link fence surrounding the silent mountain, he allowed his thoughts to stray away from the secret, still invisible base and wander.

What was he doing here, face-down among frosted lichens in a desolate, inhospitable country, working for a man he knew to be a phoney?

What unrelated chain of events, what sequence over which he had not the slightest control, had led – inevitably – to his presence here, this day, this minute, this second now already past, in a situation of danger and indecision?

A goldfish, they said, flicking its tail at the North Pole, will ultimately – however indirectly, however minutely, ripple by diminishing ripple – provoke a reaction at the South Pole.

Well, he was not all that far from the North Pole. Who was his goldfish? Who or what had forged the chain?

Might it have been Aline, protesting once too often that he was spending too much time with 'Monsieur Huefer' and not enough with her? Or the fit of coughing outside Madrid which had caused him to duck his head so that the bullet from Franco's sniper nicked his shoulder-strap and not his heart? Or the hostility of his father when he left the farm to fight with the rebels in Dublin in 1916?

Come to that, why not the very fact of being born?

Cause and effect multiply, geometrically rather than mathematically, backwards as well as forwards. If I hadn't stepped into that shop doorway to light a cigarette, I'd have been there when the bomb went off; if I hadn't called her back for a final kiss, Sonia's car would have been safely on the far side of the river when the bridge went up.

But it is impossible to fix on any *individual* action that has a *specific* effect on our lives. Or on our deaths. When at last the bullet speeds from the gun to smash into the bared chest, can one even call that a bullet . . . and not rather the physical effect of some past action? And the thought leading to that action? And the state of mind provoking the thought? To say nothing of the third parties who may or may not have been responsible for the state of mind . . .

In any case, Riordan thought crossly, a goldfish at the North Pole wouldn't survive long enough to flick its tail.

Survival here was the problem too, let alone the military action which would have to be organized once the base had been properly surveyed. For all they knew so far was that there *was* a base; they still had no idea exactly what it produced or how it worked.

The most difficult part of the mission so far had been the unending, back-breaking journey south from the Tana and the Finnish border. It was no more than fifty miles, but it had taken them six days.

Six days. One hundred and forty-four hours of unremitting physical hell, with no roads, no tracks or paths, no houses, farms, shacks, not even a landmark to point the way and break the soulless monotony of the arid tundra.

The succession of exhausting hours, the relentless slog over rough country where the ground was hidden and a careless step could result in a twisted ankle or a shin barked on a concealed rock, had coalesced in Riordan's mind into a single timeless ordeal, with no beginning and no appreciable end.

Thinking of the expedition, he was unable to impose a chronological order on events but saw them singly, as isolated snapshots – the photograph album of memory.

Perhaps the strongest impression was the least typical: an unexpected valley, deep enough at this season to support a fringe of ragged pines, beneath which water, mauve from the upland peat, cascaded between frozen banks of late snow green as the flesh of a honeydew melon. And in a space sheltered by these black trees a camp of nomad Lapps, standing in front of their reindeer-hide wigwams impassively studying these foreign arrivals, wizened Mongolian features showing no hostility, just mild curiosity. Behind them, where the trees grew more thickly, their small reindeer herd plucked branches and nibbled.

Riordan greeted them in Finnish. If they were hunters looking for the great elk, a man who seemed to be the leader said, it was too early and still too far north. There were bear, certainly, and perhaps wolverines and foxes, 'but further south, by the great lake'. Riordan thanked him and said that they were not hunters; they were prospectors, seeking metals in the ground. But first they had to report to a military base, somewhere between the smaller lake and the frontier. Did the Lapps know in which direction he should travel?

The leader shook his head, drawing his dogskin coat closer around him. 'It is far, far away to the west,' he said. 'A dangerous place, where men make their own thunder. It is wiser not to go.' He turned to his companions and broke into a diatribe in his own language. Riordan was unable to get another word about the base out of them.

Did they too pass the short night in that dell . . . or did they press on as soon as the darkness had fallen? That was another thing Riordan could never make up his mind about.

The first lecture Daniels gave on survival food in the Arctic was also imprinted indelibly on Riordan's mind.

It was at the end of the second day. Everything they had started out with, even the most condensed items, even the glucose tablets — most of which had been in Zabrisky's pack — everything was finished. 'From now on,' the hardbitten, ginger-haired little Romany told them when Riordan called a halt, 'we're in a survival situation. It's not a disaster situation, such as you might get after a plane crash, or if your vehicle was wrecked in the middle of the Kalahari desert; we do after all have tools, implements, utensils, weapons, the means to make fire. But it's survival inasmuch as we have to live from now on off the land. And right here' — he swept an arm around the barren, featureless tundra — 'the land's in no generous mood!'

They were sitting huddled together in a hollow between two rock outliers, leaning against the piled backpacks. There was no warmth in the pale sun, which was still high above the horizon, although it was almost nine o'clock. Above their heads an icy wind whistling down from the north stirred the crisp fronds of tundra vegetation.

'From now on,' Daniels told them, 'you guys forget 100 per cent the concept of *food* — that is to say, something you might enjoy eating, something that might have taste or flavour, something that might even feel good in the mouth. There's nothing in this landscape that can provide any of those luxuries.

'There are, all the same, products – plants, insects, worms, an occasional bird or small animal – that can provide between them the carbohydrates, fats, vitamins and proteins your bodies need. Even here.'

'I did hear you say insects, old chap?' Hills said faintly. '*Worms?*'

'Certainly. One of the most concentrated forms of protein. You squeeze out the muck, dry them on a rock in sunshine, then pound them into a paste to flavour boiled roots and leaves. The same goes for snails, slugs, snakes.'

'I knew I should have called by Schraft's delicatessen,' Aletti said mournfully.

'It's vital that you understand,' Daniels said. 'You will all know something about calories. A calorie is a unit of heat – the amount of heat energy needed for your body to perform a given function. An average human in a state of total rest needs normally seventy calories per hour just to keep the heart and lungs and circulation going. The simplest activity – standing up, sitting down, washing up – demands a further forty-five calories per hour – that is to say around 2040 calories a day without any actual physical work. And that, in a case like ours, could add anything from 3500 to 5000 more.'

'And you can supply this from all the crap we're tramping over?' Frenchie asked.

'Animals would be better,' Daniels said. 'But we're not static; we're pressing on and we have no time to lay traps and wait patiently. Best of all would be a large animal, a reindeer or an elk or even a wolverine – the contents of their stomachs, being already half digested, are the most nutritious, the most quick-acting food of all.'

'Oh, Christ!' Hills said disgustedly.

'What I have to do, you see,' Daniels continued imperturbably, 'is to *refuel* you guys sufficiently with vitamins and proteins and suchlike, so that you can continue to work efficiently. That's why I say don't think of it as food; think of it simply as fuel for an engine. It's no worse than a hospital patient being fed by a drip, when you come to think of it.'

'They don't have to choke down the fucking stuff!' Hills said.

'Here in the Arctic tundra,' Daniels said, 'we have a choice of ten edible plants. Three evergreen shrubs – two spruces and a Greenland ledum – all of which have leaves that can be used for making a revitalizing tea; ferns, which can be steamed, but only when the fiddleheads are young; salmonberries, cloudberries and bearberries, the first two of which can be eaten raw and the last cooked. The Finns make a liqueur out of cloudberries.'

'I wish one of them was here now!' Aletti grumbled.

'And finally the three local mosses – more properly lichens,' Daniels continued. 'They are the most nutritious. One of them, known as rock tripes, has kept a group of explorers alive for months. Like all of them, this has to be well soaked overnight to remove certain acids, and then thoroughly boiled. After that, they're roasted to crisp up like cornflakes.'

'And these shrubs we lie under, the ones that are all of two feet high?' somebody asked.

'Salix, the Arctic willow? Well, of course you're perfectly right,' Daniels admitted. 'The young shoots, leaves, inner bark, and young peeled roots are all edible, boiled or steamed. The leaves have ten times more vitamin C than oranges.'

'What about fish?' Hills queried.

'There will be some fish certainly in certain streams, but studying their movements, locating the right pools, organizing the right kinds of trap, net or line would require time, patience, and . . .'

'We have neither,' Riordan interrupted brusquely. 'This is not a Boy Scout excursion. We live on what we can harvest on the move. And that goes for birds too. There'll be no Twelfth of September on this tundra!'

Riordan could not remember what botanic and insect species provided the raw materials for Daniels's first living-off-the-land dinner. But he could recall the rank, weed-like stink of a curious, grey-green slime served hot in a skillet and sprinkled with a nameless powder reputed to be rich in protein, the roasted, crisped-up portions of rock tripes that looked more than anything else like the droppings of goats, a boiled, stringy root entirely lacking in flavour. But most of all the expressions on the faces of his team when first they saw and smelled what Daniels was offering.

One of the slightest – and one of the quick-fire snap-shots he remembered with the fondest smile – was a short exchange between Van Eyck and Aletti overheard when their route was inexplicably barred by a twenty-foot ravine snaking away across the tundra slopes. The crossing involved an abseil by Hills, who had Alpine experience, and the use of ropes to ferry men and supplies across. Van Eyck and the Italian-American had, with Riordan, been the first over. While they waited for the first pack to swing across, the Dutchman, himself no mean manipulator of the language, asked conversationally: 'Tell me, Alex: you learned your English Stateside, no?'

Aletti shrugged. 'Where else?' he said.

'And . . . you don't mind my asking? – you are from a family that is basically Jewish?'

'I should be a *goy* with a mother she is called Esther and a father Jacob?'

'So you are in fact Jewish?'

'What if I am? This is becoming a misdemeanour now?'

'No, no, don't get me wrong, Alex. It was just that . . . it's a small thing, but I often wondered: why is it that you Jewish people always make a statement into a question?'

'How else should one make a statement?' Aletti said.

The first firearms talk was given by Beverley Hills, not so

SOLDIER OF FORTUNE 5

much because it was necessary as to provide at least some form of diversion after a particularly tough – and especially boring – day's work.

It had been their first full day alone on the tundra. The alarms and excursions of the 'sugar beet' escape from Lebesby with the help of the Norwegian patriots, the perilous transfer to a small boat on the Tana, the journey upstream during the few hours of darkness, were all behind them. The worst moment had been on the waterfront in Tanakirke, when a German patrol with orders to search all vehicles had ruthlessly bayoneted the root crop through and through. The mercenaries had in fact been packed like sardines in a shallow false compartment beneath the normal floor of the flat-bed lorry loaded with the produce. But it wasn't only the penetrating north wind that chilled seven foreign spines while the search was taking place.

Now the lorry, the town and the river towpath were one short night and one interminable day's foot slog behind them, and Riordan called a halt although there were still three hours of daylight left. It would be worse than stupid, he knew from previous experience, to push an untried team too far – especially on the first really difficult day.

No planes had flown over the desolate landscape during the hours of daylight, and they had heard the sounds of no sled or vehicle, although each man in his camouflaged parka was prepared to throw himself face down the instant Riordan gave the word. Once, perhaps three or four miles away, they had glimpsed a herd of reindeer moving like the shadow of a cloud beneath a summit still pocketed with snow.

Daniels had rigged up the bivouac, and the last iron rations had been consumed when Hills laid out the various weapons in front of the men. 'Of course you all know how to fire the bloody things,' he began. 'Point it, press the tit . . . and bang she goes. But you may not be so familiar with the stripping routine, the possibilities of jamming, how to put the bally machine right when it goes wrong – and they do – and so on and so forth.'

He picked up a SIG-Sauer P-220 automatic pistol. 'This is the most familiar. We all have one – all except the boss with his P-38 Walther. It's well balanced, and weighs less than two pounds. This is a recoil-operated, mechanically locked weapon with automatic firing-pin lock, double-action trigger, de-cocking lever and outside slide catch lever. The magazine, as you know, holds nine 9mm Parabellums.' Hills looked around the circle of faces, some attentive, some bored, and grinned. 'There's no safety as such, so the gun has a first-shot capability as good as a revolver's, but there's a built-in device providing a total lock even if it's dropped accidentally with the hammer cocked or half-cocked. So you can't shoot yourself in the foot!'

He dismantled the pistol as far as was possible without an armourer's bench, and showed them the fastest way to reassemble it. 'Now you can forget about Westerns, gunmen on horseback and hoods knocking each other off from speeding Lincolns,' he said. 'This is a *short-range* tool. Factory-adjusted sights allow for a round, with a six o'clock aim, hitting the centre of a three-inch circle at *fifteen yards*, no more.'

Hills laid down the P-220 and picked up his own Steyr SSG sniper's rifle. 'This is right the other end of the jolly old spectrum,' he told them. 'I mean to say, according to the bods who turn it out a skilled type can make a six-inch group with ten shots at five *hundred* yards! Even at the maximum range of eight-fifty, you can get ten rounds into a twenty-inch group. This is a single-shot arm with a Star-Tron image intensifier, a rotating bolt, and a five-round Mannlicher-type magazine which rolls the cartridges around a horizontal spindle and up into the breech.'

Hills picked up the second specialist rifle, a Mosin-Nagant Dragunov M1891/30 designed by two Belgian brothers and a Russian artillery general and sometimes referred to simply as a Dragunov. 'Different again,' he drawled, 'but our friend from the Low Countries can tell you more about it than I can.' He tossed the weapon to Van Eyck, who caught it one-handed, low down by the bivouac floor.

'Semi-automatic, with a ten-round magazine,' the Dutchman said with a glance at his fellow-sniper. 'Gas-operated, with 7.62mm rim-fire cartridges and the cylinder above the barrel.' He grinned. 'According to the makers, with a PSO-1 × 4 telescopic sight – one quotes – "the gun will produce very accurate shooting with first-round hits at up to *one thousand* yards". In skilled hands, of course.'

Riordan had been amused by the barbed rivalry implicit in the exchange, but he was not going to allow it out into the open. He picked up the Garand M-1 carbine. 'Who can tell me about this?' he asked.

'Semi-automatic, eight-round clip, gas-operated, rate of fire twenty rounds per minute,' Aletti recited woodenly. 'And if any schmuck he should ask me to fire one, the clip is around his ear already!'

'That leaves the Schmeissers,' Riordan said. 'Advantages?'

'Superb knock-down power,' García said. 'As long as it's at close range.'

'Maximum effective – that is to say *accurate* – range, one hundred yards,' Daniels put in. 'Twice that if you're just waving it about, hoping to hit *something*.'

'There's the difference,' Riordan said. 'Horses for courses. Very high-velocity, small-calibre bullets travel great distances. In expert hands, hitting the vital spot, they're fatal. Fired by the less skilled, they travel right through the target . . . and don't necessarily halt him; he – or it, if it's an animal – can keep coming, maintaining the attack. García's right: at closer quarters knock-down power, even if it doesn't kill at first, is the answer. A weapon like this, firing heavy slugs at a rate of five hundred shots per minute in very short bursts, can practically cut an enemy in half using the S-manoeuvre, left to right.'

'Brute force against craftsmanship and skill,' summarized Hills.

It was immediately after the snow, Riordan remembered, perhaps on the fourth day, that they first saw the girl.

It was late in the afternoon. The humping of heavy packs over the endless highland wastes was beginning to tell; Riordan heard subdued grumbles, orders were queried *sotto voce*, even the taciturn García had been heard to complain. It was nevertheless a fine day by northern standards: brisk, cold, sparkling on the summits where snow lay thick. And suddenly there was more, falling incredibly from a sky that was clear – it was snowing from a clear blue sky!

Carried by the chill north wind, perhaps from a bank of cloud away to the east whose upper edges were silvered by the low sun, the snow whirled down in big flakes. It eddied around the tramping mercenaries, frosting eyebrows and blueing the tips of exposed ears, blurring the irregularities in the slopes of tundra, obscuring the compass face. Finally, when the sky had darkened and the flakes whipped horizontally at a blizzard rate, Riordan called a halt.

'Useless to continue,' he decided. 'There's a bluff off to the left. On the far side of that slope. We'll pack it in for today, make camp there, and hope it will have blown over by the time we're ready to start tomorrow.'

In fact by the time they had battled their way to the top of the bluff and slithered down the far side, the snowstorm had stopped as suddenly as it had begun. There was a carpet of perhaps six inches covering the tundra lichen and moss. The hollow below the bluff, however, was still packed with frozen snow from a previous fall. And on the side nearest the rock outlier this had been gouged out to form a cave perhaps four feet high and seven or eight feet deep. Pegged out beneath this was a single sleeping tent with a polar bedroll stowed at the far end.

And at the entrance to the tent a figure swathed in silver fox furs sat cross-legged in front of a smokeless fire battened down with flat stones.

It was only when the fur-fringed hood was lifted so that the wearer could stare at the newcomers that Riordan became aware that the stranger was a woman.

The situation was so totally unexpected, so ludicrous even, that the astonishment cancelled itself out, as it were, and there was nothing left to do but accept it as normal.

Riordan smiled. 'Mrs Livingstone, I presume?' he said.

The young woman smiled. She was in fact younger than he had thought – not a day over thirty, he guessed, and pretty in a pink-cheeked, high-cheek-boned Nordic way. A tendril of blonde hair had escaped the fur hood. 'Dr Sigurd Hasso,' she said. 'A naturalist. Senior Research Assistant in the Botanical Department of the University of Vaasa.'

'The port on the Gulf of Bothnia?' Riordan was surprised. 'I should have thought aquatic plants were more in that department's line. What are you doing so far north . . . and so far from the sea?'

'They have marine biologists up to here,' Sigurd said. 'I'm outposted here for a two-month controlled experiment: pre-summer soil conditions, and what supplementary flora might be persuaded to multiply in ground that risks remaining frozen all the year round at depths of more than two feet. And an additional chore for the Zoology Department: to discover what animals, if any, could adapt to these conditions, solar, climatic and vegetal, if the ground cover could be altered, the plant civilization broadened. And would their activity in itself encourage a proliferation of species, the emergence of hybrids by cross-pollination, and so on?'

'Kind of specialized! Especially for a woman on her own.'

'It's interesting. In conditions such as these' – she gestured towards the pocket of frozen snow – 'even the smallest success is exciting. It is lonely, of course, but solitude sharpens the concentration wonderfully: there's nothing else to do but work! And of course it's not for ever.' Sigurd looked up at him from beneath arched brows – with eyes of a clear and brilliant blue – and asked in her turn: 'And what exactly are you all doing here, so far from the battlefields of the world?'

Riordan hesitated. He and his men were clearly heavily armed; they wore Arctic camouflage clothing; they carried bulky supplies. Whoever this attractive young woman was, she wasn't going to swallow any glib fabrications concerning surveyors, winter initiative exercises or long-distance route marches.

Tell as much of the truth as possible, avoid inventing and over-embroidering, and if you must lie, lie by omission. Those had always been his personal precepts in awkward situations. 'We're nothing to do with the battlefields of the world,' he said. 'We are in fact mercenaries of a kind. Industrial, not military. But since we are operating in the country of a belligerent, we naturally have to take precautions, although we do everything we can to avoid contact with your countrymen and with the Germans.'

'Yes, but what are you *doing*? There are no secrets to steal out here in the wilds – no factories , no industry. I fail to see . . .'

'Our interest,' Riordan said carefully, 'is with the period immediately after the war. Beneath these hills there lie deposits of nickel, copper lodes and iron ores. The people who employ us – a consortium of Swiss businessmen – would offer huge sums of money to Finland for the concession to mine these minerals once the fighting stops. But they would have to get in first; many others would be interested. Which is why they have sent us secretly to prospect, to locate these valuable sites *now*.'

Sigurd still looked dubious. 'You don't have any boring equipment,' she said accusingly.

'Not at this stage,' Riordan said. 'Much too obvious: a scintillometer and magnetometer recorders will do for this first cast. Later, if the readings are positive enough, we may come with more comprehensive equipment.'

'I should be interested to see your readings,' Sigurd said.

'For the moment that's classified information.' Riordan smiled. 'Maybe later, when we're further on. If we still share the same territory.'

'They must be . . . interesting . . . if they're that secret.'

'Very,' Riordan said.

He turned to Daniels. 'Meanwhile we'd better prepare to bed down for the night. Perhaps another cave on the far side.' And to Sigurd: 'If we're not intruding?'

She smiled. She *was* pretty . . . beautiful, in fact, with the silver fur framing that face with its curl of hair. 'There's plenty of room in the bedroom,' she said with a wave of her hand at the rolling swells of tundra surrounding them.

There was little conversation after the forage master's root broth and lichen mousse had been swallowed. Hills and Van Eyck each attempted in a mild way to chat up the young woman, who was eating some kind of pemmican, which she took from a leather pouch. But she was only willing to talk about her work, in particular an idea for the introduction of small burrowing creatures in the hope that their subterranean labours might encourage plant species to proliferate.

By the time darkness fell they were all deep in an exhausted sleep.

It was still dark when Riordan felt the small but insistent tug at his insulated bedroll. At first, still half asleep, he ignored it. But when the movement grew imperative, demanding, he unwound his head from the covers and squinted through the freezing air. The moisture from his breath formed instant icicles on his eyebrows. There was still enough snow on the ground, and reflected light from the glazed bank opposite, to show him the entrance to the naturalist's scooped-out cave. And Sigurd, one finger to her lips, urgently beckoning him with her other hand.

He pulled himself into a sitting position. The come-hither wave was now wider in scope, almost peremptory. He crawled over to the cave. She pulled him in, allowing one of her furs to drop down from a couple of nails driven into the ice and block the entrance. 'What is it?' Riordan whispered. 'Is there something wrong? What's the matter?'

Sigurd smiled – a wider, much warmer smile than she had permitted herself when they were eating. A tiny wick, floating in a mussel shell full of oil, provided a flame bright enough to glisten on the iced walls of the cave and brighten the twin gleams of her blue eyes. She was wearing a rough-cut pair of woodman's trousers tucked into fleece-lined boots and a loosely knit Norwegian fisherman's sweater. There was a heavy gold chain around her neck, and the pale hair, cut off square at the ends, fell down her back in a gleaming cascade.

'What is it?' Riordan asked again. 'What can I do?'

'Two months can be a long time,' she said. 'Especially when one is alone.'

'But solitude sharpens the concentration wonderfully?' he could not resist saying.

'There are other things that remain nothing like blunted. Anyway, you are here' – she smiled very widely, brilliantly – 'and, since we are quoting me, I repeat: even the smallest success is exciting!'

Riordan didn't know what to say. The implied invitation – the whole routine of awakening him and dragging him over here – were so forward as to seem almost brazen. It was so totally different from the impression he had gained of her before. There was nevertheless such an air of candour, of honesty about her that the behaviour was robbed of any vulgarity or offence.

And yet . . . and yet . . . in this position . . . under these circumstances . . .

Sitting on her bedroll, she shifted slightly, allowing him to see that the breasts moving beneath the heavy sweater were constricted by no brassière.

Riordan's pulses were hammering. He ran his tongue over his upper lip.

'There was a poet,' Sigured said, 'an American, I think, who once wrote something like "ridiculous, our wasted time, extending before and after". The only important time element, he thought, was the moving *now* – the instant to be seized and stopped, to be preserved in crystal, a motionless centre in a whirling world.' Suddenly she crossed her arms, seized the loose hem of her sweater, and dragged the garment over her head. 'Don't you think he was right?' she asked softly.

Riordan stared, speechless. She was naked from the waist up. The breasts were marvellous, deep and firm and golden, an exquisite balance between lightness and weight. Tiny hairs surrounding the dark flesh of the right nipple shone silver gilt in the wavering illumination from the oil lamp.

Sigurd shook loose the mane of pale hair. She held out her arms. 'Come into my crystal world,' she said.

Riordan was naked. His thumping heart was trying to escape from his chest. The girl lay beside him in the sleeping bag, the whole warm, lovely length of her tinglingly close. Her hair smelled of honey; her lips were sweet as strawberries.

The taut pressure of those breasts against his chest, shifting slightly as Sigurd's breathing quickened, the hot breath on his cheek, the cool fingers wrapped around him stimulated in Riordan an ecstasy that was almost unbearable. He reached down eager fingers to feel warmth, and then a wiry wetness . . . and at last the scalding swallow that told him he was home at last.

'Oh, baby,' Aline said drowsily, 'it's been so long . . .'

The whipcrack report of the rifle shot was frighteningly loud. It was followed at once by another, and then a third, echoing away among the upland ridges. Riordan swore, struggling awake in the sleeping bag, disentangling his face and head. It was full daylight and penetratingly cold. Daniels sat below the bluff nearby, coaxing smokeless flame from dried stalks beneath a flat stone. The sky was clear but there was still snow on the ground.

Riordan turned his head. The ice cave opposite was empty.

'She left half an hour ago,' Daniels reported. 'She said she had a long way to go, and to tell you goodbye.'

Hills came leaping down from the bluff, scattering dry snow. His rifle was slung and he carried one of the canvas rucksacks they used for collecting lichens, mosses and firewood. His boyish face was shining with good health – and excitement. 'Eureka!' he cried.

'Did you fire those shots?' Riordan demanded.

'Well, yes, old boy.' Hills stopped three yards from his leader. 'I was up betimes, as the old johnnies used to say, and I thought I'd try . . .'

'You stupid, fucking imbecile,' Riordan shouted with a ferocity not entirely due to his fury at the destruction of his dream. 'Don't you bloody know, you fool, how far a rifle shot carries in this kind of landscape, in these dry air conditions?'

'Well, gosh, I'm sorry. You see, I saw these . . . I mean, I thought . . .'

'You thought!' Riordan's voice was tight with anger. 'You never bloody think – that's your trouble. I've told you before: this isn't a Baden-Powell boys' initiative test; it's a mission. I'm not running a fucking pony-trekking club; I'm heading a seek-and-destroy squad. And any thinking that's to be done, I'll do myself. What you're here for is to take orders.'

Hills looked crestfallen. 'But you don't understand . . .' he began.

'I understand one thing: you're a thoughtless, conceited cunt, prepared to endanger the lives of your companions and risk fouling up the mission – because of some damn schoolboy show-off stunt, I suppose.'

Hills tossed the lock of dark hair back from his forehead. 'There was no question of a stunt . . . sir,' he said stiffly. 'I was on watch, and I happened to spot these bally birds.'

'Birds? What birds?'

'Ptarmigan. Three of them, for God's sake! I mean, dash it all, with the state of our jolly old larder, who could resist? I got two of them; one' – the young man couldn't resist boasting – 'on the wing. At about forty feet, with a single 7.62 round!' He delved into the rucksack and produced the two bloodied birds. 'At least, tonight, we can actually *eat*!'

'Let's hope you don't *actually* choke on it,' Riordan said venomously.

'One doesn't imagine, you know,' Van Eyck said in placatory tones, 'that a rifle shot – even three shots – could be accurately pinpointed, triangled, or whatever, in this kind of landscape, echoes and all.'

'Probably not,' Riordan said. 'But there's a principle at stake here. Irresponsibility, confidence, reliability, those kind of things. And anyone who did hear the shots would now at least know there was *somebody* in the area, even if they didn't know precisely where.'

It was better, he said, if they struck camp immediately and set off at once, leaving no trace whatever that anyone had been there. Sigurd Hasso had certainly allowed no single clue to her presence to remain.

Correction, Riordan thought, making a final check. There was one tiny trace, not far from the ice cave, half hidden by last night's snow: a brittle, blue-black oval, with highlights of mauve and cream. He picked it up.

It was half a mussel shell, greasy on the inside.

How strange, Riordan thought, easing his cramped limbs

uncomfortably on the cold ground beneath the Arctic willow, how strange that the most vivid – if not necessarily the strongest – impression out of all his 'snapshot memories' should have been that of a waking dream, of something that never happened at all. But perhaps no stranger – he refocused the binoculars on yet another circuit by the motorized patrols – than the way the mind wandered at such moments of enforced inactivity, no matter how fraught the present situation.

For him, in all of his many military exploits, it had always been the same: certain things he remembered precisely as they were. Time, perhaps, had discoloured them a little, like tarnished coins discovered in an old purse at the back of a drawer. But the dates were still readable, the royal heads could still be recognized. It was the order in which they appeared, their relationship one to the other which had changed – and these would long ago have been rearranged. Some now might even be counterfeit.

But these, the forgeries and the worn-smooth, anonymous discs, were in fact no less important. They were equivalent, Riordan decided, to the false values memory gives the past in the hope that this might improve the future.

He moved again, lowering the binoculars and supporting himself on his elbows. For the moment there were no half-tracks visible behind the perimeter fence. The cold was suffocating him: no wonder his mind was playing tricks, leading him down half-conscious culs-de-sac straying far from the task in hand.

He wished though, among this chaos of recollections, that he could say with conviction whether it was in the dream or in reality that he had glimpsed the powerful radio transceiver half hidden behind the bed roll in Sigurd Hasso's cave.

17

The base had been located, indirectly, through Sigurd. During their conversations on the night they met, Riordan, playing his role of secret mineral prospector, had confided that he had heard of some kind of military base in the area. He wanted to know roughly where it was, he said, solely so that he and his fellow-prospectors could keep well away from it. 'The last thing we want,' he had said, 'is to run foul of some damn patrol, who'd probably take us for spies or something.'

Oh, there was a base all right, she had told him. And indeed there were patrols. 'But it's a long way south of here; perhaps two days' march, with all your stuff. Which way did you come up, anyway?'

Originally from Switzerland, he had replied. And then, lying: 'After Helsinki, via Rovaniemi and the bridge at Ivalo.'

'My God,' she had said, 'that's some trek! Getting on for a thousand kilometres?'

'Something like that.' Riordan smiled. 'But we had samples to take for more than half the journey.'

'If you skirted the western shores of Lake Inari, you'd still have been some way east of the base,' Sigurd said.

Riordan had thanked her and let the subject drop.

The direction they took was the exact opposite of that advised by the botanist. They struggled south for two more days, and then turned west.

The country changed here, in this more southerly part of Lapland. The landscape ran in a series of parallel ridges, angled north-east—south-west, and the lower valleys, especially those drowned by lakes, now supported thin strips of woodland – dwarf pines, spruce, an occasional emaciated fir, all of them rising like the spars of sunken ships from a tide of underbrush comprising several million years of rotted branches islanded with huge boulders dropped by retreating glaciers in the last ice age.

In fact, turning west across this infuriating terrain, they discovered, when at last they hit the tracks made by the supply lorries crossing an upland swell, that they had come too far south. They approached the base therefore from behind, as it were, with nothing but the patrolled perimeter and the rounded mountain within it to see.

Riordan was still waiting for his two flanking units to report on the far side of that bland eminence when he himself became aware of activity beyond the crest.

He was too far away to hear shouted commands, but suddenly there was mechanical noise, too varied and too complex to define. An earth-shaking rumble; a ferocious hissing noise that he couldn't identify . . . and then, abruptly, this titanic roar and a sight that was quite unforgettable.

Above the crest, an enormous finned shape, needle-sharp at the top, belching flame and blinding white steam below, rose slowly into view.

For an instant it appeared to hang there, and then, canting towards the north, accelerated up into the sky with stupefying speed. Within seconds, nothing remained but a dwindling speck at the tip of this towering column of white. And then there was only the receding thunder which had marked its passage.

Teased out by the north wind, the roiling white trail – of steam? smoke? some kind of exhaust gas? – thinned, wavered and finally dispersed. An unnatural quiet fell over the desolate landscape. In the brush somewhere behind the mercenary leader there was a sudden stealthy rustle, and a bird flapped away to the south.

Fly away, Peter; fly away, Paul, Riordan thought with

a wry smile. Because, baby, you got competition now, up there in that sky!

But what kind of artillery, for God's sake, could fire a missile of that size? No wonder a ship hit by one of those had broken up and sunk at once! Especially if the whole damn thing was filled with high explosive.

Wait, though! No, it couldn't be: isolation was blunting his power of reasoning. There was *no* artillery; there couldn't be either. He had heard no great gun firing – and it would have to have been a monumental detonation to lance a thing of that size! Over four hundred miles? Be your age, Barry!

Clearly the missile must in some way be self-propelled.

And presumably the alcohol, delivered according to the Norwegians in such huge quantities, formed part of the fuel powering whatever engine the missile had.

Quite clearly, he recalled the Norwegian agent's voice. 'A Kraut scientist . . . Specializes in powered projectiles . . . And rocketry – whatever that is.'

Riordan himself had just seen what it was.

And of course, once the point had been made, the resemblance between what he had just seen and the climactic exhibits at a firework display was clear enough.

There was just a slight difference in scale.

Riordan could see why any number of interested parties would want the installation launching it destroyed. The scientist WVB – Werner von Braun, hadn't they said? – had certainly produced what could be termed a terror weapon if it was directed against a civilian population.

The undergrowth behind him rustled again.

Another bird? One of the scout parties returning? He turned his head.

Highly polished boots. Black breeches. A tall, impeccably uniformed figure.

'Herr Riordan, I imagine?' the German officer said. 'A strange place to stumble across a neutral, I confess. Even a neutral newspaperman.'

18

Aletti, García and Hills, scouting the eastern flank of the perimeter, missed the rocket launch because they were fording a stream at the bottom of a steep ravine when it blasted off. They heard the noise, though, and above the lip of the depression they saw the upper part of the white trail it left behind it. 'What the devil was that?' García asked.

'Something, I should very much think,' Hills said, 'not unconnected with what we've come to look for.'

'You mean . . . some kind of gun? But we heard no bang.'

'It is far too low down it should be a contrail,' Aletti said.

'Then what in hell . . .?'

'Haven't a clue, old boy,' Hills said. 'But I'd swear that *is* some kind of condensation, the white gubbins besmirching old Mother N's heavenly azure. As for the rest, Lord knows what, but I'd say it was to do with ballistics. Definitely.'

It was then that they did hear an aeroplane. Or, more exactly, a float-plane. It climbed into view above the rim of the ravine and flew towards the white column – a sleek, twin-engined monoplane with a Perspex nose and the ripple camouflage used for machines flying mostly over the sea.

'*Maseltov!*' Aletti cried. 'That's an RS-14, one of Fiat's best!'

'What's an Italian seaplane doing up here?' Hills asked.

'Search me,' Aletti said. 'I should have the ear of Il Duce and his military advisers already? It's a specialized machine: I'd say it's been lent to Adolf for sea searches. If what we just saw was anything to do with the mysterious explosions out at sea, maybe this is one of the planes they send out to look for the dye and mark the spot where the thing hits.' He frowned. 'It has just about the range. A little over thirteen hundred miles.'

'It's not going to fly that far this time, is it?' García observed.

They listened. The synchronized beat of the two radial engines had altered in pitch. One of them spluttered, choked, roared to life again, and then settled into an uneven rumble.

'Ignition or feed,' Aletti said.

The float-plane had been flying north. Now it banked, turned through 180 degrees and headed back towards the base. Within seconds, the other motor cut out completely. The pilot banked again, losing height rapidly, coaxing his ailing machine, willing it to stay in the air.

The plane vanished behind the lip of the ravine.

At the lower end of the defile, the steep banks flattened out and the stream ran into a small lake. 'He can't make it to the base, so he's going to try and put her down there,' García said.

They saw the RS-14 flash past the gap between the two banks; they heard the splash and concussion as it hit the lake. The remaining engine roared one final time and then wheezed into silence.

Hills was already running down the rocky floor of the valley, racing for the lake. 'Come on!' he shouted. 'Cover me; I have an idea.'

The lake was long and narrow. By the time they emerged from the ravine, the float-plane, which seemed undamaged structurally, had been moored to a bank on the far side, about four hundred yards away. Two of the three-man crew stood on the starboard wing, removing the engine cowling. The third climbed down on to one of the floats and crouched to examine the strut housing. A thin cloud of blue smoke hazed the cold air above the exposed engine.

Hills stood among a jumble of large rocks, his rifle lying on a flat-topped boulder in front of him. 'Can you fix that machine? Can you mend it?' he hissed urgently as the other two joined him.

'I should think so,' García said. 'Though I'm not an aero . . .'

'Sure we can mend it,' Aletti said. 'Didn't I work on the Macchi-Castoldi racer? Besides I know those Fiat motors. They're A74-RC38s. Eight hundred and seventy horse-power each . . . if they're properly tuned.' He grinned. 'Leave me alone with those for a couple hours, and I'll guarantee you three hundred and ten miles per hour at ten thousand feet!'

'What had you in mind?' García asked the young Englishman.

'Well, dash it all, we're never going to get far enough today to squint round the far side of that bally mountain. And here, if we can get the thing to go, we can pull it off in ten minutes . . . and take pictures of the place too. I mean, frankly, this is a wizard spot of luck.'

'There is the matter of the crew,' García said. 'They might not see eye to eye with you on the use of their plane.'

'Don't be silly: we eliminate them before you chaps fix the kite.'

'So we steal the aeroplane, overfly the base, take pictures . . . and then what?' Aletti said. 'If we're not shot down in flames already.'

'It's *their* plane. They won't suspect anything until it's too late. Then we simply fly it back here, land on the lake . . . and walk home.'

'I hope the Krauts agree with your reading of the scene,' Aletti said.

'The ones here don't have to,' Hills said. 'They won't have time to see the bloody script.' He picked up the Steyr SSG and twisted his arm into the sling. Leaning forward, he planted his elbows on the rock and sighted the rifle carefully through the image intensifier.

'Wait,' García said. 'You can't just pick them off . . .'

'Don't bother me, Pancho,' Hills said. 'This needs concentration.' The inverted pointer within the sight's broken cross-wires floated across and then steadied on the nearer of the two men working on the engine.

'But they're not targets at a range, man. You can't cold-bloodedly shoot them down like that.'

Hills exhaled with a snort of annoyance, and looked up from the telescopic sight. 'They're enemies, aren't they? If they caught us trying to break in and destroy their installation, they'd shoot *us* down. Would you go all namby-bloody-pamby if we were creeping up on a gun-site and they were sentries?' He settled back into a firing stance and gazed through the eyepiece.

García bit his lip and turned away.

The crack of the rifle was flat and curiously unimpressive in the wide-open space beyond the ravine. A figure bent over the engine jerked upright, twisted around, slumped forward over the leading edge of the wing, and dropped into the lake.

Hills fired a second shot – so fast that the man standing on the pontoon was dead before the first crew member hit the water.

The third round winged the last man, but he had managed to drag himself halfway beneath the open canopy into the cockpit by the time the last two bullets in the magazine drilled into his back. He lay between the engine nacelle and the fuselage with an arm still raised, somehow caught up on the cockpit rim. 'All right,' Hills said coolly, 'unless anyone fancies a four-hundred-yard swim and a touch of hypothermia, we'd better leg it around the head of the lake and get to work.'

The lake shore was flat but strewn with sharp, slaty fragments of rock. It was fifteen minutes before they reached the plane.

There was a lot of blood on the starboard wing, a certain amount streaking the float beneath it. The water, stained a reddish brown, was still cloudy beneath the machine's transparent nose.

As soon as they climbed aboard, they saw why the third man's arm was hitched up to the cockpit rim: his dead hand was grasping a microphone, at the full stretch of the lead linking it to the radio on the instrument panel. 'Shit!' Hills said. 'He may have raised the base before I got him with those last two shots . . .'

The microphone crackled. As if in answer to his unspoken question, a guttural voice spilled urgent German through the static. For the last time, which lake? . . . What shots? . . . What was wrong with the machine? . . . Why did the radio remain unanswered? . . . Report back at once . . . and again what shots?

Hills jerked the lead from its socket. Aletti and García were already hunched over the starboard engine. 'Amateurs!' the Italian exclaimed disgustedly. 'Sloppy maintenance! Adjustment, cleaning, a little work with an emery paper, maybe a pipe to blow out. That should be enough – for the moment.'

'You can do it?' Hills asked.

'Of course.'

And to García: 'You take the port; I'll continue here.'

After a while, watching the skilled manipulation of wires and tubes and fuel lines and contacts, the Englishman said: 'They'll send out a search party of course. There can't be all that many lakes . . . and they will have seen the line he was taking. How far would you say we were from that blasted mountain?'

'How would I know?' Aletti shrugged. 'Two miles? Maybe three? But it's rough country, even for a half-track. We must do what we can.'

It was thirty-five minutes before he was satisfied with the starboard engine. He crossed over to help García with the port. In the distance now, still invisible but approaching, they could hear the whine of motors in low gear and an occasional clanking of caterpillar tracks.

By the time the engineers stood on the two floats to swing the airscrews and suck fuel into the cylinders, the noises were uncomfortably loud. The Fiat engines fired at once with an encouraging roar. Aletti nodded his head, smiling. With García next to him in the co-pilot's seat, he jockeyed the float-plane into the middle of the lake with alternating bursts of throttle to the two engines. Hills lay face down in the nose, peering through the Perspex observation panels.

A Hanomag scout car and two APCs full of soldiers appeared around a low bluff beyond the ravine.

At the far end of the lake, Aletti – still smiling – jabbed on the left rudder and swung the Fiat slowly west. He pushed both throttles up to full, gently, because those engines never relished a straight transfer from cold to full power, and sent the plane skimming along the lake. Twenty seconds later they came unstuck from the water and flew over the convoy at three hundred and fifty feet. Two tripod-mounted heavy machine-guns flamed, but nobody got hurt.

Aletti flattened out at five thousand feet, setting a course due west and then south. Once the bleak landscape was laid out below them like a sand-table model, Hills could see from his vantage point exactly why the German planners had chosen this particular site for their secret research installation.

From the south, where the mercenaries had made their camp, the land rose, swelling up into the hemispherical two-thousand-foot mountain with which they were only too familiar. But the primeval sedimentary strata curving to form this height had in fact been thrust up aeons ago by some subterranean volcanic catastrophe, and the far side, facing due north, had a totally different aspect. Here, a gigantic fault had ruptured the ancient beds, which now projected above a stretch of flat land in a huge overhang. It was beneath this rock shelf, over a hundred feet thick, that the working parts of the base appeared to be located.

Hills saw two gun emplacements, a number of low buildings – the serrated glass roofs of a workshop flashed reflections from the low sun – a line of dormitory huts and a camouflaged hangar. There were a number of military vehicles beneath the overhang, and yes! just as they had been told during the briefing, several curious trucks that looked like outsize fire engines, with extra-long ladders. A concrete lookout bunker was sunk into the rock on the upper edge of the shelf.

The plane banked, circling the site. Hills could see now, studying the lie of the land, how sheltered from observation the base was: in aerial terms, it was only visible from directly above and a little to the north; on land from a point between two low hills immediately in front.

Like all the members of the group, he carried a 1.1 Leica camera loaded with the recently perfected, super-fast 400 ASA 35mm film. He removed the lens cover and started to take pictures.

By now the search party at the lake would have reported. Three dead bodies and a hijacked Fiat RS-14. The aircraft could no longer be regarded as friendly.

On the site below, tiny figures scurried ant-like between the buildings. Tracer arched slowly up towards the plane, flashed past. A ragged tear appeared in the port wing. Pom-poms thudded puffballs of smoke from the gun emplacements. Smudges of brown veined with vermilion stained the pale sky behind them.

Aletti put the Fiat into a power dive, heading straight for the overhang with machine-guns blazing from the wings. 'Enough snaps?' his voice queried over the inter-com.

'One more,' Hills said. Through the open doors of the hangar he had glimpsed a slender, cigar-shaped object in gleaming metal. The nose of an aeroplane? A miniature submarine? A colossal bomb? The ants were struggling to close the doors. He finished the roll. 'Home, James,' he called.

Aletti hauled back the stick at the last moment, clearing the lip by no more than twenty feet.

Instinctively, Hills ducked back in the transparent nose as the bunker hurtled towards them. He saw chips of concrete spinning from the rounded façade; he saw muzzle flashes from the firing slits; a section of Perspex starred as a stream of slugs sped past his right shoulder. Then they were over the summit and roaring south.

There were a lot more holes in the Fiat's wings now. 'I'll have to put her down soon,' Aletti said. 'It won't take them long to call up fighters from Lakselv. We can't do what we planned: put her back where we found her. We gotta find another lake. The sooner the better. I want we should step out of the machine at ground level, not five thousand feet.'

'There's a long, narrow lake five miles to the west,' Hills reported. 'But there are huts at one end and a jetty and what looks like an oil tanker. I'd think that was the crate's home base. Complete with army.'

'I'm turning east!' Aletti said.

For the first time, García's soft southern drawl sounded in Hills's earphones. 'Is maybe a little near the tracks made by the alcohol tankers coming from the Ivalo road, but no more than three, four miles from our camp. Look . . . there! Two o'clock from the dark wood on that ridge. Not really a lake, maybe, but where the Iijärvi widens into that curve . . .'

'Got it. We'll try that one.'

The ground below was falling away, each ridge lower than the last, like waves advancing on a low-tide shore. Hills had been looking down and back through the plane's nose. 'Can't be abso-bally-lutely sure,' he reported, 'but I *think*, frankly, that the port float is damaged. The strut seems to me at a deucedly odd angle.'

'Now he tells me!' Aletti said.

19

The officer's name was Rudi Höhner-Lanz, SS Obersturmbannführer in charge of base security, directly responsible
to Leutnant-General Erich Heinemann, whose 66th Corps
had been specially formed to promote and perfect new
inventions in the field of weaponry.

Höhner-Lanz was a tall man, perhaps forty years old,
with very pale hair and light-grey eyes that were almost
lashless. Everything about the rest of him shone: his
boots, his buttons, his belt and its buckle, the Knight's
Cross above his campaign medals, even a gold tooth that
gleamed in the right-hand corner of his mouth when his
lip lifted in a smile. Which it did more often than Riordan
expected.

He was suave, quite polite, clearly intelligent. But there
was a certain steely quality behind the superficial manners
that told Riordan instantly: here is an opponent neither to
be trusted not underrated.

Bundled at first into a rear-engined scout's *Kübelwagen*
already overloaded with a Madsen machine-gun and four
greatcoated soldiers carrying Schmeisser machine-pistols,
Riordan had subsequently been transferred to an open
Mercedes-Benz and driven around a rough track to a
guarded opening in the perimeter fence. The SS officer
sat beside him in the back seat, holding Riordan's own
Walther P-38 in a black-gloved hand.

Rounding the flank of the mountain, the staff car
approached the vast rock overhang and the complex of
buildings beneath it. Riordan's professional eye registered
the entire scene at a glance: the hangar, the huts, the

lookout bunker, the gun emplacements, two workshops with the names Argus and Fieseler above the entrance doors. One thing only startled an exclamation from him. 'My God!' he cried. 'The fire engines!'

'Fire engines?' The German frowned – and then, following Riordan's gaze, he smiled. 'Yes, I suppose they could look like that from a distance – to a barman at a Lebesby tavern. We call them *Meillerwagens*. The ladder-like structure is to carry the *Vergeltungswaffen* to the launching pad and then raise it to the required near-vertical position for blast-off.'

'*Vergeltungswaffen?*' Riordan asked the question not so much to gather information as to gain time to study the vehicle. Behind the tractor cab, the chassis, which was forty feet long, was mounted on two double wheels at the rear, and a four-wheel bogey in front. The ladder-like framework, attached to a turntable over the rear wheels, could be swivelled and raised through ninety degrees.

'The word,' Höhner-Lanz was saying, 'means "reprisal weapon" – some would say "revenge weapon". The rockets – you will of course have witnessed a launch not long ago – the rockets are designed to punish the Englanders for their senseless terror-bombing of our cities and civilians.' He leaned forward and tapped the driver on the shoulder. 'You may drive us to the headquarters wing now.'

Riordan sat in a padded chair, facing the SS officer across an empty desk, determined not to be fooled by the apparently civilized manner of his reception. He had already suffered one severe shock, being addressed by name. He was to be subjected to four more within the next few hours.

At the moment, he was too confused by the speed with which the situation had changed to make positive plans.

'We know you, Herr Riordan,' Höhner-Lanz said. 'We know about you; we are familiar with your record. We know you really are a neutral and not some Yankee or Britisher spy. We are very well aware that neither you nor your three companions are prospectors, that you have nothing whatsoever to do with minerals or the search for valuable ores.'

A wintry smile. The lip lifted, the gold tooth winked. The smile did not reach those pale-grey eyes.

'You are a mercenary, Herr Riordan. A soldier of fortune. And so, doubtless, are your confederates. You may not be British or American, but you are certainly spying. The one thing we do *not* know is why, and for whom.'

The German took a cigarette from a silver box and lit it with a gold Cartier lighter. He blew out a plume of smoke. 'It is time now for us to examine that question.'

For a moment Riordan was silent. Höhner-Lanz, knowingly or unknowingly, had already provided him with several items of information. The longer he could keep the man talking, the more he would be able to learn.

He had only given the mineralogist line to one person: Sigurd. So that was one more person not to be trusted.

The German had mentioned spying, but had said nothing about sabotage. Presumably, then, he didn't know about the explosives among their supplies, which implied that the bivouac camp had not been discovered. But what was this 'your *three* companions' thing? Sigurd certainly knew there were six. Who else had they seen . . . and *which* three?

There had, too, been that sneering reference to 'a barman at a Lebesby tavern'. This must mean either that the SOE agent's ring was blown, or that he was a double agent, feeding information to the Germans. In either case it explained why Riordan's identity had been known when Höhner-Lanz flushed him from his observation post. But did it explain the barman's claim that the whole group had been expected, even before they left Lebesby?

'Well?' the SS officer said. 'I am waiting.'

'It is of course perfectly true,' Riordan said easily, 'that we are not prospectors, that we have nothing to do with minerals. Equally, I admit that I was monitoring the activities of this station.'

'Why? For whom?'

'Well informed as you are, you will know that I am also a newspaperman; you have already said so.'

'I know you use that as a cover for your mercenary activities.'

'What you will not know is that I was approached in Paris, in that guise,' Riordan said, thinking: Tell as much of the truth as possible; don't embroider, 'by a Swiss businessman who . . .'

'I know. A man calling himself Huefer.'

For an instant, Riordan froze. How could the man *possibly* have known that?

Not a flicker of alarm showed on his face. He said: 'It was Huefer who commissioned me to come here, with my . . . companions . . . and find out what weapon or weapons were being tested on this base.'

'What is Huefer's real name? Whom does he represent? Why should they wish to know this – assuming, as you assumed, that they are non-belligerents?'

'I don't know his real name, though I agree "Huefer" is probably false. I assumed he might have been representing such Swiss armaments manufacturers as SIG. If they heard that something revolutionary was being developed by a rival, it is reasonable to suppose they might want to know details, perhaps with an eye to post-war markets. I think they call it industrial espionage.'

'To send a highly paid group of mercenaries beyond the Arctic Circle, with all that implies in terms of logistics and expense? In the middle of a world war? Ingenious, I suppose – but I am afraid I cannot even call that a good try. Herr Riordan, you insult my intelligence.'

'The fact that it's such an unlikely story militates in favour of its being true,' Riordan said. 'If I was inventing something, I'd present you with something far more plausible.'

'Better,' Höhner-Lanz approved. 'The double double-bluff routine. It's like watching a game of tennis: this way, that way; this way, that way. But I still do not believe you.' He stubbed out his cigarette in a thick green glass ashtray and rose to his feet. He walked to the window of his office. 'Come, I will supply you, gratis, with the information you seek; in return, perhaps you will tell me what I want to know?' He beckoned Riordan to the window.

Over a line of steel filing cabinets, the mercenary leader looked out past administration huts, past the workshops and the hangar, to a concrete-lined depression in which one of the *Meillerwagens* was parked with a huge, finned, sharp-nosed missile attached to its 'ladder'. As they watched, hydraulic pistons raised the projectile slowly from the horizontal to the near-vertical.

'A beautiful piece of streamlining,' Höhner-Lanz enthused, eyeing the slender, deadly silhouette. 'Fourteen metres from nose to tail. Do you know what that thing weighs? With nine tonnes of fuel and a one-tonne warhead, it tips the scales at thirteen tonnes! And yet it accelerates to Mach-1 – the speed at which the sound barrier is ruptured – in less than thirty seconds.

'That must be very special fuel,' Riordan tempted.

The SS officer nodded. 'The Herr Doktor von Braun. A mixture of alcohol and liquid oxygen. Carried in two separate tanks which occupy most of the missile's body. Above are the guidance controls, the fuses and the warhead. Below, between the fins, the fuel feed and rocket motor.'

'It is directional then? I mean, not random over a given distance?'

'Of course it is directional.' Höhner-Lanz sounded personally affronted. 'There are, naturally, certain problems with regard to precise targeting to be solved. Teething troubles, as the Englanders say. But since the weapon reaches a peak trajectory height of some ninety-six kilometres, with a range of nearly six hundred and fifty kilometres and a maximum burn-time of seventy seconds, our engineers and scientists, I think, have already taken a great stride forward in the direction of sophisticated weaponry.'

He reached behind him for the silver box and lit another cigarette. 'Much greater heights, of course, can be attained if range is no object.'

'Remarkable,' Riordan said. 'What do they call this . . . triumph?'

'I told you. *Vergeltungswaffen*. V-2 for short.'

Riordan raised his brows. 'There was a V-1, then?'

'There will be. It is less sophisticated. Basically a small, pilotless aircraft with a rocket motor and the fuselage filled with explosive. A flying bomb, if you like. But that is being developed, with problems, elsewhere. So far it remains at the prototype stage.' The gold tooth reappeared. 'The Herr Doktor here,' he added proprietorially, 'likes to meet his deadlines.'

'You choose your words well,' Riordan said, staring at the rocket.

Höhner-Lanz sat down at his desk again, indicating the vacant chair. 'You are familiar with Hollywood films? *Ja*, I thought so. Well, now we come to the part where the wicked Gestapo man snarls: "*Ve* ask ze qvestions." After which he adds: "You realize *vy* I am tellink you all zis?"'

'"Because you will not leave here alive to tell the tale",' Riordan supplied, although he didn't think the joke was very funny. Or in very good taste. Heavy, in fact. Rather Germanic, really.

'Exactly,' Höhner-Lanz said, showing the largest area of gold tooth yet. 'This is, after all, still a secret project. We cannot risk the possibility, the certainty, that you would pass on what you know already. Far too much for the Führer's comfort.' He pushed back his chair.

'I have to leave you for a few minutes,' he said. 'Perhaps you could usefully pass the time reflecting on the exchange of information I suggest. I have done my part. Now I expect Huefer's real name, the precise details of your mission brief, and of course the identity of the organization employing you both. I should add that there are two armed guards outside the entrance door.'

Höhner-Lanz rose to his feet and walked to an inner door. He opened it and went through into what looked like some kind of operations room. Riordan saw a team of uniformed *Hilferinnen* girls bent over charts and drawing boards, the dials and switches and pilot lights of a complex radio installation, men with calculating machines.

The door was closed automatically by a piston and compressed-air cylinder. The piston worked slowly. Before the door sighed shut, Riordan also glimpsed a very large-scale wall map of northern Scandinavia and the Barents Sea. Pins with coloured heads, red and green, dotted the map. The green ones, perhaps a couple of dozen, scattered the area representing the sea; the red, a smaller group, were all on the land mass. Hits and misses, Riordan thought, or more properly hits and shortfalls.

The most electrifying revelation, however, had little to do with the running of the base or the operation of its lethal projectiles.

He heard the SS officer's voice saying: 'We are most grateful, Fräulein, for your help in this matter. There would be a great deal less terrorist activity if more people were as conscientious and co-operative as yourself . . .' And then, in the narrowing crack as the door closed, fur parka over one arm, a snapshot of the woman whose hand Höhner-Lanz was shaking.

Sigurd Hasso, smiling. And her blonde hair didn't fall in a cascade down her back: it was cut quite short and curled around her ears.

So much for dreams! Riordan thought bitterly.

He walked across and stared out of the window, concentrating on the glass-roofed assembly shops behind the huts. Argus, he knew, was an organization specializing in experimental engines. They were responsible, he supposed, for the rocket motor. Fieseler, the builders of the

Storch spotter plane, would be designing, fabricating and assembling the streamlined rocket hull.

How – assuming he ever escaped from the base – could both sets of workshops, and all the data and design material stored in the operations room, be destroyed?

The third, and most shattering, surprise of the day lay literally under Riordan's nose.

On a narrow table below the window lay a German army newspaper published in occupied Norway, folded back to an inside page. Glancing idly at the headlines, he saw that the American aircraft-carrier *Lexington* had been sunk by the Japanese during the battle of the Coral Sea. Hitler and Mussolini had met in Salzburg, but the Führer was unwilling for the moment to give the go-ahead for an Italian invasion of Malta, despite the fact that the Luftwaffe had destroyed every single Spitfire sent to reinforce the island's depleted force of Hurricanes. At a gathering of high-ranking officers in Tromsö . . .

Riordan stiffened, gazing in disbelief at a photograph and caption accompanying the last story.

The picture showed Höhner-Lanz, smiling, in full dress uniform with medals glittering, sitting at a crowded table beside a glamorous young woman wearing a low-cut evening dress and a five-strand pearl choker. The caption read: 'At the Mayor's table: SS Obersturmbannführer Rudolf Höhner-Lanz with his charming French companion, Fräulein Aline Pacquot from Paris. An earnest of the international accord characterizing the New Europe?'

Riordan was rigid. It was his Aline all right. The auburn hair registered as black in a newspaper photo, but no grainy newsprint reproduction, no flash-bulb stare, could disguise those cheek-bones, that wry, quizzical smile with its hint of complicity.

He was staggered. And of course a great number of puzzles, quite suddenly, solved themselves.

If Aline was in fact a *collabo*, a darling of the occupiers, it was no wonder that he had been followed when he went to

Holland to recruit Van Eyck, no wonder that his apartment was staked out and Zabrisky's phone tapped after he had shaken the tails and returned to free Frenchie Delorme. Although he had told her nothing of the mission, she could have been eavesdropping on his conversations with Huefer ever since that first meeting when she had supposedly retired to the kitchen to make coffee, listened to his telephone calls, noted all the arrangements he made, reported everything. He had had no reason to distrust her.

Most satisfying of all – in a perverse way – was the fact that now the inexplicable was explained. With what Aline had reported, an intelligence agent who knew Riordan's background could easily enough have deduced that he had been commissioned to recruit helpers and go to Finland – even, if a German agent had been sent to Fribourg, that it was the north of the country. He had made no secret of his visit to Switzerland, telling Aline that it was connected with the articles he was to write for Huefer.

And once the Nazis suspected that a group of mercenaries were being sent secretly to that bleak and inhospitable northern area, what other project worthy of such attention was there apart from the rocket research installation?

The SOE man had been right when he reported that Riordan was the subject of a Berlin warning alerting local commanders.

Perhaps it was because this was on his mind that he noticed, leafing through the paper, a small item at the foot of another inside page. The story, set in a bold-face panel, repeated a communiqué issued by the Finnmark Propaganda Abteilung. Five days ago, the statement said, Otto Knudsen, a Norwegian working as a barman at Lebesby, had been arrested, together with six companions, on charges of sabotage and treasonable activities prejudicial to the Reich. Found guilty by a military court, the terrorists had been sentenced to death and summarily executed the following morning.

Riordan shook his head gravely. Some risked everything for a principle – and lost out just the same.

There was activity now on the launching pad. The missile was in a near-vertical position, inclined slightly towards the north. Steam wisped from a vent between two of the fins. Some members of the workforce had already retired behind the concrete anti-blast walls. An officer ran into a command hut sunk into the ground some way from the pad.

Riordan picked up the paper again. He looked at the photo of Aline. Was it some subconscious premonition of this betrayal which had provoked his sleeping mind, substituting her for Sigurd at the end of his dream?

'A charming companion, our mutual friend, don't you think?' Höhner-Lanz said genially at his elbow. 'One of our most successful agents. We – shall we say? – engineered your meeting with her as soon as we learned your case history.'

'I do not propose to comment on that situation at all,' Riordan said stiffly, feeling pompous and a little stuffy but able to do nothing about it. 'But there is one thing that puzzles me a great deal.'

'Namely?'

'The ... commitment ... which brought me here, like my meeting with Monsieur Huefer, is comparatively recent. You have said you know all about me, and my record, and my relationship with that gentleman – no doubt through the woman we are discussing. You say, indeed, that you engineered our meeting. Yet my relationship with that person dates back long before, many months before, I had ever heard of Monsieur Huefer. How do you account for this discrepancy?'

Höhner-Lanz laughed. 'Poor Riordan. Male pride, once wounded, is seldom able to hide its scars. But of course you are quite right. It is funny, really; certainly ironic. Our original idea, bringing the two of you, as it were, together, had nothing to do with Huefer or whatever he is called. We were hoping, once the affair settled down, that Fräulein Pacquot would be able to persuade you in fact to work for *us* ... much in the way you finally chose to work for this Huefer. You have to admit there's at least material for a French farce there! ... But watch. Today's last blast-off is about to be organized.'

The launching pad was deserted now. A loud hissing, underlaid by a growing, earth-shaking rumble, manifested itself from outside the headquarters building. And suddenly, shockingly, pale smoke boiled from beneath the missile. The smoke seethed, darkened, rolled out to fill the depression and churn against the anti-blast walls.

From the operations room next door, Riordan heard a disembodied loudspeaker voice declaiming what was presumably a countdown.

The glass panes of the window shivered.

'... *Seven ... Six ... Five ... Four ... Three ... Two ... One ... Zero!*'

A roar of flame and a thunderous assault on the ears. The entire building was shuddering.

'*We have lift-off!*'

And suddenly, unbelievably, above the turbulent smoke, the monstrous finned cigar moved. Trembling, the whole sinister length rose into the air. For an instant it appeared to hover there, balanced above a smoky inferno ... then it was streaking away with the fires of hell belching from its tail.

Riordan and the German watched it go. Almost at once the startlingly white vapour column etched itself against the blue sky, linking the rocket to the earth it was leaving with such velocity.

The acceleration was astonishing. Within seconds, the slender silhouette spearheading the snow-white contrail dwindled from a cigar to a pencil to a pin to a speck.

When the speck could barely be distinguished among the moving cells of the fluid sheathing the eye – Riordan estimated the height at between sixty and seventy thousand feet – the missile died.

A white flower blossomed obscenely at the head of the trail, expanded at once to a huge and hideous puffball, and spewed out subsidiary trails which arched into the sky or snaked earthwards streaked with flame. Northwards in the direction of the Norwegian frontier, smoking fragments spiralled down to the tundra wastes.

Seconds later they heard the distant thunder of the explosion.

From the command hut, the hangar, the operations room, from behind the blast walls and dormitory buildings, men had run out to stare at the sky, shielding their eyes against the glare of the setting sun.

Höhner-Lanz shook his head. 'Very volatile fuels,' he said. 'There remain, as I told you, certain obstacles to overcome . . .'

He went back and stood beside his desk. 'Sit down,' he said, pointing to the vacant chair.

Riordan sat.

'The entertainment is over,' Höhner-Lanz said. 'Tell me now, at once, Huefer's real name, the organization employing you, the mission brief.'

'I thought I had made this clear,' Riordan said. 'I only know the man as Huefer; I don't *know* his real name. I have no idea what organization he represents. That was the whole idea: that none of us should know who we were working for. So that if we were caught and questioned we genuinely couldn't answer questions such as yours.' He paused for a moment, and then went on: 'So far as the briefing is concerned, it was given by Huefer himself, and I have told you already what it was. I have nothing to add.'

The attack was as violent as it was unexpected.

The SS officer had been standing with his right arm held across his chest. Now, stretching it out to its full length, he struck Riordan viciously, backhanded, the top of his fist cracking against the side of his unprotected face.

The speed and ferocity of the blow were enough to knock Riordan out of his chair and send him sprawling to the floor. The flesh of his cheek was split, and blood ran from his nose. He realized from the stunning impact that the hand inside Höhner-Lanz's black leather glove must be artificial, probably made of steel. Licking blood from his lip, he raised a hand to touch his savaged cheek.

The German was white with fury. 'You are a fool, Riordan,' he rasped. 'Do you know what sharpened interrogation is? Well, you will soon, for I do not give second chances. By dawn tomorrow I shall have the answers to my questions.'

He strode to the door, jerked it open, and barked to the armed Wehrmacht guards outside: 'Take him away. Chain him to the others, and deliver them all to Gestapo headquarters in Lakselv.'

20

Captain O'Kelly strode into the CO(S)E operations room in the Citadel and shrugged out of his immaculate jacket. 'Tell you one thing, Archie,' he growled, draping it over the back of his chair. 'It's still bloody cold for the time of the year up there. Thank God the Ministry of Works allows us to keep the bloody radiators on a bit longer than those for the official Civil Service wallahs in Whitehall!'

Commander Lang smiled. 'Yes, sir – like the song says: Spring will be a little late this year. Winter doesn't seem anxious to leave.'

'At least it's better than being out in the North Atlantic on some blasted convoy duty. Or, worse, in the bloody Arctic. Any news, by the way, on Operation Icicle?'

'Yes, sir. A signal came in during the night.' Lang turned to a telegraphist wearing earphones, who sat beneath a battery of radar monitor screens, watching coloured lights blink among the dials of his transmitter. 'Finished decoding it yet, Ford?'

The man lifted a phone away from one ear and looked enquiring. Lang repeated his question. The telegraphist nodded and tore a sheet of paper from a pad attached to a clipboard on a shelf in front of him. Lang took the message and scanned the neat capitals.

He shook his head. 'Bad show.'

'What is?'

'Knudsen's ring – the SOE group servicing the northern fiords – has been rolled up.' He read more. 'But it seems our chaps got away first . . .'

'Good show.'

'They've actually located the base . . . and there's something here about . . . what is this, Ford?'

'Spot of poor reception there, sir. Lot of interference. The word could be pocket, docket, or rocket, and the next few are garbled. Unfortunately the sender was unable to repeat. Bit of a dicey situation, I gathered.'

'Anyway,' Lang said, 'the signal goes on to say that four of them have been taken actually into the base – why *taken*, I wonder? – but that efforts are being made . . .' He frowned, reading the line again. 'I don't understand this. Efforts are being made to get them *out* – so that they can go back *in* again and "complete the picture", whatever that means. That's what it says.'

'Well,' O'Kelly said, 'there's nothing we can do but wait for the next transmission and ask for clarification.' He sighed. 'That's all we do half the time in this bloody job: sit and bloody wait!'

Van Eyck was waiting. Together with Daniels and Frenchie – helped by a dried-up watercourse and a line of ragged birch trees – he had succeeded in making a flanking movement wide enough for them to see the far side of the mountain, together with the colossal rock overhang and the research station it sheltered.

They had been on the way back to the bivouac, complete with photos, when they heard the firing of machine-guns and pom-poms, then saw the crippled Fiat float-plane pass overhead, going south. 'Christ,' Daniels said, 'we already saw that rocket thing take off and vanish into the far blue fucking yonder. What the hell goes on here? What else have they got to show us?'

They were back at the bivouac when his question was dramatically answered. A little awed by the splendour of the scene, they watched the second missile auto-destruct. 'One is really being spoiled by these fellows,' Van Eyck observed. 'Three pyrotechnical displays in one long afternoon! Can one seriously expect anything more?'

One could.

It was Frenchie who found the paper. A wadded square between two of the stacked skillets in the forage master's neat collection of survival kitchen equipment – a place where it was sure to be found before the end of the evening, when the next meal was made.

There was a message on the paper: half a dozen hand-written lines scrawled with a soft lead pencil. The message read: 'Your leader has been taken. He is a prisoner within the base. It is possible that the others too, those who took the plane, may have been arrested after the crash landing. In any case, there are no interrogation facilities, no cells, on the site. Any prisoners will surely be sent back to the Gestapo on the far side of the border, probably tonight. You should watch the tracks made by the fuel convoy tankers.'

It was unsigned.

'I give up,' said Daniels in disgust. 'I don't understand any of this. I mean I give sodding *up*!'

'One watches, nevertheless, these tracks, no?' Van Eyck said.

'I would think. In any case I don't want to organize chow twice!'

So they waited. Taking advantage of a rocky gully over-looking the track churned out by the forty-ton Büssing-NAG overlanders, Van Eyck posted Daniels and Frenchie among a cluster of rounded boulders which had once formed part of a glacial moraine. Daniels was armed with a Garand carbine; Frenchie had one of the machine-pistols in his powerful clasp. Van Eyck himself took his sniper's rifle to the far side of the defile and concealed himself among the lower branches of a snow-damaged pine.

The sun balanced like a flaming coin on the rim of the nearest ridge. The sky paled but the light failed to thicken. Somewhere overhead, a bird of prey floated darkly on spread wings.

Van Eyck was aware of the ticking of his watch. A breath

of cold wind caressed his cheek. Were they waiting here for nothing? Had the convoy with the prisoners passed already?

If there *was* a convoy. If the others *had* been taken prisoner.

Forced inactivity in a tense situation, he knew as well as Riordan, could induce a panic state as irrational as it was acute. Too much adrenalin, perhaps, with nowhere useful to go. Yet certain questions clamoured for an answer.

The pencilled message between Daniels's skillets was the only evidence they had for any of this. Suppose the whole thing was a plant, a ruse to get them away from the bivouac so that their supplies could be plundered? Or sabotaged? Or the food spiked?

Suppose the aim of the plant was to tempt them out into the open, where they too could more easily be captured? Or shot down? Suppose Riordan and the others had never been captured at all?

The minimum of logic disposed of all such hysteria, Van Eyck thought. If Riordan and the others were still free, they would have returned to the bivouac hours ago. If the message was a trick to get them away from the bivouac, any sabotage or theft could just as easily have taken place when the message was left: after all, they had *already* been away from the bivouac then. And other than that which grew in clefts among the rocks, there was no food to spike.

So far as tempting them out into the open was concerned, they were far better protected here than they would have been there.

Whoever left that message was either a friend or an enemy, in any case someone who knew this was their hide-out, the Dutchman reasoned. If it was an enemy, there would be no point to the message: it would be easier either to eliminate them or capture them without tipping them off first. A friend, then. In which case there could only be one point to the message: that it was true, that the others *had* been taken prisoner, that they *would* be brought along this track.

Or had been brought already.

Only time could tell them if that one was true.

There remained the one principal, and baffling, question: Who had left the message, and how had they known?

Van Eyck shifted restlessly. In some places, resin had leaked out between the lozenges of the pine bark, sticking to his fingers, smearing an aromatic, translucent glue on the material of his parka. Desperate suddenly for a sign of life to break the brooding silence of this dead land — anyone's life, most especially his own — he shouted aloud. What did it matter? There was no one to hear.

'*How far would you say we were from the perimeter?*'

'*Three miles, maybe four,*' Daniels's voice echoed back reassuringly from among the rocks.

'*So we should hear them when they're halfway here? Between one and a half and two miles away under these conditions?*'

'*I would think. There's nothing to mask the sound, no other noise whatever.*'

'*One had noticed,*' Van Eyck called.

But it was precisely then that there *was* an alien sound.

The whine of powerful, heavy-duty engines in low gear, a distant rattle of caterpillar tracks. A burble, perhaps, of motorcycle exhausts?

Van Eyck repeated the instructions he had given his companions earlier.

Once more they waited.

The track was exceedingly rough. In this particular defile, it was naked bedrock scattered with slaty stones, running beside the loose gravel of a long-dead watercourse.

It was half an hour before the complex mechanical clamour of the approaching convoy had swelled in volume enough to signal that the moment of truth was near.

Around a bend in the ravine, quite naturally, as if

ACTION IN THE ARCTIC

it was the most normal thing in the world, the long northern twilight revealed a pair of motorcycle combinations, skating uneasily over the rock-strewn floor, a heavy half-track command truck with barred windows, a Hanomag scout car with a crew of four, and two solo motorcyclists bringing up the rear.

The sidecars and the scout were armed with Madsen machine-guns.

Van Eyck eased back the bolt of his Dragunov and then pushed it gently forward to lodge one of the ten rounds from his magazine in the breech.

Riordan's final surprise on that fateful day was delayed until he was dragged away from Höhner-Lanz's office. When they came in, he had taken off his parka and dropped it over a chair near the door of the operations room. Now, as the guards advanced on him from the outer door, he scrambled up and shrugged it on before they reached him. Nobody tried to stop him. Astonishingly, he wasn't searched again. The Walther P-38 and the binoculars had been taken from him, along with the notes he had made on the perimeter patrols, when he was captured. He supposed the men hustling him out assumed that he must be clean; and anyway, they had received no orders to search him. Initiative in ordinary soldiers was frowned upon.

Höhner-Lanz stood with his back to them, staring out of the window, his hands clasped behind his back. The gloved fingers of the good hand clenched and unclenched as he waited there, ramrod still, apparently furious that his man-to-man, placatory approach had produced no tangible results. In any case, the role he had written for himself required him to be distanced from the scene once his decision had been made. No second thoughts; even to glance at the prisoner again would be beneath him.

It was one of the techniques, Riordan knew, that they used to diminish and dehumanize their prisoners and tacitly assert their own superiority. The prisoner was an object beneath contempt, to be ignored now until the executioners, the experts, had squeezed the truth out of him, when the manner of his death could be decided.

If a little more attention had been paid, nevertheless, his captors might have discovered what it was that weighed down the inner right-hand pocket of this particular prisoner's parka.

Riordan himself had no idea; he only knew that it had not been there when he took the garment off.

He had no chance to find out until he was thrust into a guardroom that formed part of a sandbagged building at the perimeter entrance. García, Aletti and a crestfallen Hills were already there, handcuffed to a steam pipe that fed a radiator. The room was stiflingly hot, the atmosphere tainted with sweat and cigarette smoke and boot polish, the components characteristic of any institutional army office the whole world over.

Scientific teams, *Hilferinnen* and members of the crack 155th Flakregiment had glanced curiously at Riordan as he was led through the compound to the guardhouse, but inside, the Wehrmacht detail instructed to take them to the Gestapo headquarters at Lakselv virtually ignored them; they were just another batch of criminals headed for the camps or forced-labour factories.

With one wrist locked to the pipe, Riordan tried stealthily to explore his pocket with the other hand. Hills, standing next to him, murmured: 'Bit of a black, actually. Got hold of this bally seaplane, overflew the base and took lots of jolly snaps – then bought it when we crash-landed in some bloody marsh that looked like a real lake. After which we were fished out by the boys in grey who'd been sent to look for us.'

'No talking!' shouted the *Feldwebel* in charge of the detail.

'They got the cameras, I suppose?' Riordan asked.

'Well, actually no. We had time to junk them in a bed of reeds. Easy enough to find again, if we . . .'

'*I said no talking!*' the NCO yelled, drawing back a heavy fist to punch first Hills and then Riordan in the face.

Blood had already blocked Riordan's nose and the gash over his cheek-bone was badly swollen. Now he had a split lip and a broken tooth. For the moment though he was sublimely unaware of this. *The object weighing down his pocket was a handgun.*

Not the heavy, long-barrelled Walther which had been taken from him, but a compact, lightweight automatic, shiny to the touch, which he guessed to be a small-calibre weapon, probably with a seven-round magazine, possibly Italian.

It was impossible to examine it properly here. But it was comforting to know it was there, and his expert touch told him that the weapon was almost certainly loaded.

He put totally out of his mind the mystifying questions connected with the find. Questions like: How did it get there? Who put it there? And what did whoever-it-was hope to gain? What was *he* supposed to do? He couldn't answer any of them anyway. The time for questions and answers would be after he had used the gun, if he found an opportunity.

If, as seemed likely, he had a friend in the camp, the least he could do was play it by ear and profit from his good luck as best he could. Maybe then he would even find out who the friend was.

The prisoners were being marched out to the armoured lorry which was to take them back to Norway. Each man was released from the steam pipe and had his wrists handcuffed behind his back. Once in the lorry, the cuffs themselves were locked to a heavy chain stretching from the front to the rear of the body, along one wall and opposite a row of benches.

Two guards climbed in the back with them, one posted at each end of the chain. The driver's mate carried two dossiers, one concerning Riordan's arrest and interrogation, together with the notes he had taken, the other detailing the exploits of his men, including the 'murder' of three aviators.

Very slowly, the convoy rolled off the smooth macadamed surface of the research base and took the rutted, potholed, rock-strewn tanker track.

Shackled to the taut chain as they were, and unable to sit on the wooden benches, Riordan and his three men, thrown often together, struggled to keep their balance as the lorry lurched and rolled across the rough ground. Through small window grilles they could watch the bare ridges, the occasional lines of ragged trees moving past. On particularly sharp curves, the two motorcycle combinations riding ahead could be seen. And once, rounding an acute corner, the vehicle slewed across a patch of gravel to reveal the Hanomag and its outriders behind.

On one of the occasions when the four prisoners were hurled against one another, Riordan succeeded in a double contortion which permitted him to grab the gun and bring it half into view. 'Stay off balance, leaning in to me!' he hissed to García. Hills caught on at once too, staggering against them as the lorry rocketed over a section of shale.

'No talking!' the guard bellowed. But by the time they had extricated themselves, the gun was in Riordan's outer pocket.

It was indeed Italian, a Beretta Modello 1935-C, only six inches long, weighing less than one and a half pounds and chambered for the .22LR cartridge. There were in fact eight of these tiny rounds in the non-standard, transparent, pistol-grip magazine.

Riordan was unaware, with the present odds stacked against them, when and if he would find an opportunity to use it. But it provided a barely discernible light at the end of what had been the darkest of tunnels.

The opportunity presented itself far more speedily than he could have hoped for.

The convoy was bouncing downhill into a rocky valley.

Winding around a bluff which blocked half the route, the combinations entered a long, narrow defile. The armoured lorry and the others followed.

Even in the vehicle's noisy, metallic interior, they heard the sharp snap of the rifle, echoing off the rock walls.

Through the forward grille, Riordan saw the rider of the leading combination slump forward over his handlebars, swerving bike and sidecar off into the loose gravel, where it tipped over on to its side, with the bullet-shaped sidecar in the air.

The gunner leapt out and tried to heave the combination back on to the level, so that he could crouch down and operate the machine-gun. But a second rifle shot had followed quickly on the first, and the man fell flat on his back, blood running from a hole just below the brim of his helmet to stain the rounded pebbles.

'Our cue, I think,' Riordan murmured.

The trigger mechanism of the gas-operated Dragunov, with its short-stroke piston, was simple. Geared for single shots, it involved nothing but the rifle's hammer, a safety sear controlled by the bolt carrier and a disconnector which ensured that the trigger must be released after each shot to reunite the trigger bar and the sear. In hands as expert as Van Eyck's, however, it was as lethal as any high-precision, long-distance killer in the world. And, because of this simplicity, as quick, even when it wasn't in semi-automatic mode.

At his first shot, the surprise was total. By the second, the convoy had slithered to a halt with brakes squealing. The driver and his mate were out of the cab and under the chassis, holding Walther automatics.

Van Eyck dropped from the tree, squinted for the third time through his PSO-1 sight, and drilled the gunner of the second combination. The rider threw himself from the saddle, pushed up the body of his companion as a shield, and manoeuvred the sidecar machine-gun on its mounting to blast a searing stream of bullets up into the tree where Van Eyck had been hiding. A branch snapped and fell. Pine needles and twigs showered to the ground. Several cones dropped and bounced down on to the track.

The Dutchman himself was already on his feet and running . . . away from the stalled convoy, scaling the steep, rocky bank, dodging between the trees. The maximum effective range of the Schmeissers carried by the escort would not exceed two hundred and fifty yards. For the Madsens, add perhaps another hundred. Once he had put five hundred yards between himself and the Germans, therefore, he could safely show himself – or show where he was – in a position where he could reach them, but they couldn't reach him.

Unless they tried to creep up and enfilade him.

And that was where Daniels and Frenchie, with the machine-pistol and the longer-range carbine, were to play their part.

The *Feldwebel*, riding beside the driver in the Hanomag, had by now deployed his men: the driver and the two solo motorcyclists, who only carried automatic pistols, sheltering behind the lorry but ready to fire at anything that moved; the four soldiers with their Schmeissers among the rocks flanking the defile behind the Hanomag. The NCO himself was going to make a rush for the unused machine-gun in the first sidecar while the surviving outrider continued to blast out short bursts after Van Eyck.

It was at this point that Daniels and Frenchie opened fire.

After three individual rifle shots and a few bursts from one machine-pistol, the cannonade erupting suddenly outside was deafening to the mercenaries locked inside the lorry. Clearly the guards' orders were to stay with them. Riordan had slipped the small automatic from his pocket, and now held it two-handed behind him, with his back to the chain. It had not been too difficult, making unobtrusive movements when the lorry was jolting over rough ground, much more likely to attract the guards' attention now they were at a standstill. He spoke over his shoulder to Hills, who had been last into the vehicle and stood nearest the guard by the rear doors.

'Watch me. When I move, try to kick his gun away.'

'*No talking!*' the front guard shouted in German. 'The next man utters a word gets a ball in the guts!'

'Jolly convenient. Couldn't find a better place,' Hills murmured.

The guard raised his gun threateningly – both men carried normal service revolvers – but the last half of the Englishman's remark was drowned by a fresh outbreak of shooting in the ravine.

Riordan took advantage of it. One tiny report from inside the closed truck wasn't going to be noticed among the rasping bursts of rival machine-pistol fire outside. Twisting away from the chain and down, the mercenary leader brought up his fettered hands behind him and shot the forward guard.

The small-calibre bullet penetrated his diaphragm. For an instant he stared in disbelief, then choked up blood, pitching forward first on to his knees, then flat on his face. The heavy revolver fell from his hand. Aletti lunged forward and kicked it away.

Hills meanwhile had stealthily inched forward until he was as far from the chain as the full stretch of his arms would permit. As Riordan ducked down to shoot, he lashed out a long leg and kicked the gun from the rear guard's grip. A second blow, delivered with lightning speed, buried the toe of his boot in the German's crotch. The guard folded forward, gasping, hands clutching his lower belly. Before he hit the floor, Riordan had turned, contorted himself in the other direction and fired again. In such conditions, it was impossible to aim accurately. But hard, too, to miss.

The bullet caught the man in the left shoulder, four

inches from the armpit, slamming him back to sit against the armoured doors. He slumped there, trying to master the pain twisting his guts. But one hand was creeping towards the revolver, which had thumped against the metal wall and dropped to the floor.

'I wouldn't,' Riordan warned. The hand continued to creep.

Riordan shot for the third time.

The guard cursed. The slug had seared through his upper thigh. He rolled over on to his face. And still he continued to inch towards his gun.

Riordan bit his lip. 'I don't like to do this,' he said tensely, 'but you leave me no choice. Stop moving that way or I continue shooting.'

Bullet number four smashed the fingers of the outstretched hand.

The guard reached out his undamaged hand. Trails of blood around him gathered dust from the metal floor. He looked over his shoulder; a travesty of a smile contorted his white face. 'You're fucked, and you don't know it,' he said. 'You fired four times already. How many rounds have you got left in that thing? Two? Three? Four at the most. What use are they to you? What can you do with them? Only two things: blow me away, or use the threat of that to make me stop trying to reach my own shooter. I already showed you that threats don't work with me. So you're going to have to kill me – or allow me to reach that gun and kill you.'

'And so?'

'So there was one other thing. You thought maybe a gun would intimidate me, that I could be "persuaded" to hand over the handcuff keys.' Very slowly, he shook his head. He was losing a lot of blood. 'No way,' he said. 'No way at all. I have my duty to the Führer, to the Reich: one does not release prisoners who have acted against the Reich – even at the expense of one's own life.'

'Do it,' Hills urged. 'You have no choice.'

'So when you've got rid of me,' the guard continued,

his voice weaker now, 'where are you? Exactly where you were before the shooting started: two German soldiers are dead and you are still manacled to a chain. Even if you contrive to move our bodies closer, you cannot reach the keys, because the chain is waist-high and *both* your hands are attached to it. There is no way you can reach down far enough to rifle our belts.'

'There are friends outside who can do that for us,' Riordan said.

'I do not think they will reach you. There is no way of opening this lorry from the outside.'

There was a sudden thumping on the doors from outside. The *Feldwebel*'s voice: 'What the devil goes on in there. Open up, Schultz. I want the prisoners as hostages, to act as a shield.'

'He's just stalling,' Hills said. 'Better to get it over.'

Riordan felt a chill at the nape of his neck. The guard was quite right. With both men dead, they no longer risked being shot – but they were as much a group of prisoners as ever, helplessly chained and prevented from reaching the device that would free them.

'You are a brave man,' Riordan said, 'and I salute your sense of duty. Nevertheless . . .' Twisting, he fired for the last time. The German's hand had already closed around the butt of his gun.

The .22 slug hit him between the eyes, and he died instantly. He slid again to the floor, leaving a smear of blood and brains on the reinforced wall.

'All right,' Riordan said. 'The guy was right and we're no better off. So we improvise. García, Alex, reach out a foot as far as you can and see if you can shift the one at the front. If you can, shove him towards the bulkhead so that the body's stable, then hook a heel or toe into a crease in his uniform, a pocket, his belt, anything, and slide him my way.'

Aletti, at the front end of the chain, could only just touch the body with his heel; García, straining his arms away from the chain, managed to wedge an instep against the top of a thigh. Between them, heaving and sweating despite the near-freezing temperature, they manoeuvred the dead guard, inch by inch, until his frame was hard against the partition separating the cab from the rear of the lorry. After that, with proper purchase for heels and toes, they pushed the body towards Riordan.

They had established that the guard's keys were on a ring clipped to his belt, with the keys themselves in his trouser pocket.

Riordan explained what he wanted. 'It's no good,' García, the shortest one, said. 'Bent double, at the full stretch of my arms, I can't even get my *teeth* near his pocket!'

'You will if we all work together,' Riordan told him.

Stepping away from the chain and over the body, they heeled it back until it was lying along the foot of the wall, below the chain. Then, balanced on one leg, each of them lodged the heel of the other beneath the dead German and eased him up until he was level with the chain. It was not easily done. The effort had to be co-ordinated as it would in a tug-of-war; Riordan called out the one-two-three-*go*! that preceded each concerted heave, but on several occasions the body slipped, and once it jackknifed and collapsed back on to the floor. Finally, however, it was held in place by the pressure of their bent legs, steadied by their hands. García unclipped the key ring behind his back and pushed it towards Riordan.

The bunch of keys dropped to the floor.

Over the unison gasp of dismay, Riordan's cool voice called out: 'All *right*. No panic. We don't have to go through the whole scene again, or try and fetch the other fellow over. The keys are not in a pocket now; they're a pretty solid bunch. Who's got big feet? . . . Hills! Wedge the side of one foot against them, and work them up the wall until they're at the level of the chain. And keep them there until you're *sure* someone's grabbed them!'

The three other members of the team held their breath as the tall, fair marksman splayed out a foot, trapped the keys, and twisted himself to slide them up the smooth wall. For the final eighteen inches, the top half of his body was bent forward almost horizontally, and his knee cocked like a champion hurdler's. The *Feldwebel* was still thumping on the rear doors and shouting.

Hills was panting. Sweat dewed his upper lip. With infinite concentration, he forced aching muscles to slide the keys a final few inches, forcing them at the same time hard against the wall. They were level with the chain.

Pushing his manacled wrist through the steel circlet as far as it would squeeze, García found he could touch the keys. Flipping fingers to displace the top few so that he could grasp a solid one, the nut-faced little Spaniard lifted the bunch from Hills's foot with a cry of 'Got it!' He rattled the handcuffs the other way and lowered the keys gently into Riordan's waiting palm.

Two minutes later, all four of them were free, rubbing sore wrists to bring back the circulation.

Riordan had seen that there was a locked door communicating with the driver's cab. 'We'll go that way,' he said. 'The guy won't just be sitting there, after all.' At the third try, he found the key that opened the door.

'For the moment I'll stay with this little toy,' Riordan said, hefting the Beretta. 'Hills, you and García take the guards' revolvers. Right now, Alex, all I can do for you is advise you to keep a low profile. As soon as we bump off some Kraut, you can have what he's got.'

'Just so long,' Aletti said mournfully, 'as we don't pick the Kraut thinks *he's* the one chosen to blow away *me*!'

The shooting had grown sporadic. Some of it, clearly, was now more distant from the convoy. Riordan slid open the door, dropped to his hands and knees, and crawled forward, leading the way into the cab.

* * *

The situation outside was now confused. Daniels and Frenchie, blazing away at anything they could see from the safety of the boulders, were out of touch with Van Eyck, who had found an eyrie behind a fallen pine on the lip of the ravine – but several hundred yards away from his companions.

Without Riordan to co-ordinate them, they were like a rudderless ship: afloat, sheltered, with cannons primed – but nobody at the helm.

The surviving outrider, firing the second Madsen machine-gun towards Van Eyck, had quickly been picked off by Daniels with the Garand, once the two men concealed in the moraine revealed their presence. A warning burst from Frenchie's Schmeisser had discouraged the *Feldwebel* when he tried to crawl out to the abandoned combination and take over the gun. Now both combinations, with their armament, lay in the no man's land in front of the lorry, too vulnerable to be reached by anyone.

The driver and his mate lay beneath the chassis with their handguns, ready to fire at anything that appeared; the *Feldwebel* was still lurking behind the lorry, but his driver was dead. A foolhardy dash for the cover of a rock fissure, from which he could have menaced Frenchie and Daniels, had been ended by a two-second burst sprayed from the Schmeisser. He had made the cleft all right, but most of his blood was splashed across the smooth slate face of an outcrop overlooking the gap in which his body lay.

The four soldiers were pinned down on the far side of the ravine from the mercenaries. Hoping to climb higher among a jumble of boulders at the foot of an ancient landslide, one of them had been shot and wounded in the belly by Daniels, and now the remaining three were threatened from a distance by Van Eyck.

In the lull between bursts of small-arms fire, the injured man's groans echoed off the rock walls. Above him the black bird, coasting in slow circles on its spread wings, settled lower as the cold northern light dimmed.

It was when he received no answer to his thumping on the locked rear doors of the lorry that the *Feldwebel* decided enough was enough. He ordered the two solo motorcyclists back to the base with a request for reinforcements.

That was when Van Eyck pulled off perhaps the most brilliant piece of marksmanship in his life.

The two men had reached their machines, kick-started and roared off. Van Eyck cradled his Dragunov, steadied his elbows on the trunk of the fallen tree, peered through the PSO-1, curled a trigger finger, held his breath . . . and squeezed. The shot startled the black bird higher up over the ravine.

Over a distance of more than 750 yards, in poor light, with a bouncing, swaying target, the Dutchman scored between the shoulder-blades of one of the riders. The man threw up his arms and plunged off his machine; the motorcycle corkscrewed into the soft gravel beside the track and cartwheeled to a standstill, engine screaming and rear wheel spinning because the twist-grip was blocked open among the constricting stones.

The second rider vanished safely around the corner in the defile and roared back towards the base.

The mechanical bedlam in the ravine was augmented almost at once when the lorry's motor burst shatteringly to life, shaking the body on its springs.

Windscreen and glasses vanished instantly in a hail of shining splinters as the soldiers opened fire. Riordan, García and Hills replied, shooting blind over the top of the armoured doors, the heavy reports of the two revolvers drowning the crack of the Beretta as the mercenary leader exhausted the last few rounds in his magazine. At the same time Aletti, who had started the engine, crouched in front of the driving seat and used both hands to declutch, haul the gear lever into reverse, and lean on the accelerator.

The lorry shot backwards, exposing the driver and his mate, who had been lying prone beneath the engine. Before they could react, Frenchie sprang into sudden view on top of a boulder, hosing death in blazing bursts, crumpling up the two men in a smother of blood, dust and jerking limbs.

The soldiers, reloading out of sight, were too late to reply. Frenchie vanished from view again to reload in his turn.

It was hardly necessary. There was a loud cry from further along the ravine. The *Feldwebel*, taken by surprise when the lorry reversed so abruptly, had been knocked down and then run over. He lay now with one leg beneath the caterpillar track and the whole weight of the vehicle pinning him to the ground.

Gritting his teeth, he was bellowing instructions.

On the far side of the ravine, the tip of a rifle appeared above a rock. The scrap of white material tied to it fluttered in the chill Arctic breeze.

Riordan stood up in the cab. He opened the door and stepped down on to the running-board, covered from behind by Daniels and Frenchie. Van Eyck, in the distance, was sliding down the shale to join them. 'Very well,' Riordan called. 'Throw out the guns, far out, and step from behind those rocks with your hands held *high*. Come down quietly and no one will be hurt. Try anything tricky and everyone dies. Now . . . *move!*'

Four weapons clattered on to the rocky slope and skated down towards the track. The three Germans, white-faced, emerged. 'There's a wounded man up there,' one of them said hoarsely.

'He will be attended to,' Riordan said.

The rest was routine. The *Feldwebel*, released from his torment, was laid with the wounded soldier on the floor of the lorry. The three soldiers were handcuffed to the chain inside. Aletti took a water bottle from one of the men and sabotaged the vehicle's petrol tank and the three remaining bikes. The dead could be left to the reinforcements . . . when they came.

'Take the biker maybe fifteen, twenty minutes to get back,' Daniels said. 'Another half hour to round up a posse and get here. If we use the Hanomag and take to the hills, we should have a good twenty-five minutes' start. Besides which, they won't know which way we went, and it'll be dark anyway by then.'

Riordan, who had been calling instructions to non-existent companions above the ravine, and using the echoes as replies, was anxious that the Germans shouldn't know how very small his team was. 'Thank God,' he said, 'that this was only a routine, take-'em-to-jail, MP escort. If they'd been in radio contact with the base . . .' He shook his head. 'Good shooting, anyway, all you guys.'

Aletti was starting the Hanomag scout car. 'Good shooting, he says,' the tough Jewish-Italian muttered. 'And I should be the only one without a gun?'

The seven of them piled into the scout car with what arms they could recuperate, and such stolen papers, passes and forms as Riordan considered useful.

Aletti turned the Hanomag round, drove back around the corner in the defile and as soon as the land flattened out, headed over the rough country towards their bivouac.

In the ravine, after the appalling clamour of gunfire and the beat of machines, the dust settled in the fading light. The northern silence, broken only by the sighing of wind and an occasional groan from a wounded man, lay heavily once again over the bare rock walls. The black bird croaked twice, soared higher, and then flew away to chase the vanished sun.

21

'One better can wait, maybe two days, three?' Van Eyck suggested. 'Then we can perhaps be taking them altogether by surprise. After all, they do not know there be orders to destroy the place. Maybe they think one is just to locate and report on this research installation, no? That once the prisoners be released, we go home with the info?'

'Yeah,' Riordan said. 'I'd agree with you, Piet, except for one thing. Whether or not they know our brief is seek *and* destroy, they'll be looking – looking for the brigands who dared to ambush their convoy. That SS security chief will be doing his nut: *his* prisoners released, *his* escort shot up, *his* orders defied. He'll move heaven and earth to locate – and punish – the "terrorists" responsible for such an outrage. He'll order the frontier and the road to Lake Inari blocked – in case the aim of the ambush operation was simply to rescue us and scoot. But he'll also search the area around the base – in case we *are* still around. The search will be in widening circles . . . and if we wait two or three days, they'll find us, however many times we move camp. That's why I say we strike now, today, as soon as it's dark again. Surprise, as you say, is the best weapon of all, but I prefer to hit them with surprise number two while they're still reeling from the effect of number one.'

'You're the boss,' Van Eyck said.

It was less than twelve hours after the ambush. The sun had reappeared, casting a wintry light over the unforgiving contours of the landscape. The bivouac had been dismantled and the remainder of their supplies repacked. If the person who had left the warning message had found their temporary camp, Riordan reasoned, others could do the same.

Or be tipped off as to the location.

By whom? The person who had left the message? If so, why? And would that be the same person who had slipped the Beretta into his pocket while he was a prisoner inside the base?

Who could that possibly have been?

If it was someone he knew — or knew of — or even someone who knew him, there was only one candidate: Sigurd Hasso.

Yet he had heard with his own ears that it was she who had betrayed him to the Germans in the first place . . .

None of it made sense. The girl had betrayed him — but she had lied about the size of his team; she had said there were *three* others. They had captured three when the float-plane crash-landed, and apparently assumed that was all. Otherwise the ambush would never have succeeded: search parties would have been out; precautions would have been taken.

Again, Sigurd, who had been in the next room, might have had an opportunity to slip in and drop the gun in the pocket of his parka — maybe when he and Höhner-Lanz were watching the blast-off. But why in hell would she want to help *out* a man she had just manoeuvred *in*? What the devil was this girl playing at?

Her role, Riordan reflected with a wry smile, was just about as equivocal as his own when it came to where loyalties lay!

Meanwhile, there were more important questions to be answered.

Hills and Aletti had returned to the marsh to recover the 35mm cameras they had hidden among the reeds. García was looking over the mechanical parts of the Hanomag. Daniels was cleaning and loading what weapons remained to them: the Garand carbine, the Bergmann-Schmeisser machine-pistol, three Sig-Sauer P-220 automatics, Van

Eyck's Dragunov sniper's rifle. Everything else had been taken from them by their captors, although this was more than balanced by four machine-pistols, three automatic pistols and two revolvers won from the escort they ambushed.

Frenchie had been busy with a miniature forger's kit from his pack, perfecting a document whose heading he copied from one of the papers Riordan took from the *Feldwebel*. Now he put away his inks and blades and rubber blanks, snapped shut the shallow ebony case, and rejoined Van Eyck and their leader.

'Not too happy, boss, about the explosives situation,' he said to Riordan. 'We lost a lot when Zabrisky went down and Aletti lost his pack. We're left with dynamite, gelignite, plastic and some new colloidal shit the backroom boys are apparently trying out. Not too much of any of them either.'

'We were never going to attempt more than the greatest possible damage with the smallest amount of charges,' Riordan said.

'Oh, sure. But there's ways and ways of using charges. From what you saw, I reckon there ain't too much actual *machinery* working in there?'

'That's true enough. There's chemical plant, there's an assembly shop for the rockets, but I would think it's mainly prefabricated sections delivered from factories elsewhere; you're not going to get much more than welding material, jigs, frames and lifting equipment in there. In the sense you mean, they don't *make* anything up here; there'll be no belt drives and lathes and presses and that kind of thing.'

Frenchie shook his head. 'Pity,' he said. 'The whole art of explosives in sabotage is picking your spot. The weak link, if you like. With machinery that's *working*, all you have to do is blow some heavy moving part – a beam, a gear train, a con-rod – and it'll thrash about and do your work for you, smash up the whole works in no time. A shaft with one end disconnected can do one hell of a lot of damage, far more than you could yourself with one big charge. It's the principle the Nips employ in their martial arts: use the opponent's strength to hasten his own destruction, channel *his* energy against himself. Except in this case the opponent's a machine.'

'It's a fine principle,' Riordan said, 'but it doesn't apply here.'

'So we have to box crafty. The things are bloody *driven* by some kind of explosive, or exploded gases, right?'

'Alcohol and liquid oxygen, yes. They don't need to react with the atmosphere. Combined chemically, they create a colossal amount of energy, released in the form of heat – a controlled explosion, if you like – and this shoots out of the backside of the missile and shoves it into the sky.'

'Yeah, I read up some of the theory on rockets when I was inside,' Frenchie said. 'Invented by the Chinks in AD 1200. Here you got a carburant – that's the alcohol – and a comburant, the liquid oxygen, combined into what they call a propergol. And when she ignites . . . *Whoosh!* Am I right?'

'Righter than I would ever have been if I hadn't been lectured by our friend in the black uniform,' Riordan said.

'OK,' the French-Canadian said. 'So we use the same flaming *optique*: we get the existing installation to do our work for us – only this time it's not machinery, it's another form of explosive.'

'You mean . . .?'

'I mean alcohol and liquid oxygen don't have to be stashed in a vertically oriented rocket before they go bang when combined. I mean, maybe between our small charges and their big ones, we can organize something of a display.'

'That's my boy!' Riordan said.

When they moved, it was to go closer to the base. This was for two reasons. The first concerned the Hanomag. This was an invaluable asset: not only did it take all their supplies and weapons; it gave them in addition both mobility and speed. The fuel tank, too, was almost full – and there were several hundred rounds of 9mm ammunition for the Madsen machine-gun. Riordan's first impulse, nevertheless, was to abandon it. The car, any car, would be instantly spotted by searchers in this bleak landscape, especially if the searchers had air support – and he was convinced there *would* be air support as early as Höhner-Lanz could call it up.

It was Beverley Hills who made him change his mind.

At the head of the valley from which they saw the lake and the float-plane, Hills remembered, there was a rock formation resembling a miniature replica of the huge shelf protecting the base. 'Probably an offshoot of the same fault,' he said, 'only this time the bally shelf's no more than twenty or thirty feet thick. And water running down the face has hollowed out the softer strata underneath to make a sort of open-sided cave.'

Riordan was interested. 'How deep is the cave?'

Hills shrugged. 'Search me. Three or four car's lengths.'

'And how high?'

'Not very. If you stood up in the Hanomag, you could touch the roof.'

'We'll go there,' Riordan decided. 'Apart from hiding the scout car, there's a second reason for moving in closer to the base: they'll be spreading the search the other way – further and further afield. Nobody expects the hunted to run *towards* the hunters.'

It was a tough journey over the trackless wastes. Before each rise, one of the mercenaries had to go ahead and scan the succeeding depression to make sure that the coast was clear. Even for Aletti, steering a course across the boulder-studded slopes of lichen and moss was a nightmare. It was probably not more than three miles, but it took them over two spine-jolting hours. When they finally reached the head of the valley, the Hanomag had to be skated down a forty-five-degree slant of crumbling shale before they could manhandle it into the cavern.

Ten minutes later they heard the uneven drone of a small aircraft.

Riordan peered out from beneath the rock shelf. A Fieseler Storch artillery spotter, like a gaunt mosquito circling and circling again above the desolate terrain. Soon, it flew away towards the south, where – he was certain – the search would first of all be concentrated, along with salvage operations, in the vicinity of the ambush.

When they could no longer hear the plane, Riordan and the three who had been taken prisoner drew up a chart mapping, as accurately as they could remember, the principal locations within the base.

It was bitterly cold in the gloom beneath the rock roof. Water feeding the stream traversing the valley, reduced in volume since the snows melted, nevertheless still streamed down the face of the sedimentary shelf, lay in pools on the floor and dripped in the further recesses of the cavern. The mercenaries' voices echoed hollowly as they worked out the assault on the base.

'You do realize,' Aletti said at the beginning of the discussion, 'that the only way the Hanomag she can be driven out of here is along the river-bed, out by the lake, and then west towards the base, the way the patrol comes when we steal the float-planes?'

'No problem,' Riordan said. 'That means the scout will be used north of the base – and once they know there *is* an attack, they'll expect it from the south. You've heard it before and I'll say it again,' he went on, 'the essence, the core of this thing is surprise, surprise and surprise again.'

He laid the chart on the warm, sloping bonnet of the Hanomag as they crowded around. 'By which I mean: surprise that there's an attack at all, surprise that it comes so soon, surprise at the quarter from which it comes and finally astonishment at the *manner* of the attack.'

He looked around the group. Six totally dissimilar faces: García, tense and serious; Van Eyck, alert and efficient;

Aletti with his wry smile, expecting the worst and over-coming it; Hills, affecting to be a little bored; strong, reli-able Frenchie, with his bruiser's build; hardbitten Daniels, the man of so many parts. Six men, on each of whom, in a relatively short time, the lives of all the others would depend . . .

'We shall go over this again and again until just before dark,' Riordan said, 'but I insist that you remember all the time that these are the priorities: they must *never* know how many – or how few – we are; they must *always* be wondering from which direction the next thrust will come; they must *never* realize precisely what the object of the assault is.' Riordan smiled. 'Add to that the fact that, being inside a guarded perimeter, they'll naturally assume that any attack will start outside, with people trying to get in – when of course the real danger will come from those *already* in.'

'I say, dash it all, that's a bit of a tall order, isn't it?' Hills drawled. 'Just how do you propose to organize that, sir?'

Riordan told him how he proposed to organize it.

22

'So often,' Riordan said to Frenchie, 'it's the simplest things that solve the problems, the answers so obvious that nobody bothered even to consider them.'

The two of them lay beneath a two-foot-high clump of salix and cloudberries overhanging a low rock platform a hundred and fifty yards inside the base perimeter.

'A fence like this one,' Riordan said, nodding towards the ten-foot chain-link barrier stretching as far as they could see in either direction. 'You can build it ten, twelve, fifteen feet high; you can curve the top of it over or knit barbed wire into it; you can electrify the entire circuit. And the people you're trying to keep out will do their nuts attempting to work out ways of getting over that fence. Short of an explosion or battering it down with a tank, they won't find one, especially if the fence is patrolled as frequently as this one.'

Riordan peered up through the branches. The spotter plane was overflying the area again. 'But what the fence builders won't have done,' he continued, 'is cement the foot of the fence into a concrete fillet throughout the whole length of the perimeter – in this case maybe four or five miles. It's just too much to ask. So the wise invader doesn't waste his time wondering how to get over: he looks for a place where he can get under – as we have done here.'

It was no more than a crease in the ground really; he had noticed it when he was scanning the perimeter through binoculars just before he was surprised by Höhner-Lanz. But the narrow, shallow fold must have served as a runaway for snows melting from the summit overlooking the base, for although it was dried up now, the sparse Arctic vegetation grew more thickly along its course than along the neighbouring reaches of the perimeter.

And it ran beneath the wire, snaking up to the rock sheltering the two mercenaries.

Its advantage was that the depth was not sufficient to make a noticeable difference in the level of tundra growth carpeting the hillside. But it was deep enough to hide a man flat on his face – as long as he didn't move when anyone was watching.

It had taken Riordan and Frenchie two agonizing hours to crawl beneath the wire and reach their hideaway. Behind him, each man dragged a waterproofed sack, attached to his waist by a cord, containing explosives, an automatic pistol and certain tools more familiar to Frenchie than to his leader. The conditioning factor was movement – or the lack of it. They must freeze instantly each time one of the half-track APCs patrolling the perimeter approached: a tell-tale stirring of leaves, a branch springing back into place among the low-growing clumps, could spell disaster. And as the sound of advancing engines was the only clue they had to the position of the APCs – still circling in opposite directions – the time spent stealthily crawling was considerably less than that flattened to the cold earth, the heart thudding, the watch ticking away the chilling seconds.

When Riordan finally called a halt, the long northern twilight was already dimming towards darkness. It would soon be safe to move openly, particularly as the patrolling guards should be concentrating their attention outside, rather than inside, the perimeter fence.

Riordan and his companion wore skin-tight black thermal ski suits, with soft-soled Mukluk boots and a woollen Balaclava helmet covering the whole head except for the eyes. Once the dusk had thickened enough to make outlines imprecise, they left the rock and began picking their way fast uphill towards the summit.

Below them, the APC drivers switched on their head-lamps, and spotlight beams swept the fence and the ground immediately outside it.

Riordan's plan depended on timing so precise that it was almost second by second. The two hours of darkness were all he had: if the job wasn't completed by sunrise, the odds against him and his team would be too long.

Just below the crest, he laid a hand on Frenchie's arm and murmured: 'Lookout bunker's about a hundred yards away, sunk into the ground in that hollow on the right. If you bend down and look up, you can see the flat roof against the sky.'

Frenchie nodded. 'So we do it now?'

'Check.'

Each of them buckled on a belt supporting a holstered P-220 automatic; each had a knife strapped to his left ankle. Leaving the sacks on a flat-topped rock, they stole towards the bunker.

On their left, the ground sloped down only a few yards to the lip of the rock shelf. Below that, sedimentary strata in horizontal layers dropped almost vertically to the gap beneath which much of the installation was concealed. The concourse was floodlit, although there were bars and patches of deep shadow between buildings and in the motor pool. Away out in the darkness beyond, moving points of light charted the progress of APCs around the northern curve of the perimeter.

The bunker was hexagonal, with observation slots and firing slits set obliquely in the faces looking north-east and north-west. A faint green light showed inside the slits. There was a murmur of conversation – two voices, Riordan thought – and a hint of tobacco smoke in the cold air.

Riordan opened an insulated cardboard box with a pad-ded interior and took out two fragile glass ovals from the hollows nesting inside. Handing one to Frenchie, he pushed him gently towards the further slit. The French-Canadian crept around the angled wall of the bunker.

The ovals were gas grenades containing hydrocyanic-acid vapour.

Riordan heard the soft *Plop!* as Frenchie's grenade smashed inside the bunker, waited five seconds and then lobbed his own through the nearer slit.

The coughings and retchings and choked groans which followed were not pleasant to hear, but they lasted a very short time. The two mercenaries returned to the rock and retrieved their sacks. In one of these there was a coil of thin, immensely strong climbing rope. Riordan fastened one end of this around a projection at the edge of the cliff, tested it with his full weight, and prepared to abseil down to the lower extremity of the shelf.

He passed the free end of the line between his legs from the front, wound it around his left hip, across his chest and over his right shoulder so that it hung down behind him. Then, with one hand holding the rope in front and the other behind, he leaned against the support of the rope and began slowly to walk backwards down the cliff, paying out the lifeline as he descended.

Frenchie followed with the two sacks slung around his neck. When he reached the narrow horizontal ledge at which Riordan had left it, he reached up as far as he could with his knife and sawed through the rope.

The cliff was over a hundred feet high; Frenchie was left with between seventy and eighty feet of usable line in his hands, enough to swarm down to the ground once it was attached to another projection Riordan had found at the eastern end of the ledge.

At first the floodlights dazzled them. They were at the end of the colossal cavern furthest from the guardhouse at the site entrance, fifty yards from Höhner-Lanz's office and the operations room. The workshops and the rocket assembly hangar were twice that far to the north, out in the open beyond the shelf.

Riordan waited, allowing his eyes to adapt to the brilliance. Wind whistled among the irregularities of the

ACTION IN THE ARCTIC

rock roof far above them. Someone strode across a patch
of tarmac. A distant door slammed. In one of the buildings
beneath the overhang – presumably a mess hall – there was
a rumble of voices, a sudden burst of male laughter.

'We'll take the security office and the operations room
first,' Riordan decided. 'That way, whatever else happens,
we'll be sure of destroying the accumulated research data,
the success and failure reports, details of any modifications
made on account of those – that kind of thing.'

Silently, on cushioned soles, they flitted through the
shadows at the inner end of the cavern. The outer door of
the long, low headquarters building yielded within thirty
seconds to Frenchie's expert ministrations. The operations
room was tougher, requiring the use of a small jemmy.
The splintering of wood sounded so loud that both men
expected the guard to come rushing from the gate within
seconds.

Riordan extinguished his pencil torch and they waited
in the dark, breath held and blood humming through
their veins.

No one came. The laughter from the mess grew louder.

'All right then: what's to go from here?' Frenchie asked
when Riordan ventured at last to switch on the tiny
beam again.

'Ideally,' Riordan said, 'all the paperwork. But we don't
have time to sort through it, or pile all the most sensitive
material in one place – and we mustn't waste what explosive
we have.'

'You find the best collection,' Frenchie said, 'and I'll fix
it.' He began plucking the pins from the wall chart.

Riordan slid out the metal drawers from filing cabinets,
flipping through folders to read the titles, pulling out an
occasional paper at random. 'This one seems to be the
jackpot,' he said, hovering over a folder that was thicker
than the others. 'Blueprints, charts, graphs, lab reports on
fuels, a day-to-day breakdown of problems in directional
guidance and suggested solutions.'

Frenchie nodded. He rummaged in his sack and produced a small silver cylinder with hemispherical ends. 'One of my specials,' he confided. 'The only one I have. It's a phosphor bomb. Will burn anything, eats it up, goes through wood, paper, materials, like a wire through cheese. How far ahead?'

Riordan glanced at the luminous face of his watch. 'Thirty-two minutes,' he said.

The French-Canadian nodded. He clicked around a small dial set in one end of the bomb, pulled out all the drawers of the cabinet to their full extent, and placed it among the folders in the bottom drawer. 'A small charge here?' he suggested, indicating the dials and speakers and monitor screens above the operations room workbench.

'Oh, yes, I think so,' Riordan said.

'Plastic here.' Beneath the gleam of metal and glass reflected by the light of the torch shielded by Riordan's palm, Frenchie crouched down to lodge his charge on the underside of the work surface. The delayed-action fuses were simple and efficient. One of two wires attached to a small battery was joined to the minute hand of a tiny wristwatch; the other connected to a pin piercing the face. The hand was then put back anything up to fifty-nine minutes and the watch wound up. When the hand touched the pin, the circuit was completed and the charge fired.

'How many minutes?' Frenchie asked again.

'Leave it at thirty-two. We want the fire-bomb to go off a little while before,' Riordan said.

When the hand had been set back that far and the timed fuse positioned, they returned through the outer office. 'You want the desk here stirred up some?' Frenchie enquired. 'Another pinch of the plastic maybe?'

Riordan touched his cheek where it had been split by the blow from the SS officer's steel hand. 'Yes,' he said with unaccustomed viciousness, 'blow up the bastard's fucking desk.'

While the diminutive charge was put in place, he

picked up a six-page typed folder from the desk. It was illustrated with diagrams, and the cover page read: 'VERGELTUNGSWAFFEN V-2 – Report on the past three months' theory, research and practical tests, from Colonel Wachtel, 155th Flakregiment.' And then, on a separate line below: 'For the attention of Leutnant-General Erich Heinemann, 66th Corps.'

'I'm taking this one with me,' Riordan said, folding the document and stowing it in his sack. 'It should brings tears of joy to the eyes of Monsieur Huefer!'

They left the office and Frenchie carefully relocked the outer door. 'Where now?' he asked.

'The command hut,' Riordan told him. 'I don't want to touch the hangar until after the diversion starts.' Another glance at the watch. 'Three minutes.'

The door to the hut was naturally at the back, on the side away from the launching pad with its anti-blast walls. It was locked with an ordinary mortice key: there was nothing movable inside, nothing anyone would want to steal. Twenty seconds was all the time Frenchie needed.

Inside, the hut was no more than fifteen feet square. Riordan flashed his torch around. He saw a battery of different dials, radio equipment, monitor screens, oscillographs, a teleprinter. 'Apart from firing the things,' he said, 'I reckon this place receives flight information radioed from the missile, monitoring the entire trajectory, from the off to the hit. That way, if anything goes wrong, as it did yesterday afternoon, they know precisely when – and they can work out where.'

'A big one, then?'

'Biggish. I don't want the installation here just put out of order; I want it destroyed, flattened.'

'No problem.' Frenchie had produced what looked like a bunch of wax candles from his sack. He bent down to place it beneath a wide control panel bristling with switches and pilot lights. 'I reckon this is the best . . .'

Riordan shushed him with an upheld hand. He was looking at his watch again.

In the distance, they heard a sudden stutter of automatic fire, followed by a burst from some heavier weapon. And then, in a different direction, individual shots from a rifle and – further away still – the explosion of a grenade. 'Not bad,' Riordan approved. 'Only fifteen seconds late.'

Outside on the concourse an alarm bell was shrilling.

Unhurriedly, Frenchie positioned his explosive and timed his fuses. Beneath the insistent clangour of the bell, now they could hear a hubbub of voices, the tramp of feet as soldiers turned out of their sleeping quarters, an officer shouting commands. In the motor pool, a heavy lorry engine burst into life, and then another.

Riordan and Frenchie left the command hut, locking the door behind them and then racing for the shadows at the back of the overhang. 'They'll be in radio contact with the patrols,' Riordan panted. 'They'll send people out. We wait for the moment of maximum chaos before we head for the hangar.'

Behind the sabotaged headquarters block, they crouched down with their sacks. Without the rope and the grenades and explosives already used, what remained was sufficiently light and reduced in volume to go into a single sack. Frenchie made the transfer, rose to his feet and slung the sack over his shoulder. Out on the perimeter, sporadic bursts of gunfire continued.

As the two men rounded the corner of the building, two open-sided half-track lorries loaded with soldiers were heading for the gates. The bell continued ringing.

'If we can make it to the dormitory huts,' Riordan whispered, 'we'll be behind the hangar – and hopefully in the safest place, because all the Krauts will have been called out to beat off the attack!'

They raced fifteen yards across an open space, dodged into deep shadow between two of the workshops, and skirted the motor pool. Beyond half a dozen parked motorcycle combinations was a latrine and ablutions block. It was at the far end of this that the three soldiers with machine-pistols stepped out of the shadows to confront them.

Van Eyck had been awarded the most difficult role among the five mercenaries setting the scene outside the base perimeter. Not only was he to orchestrate the movements and fire plan of the remaining quartet in such a way as to suggest there were far more attackers involved; he had also to enter the camp openly, bluff his way to the centre and evacuate Riordan and Frenchie once their job was done.

The Hanomag was crucial to the success of the plan. Like Van Eyck himself, the vehicle was to play a double role.

To help in this deception, the engine – and particularly the silencers and exhaust – had been doctored by Aletti and García before night fell, so that the characteristic rasping rattle of the machine was replaced by a softer, more refined note. This would be to disguise the fact that, on a second appearance, it was the same vehicle.

One hour before sunset, the Hanomag left the shelter of the overhang, traversed the rocky valley floor as far as the lake, and then turned west to follow the route taken by the patrol searching for the Fiat float-plane.

At the time Riordan had chosen, the scout car was hull down behind a swell in the landscape, a quarter of a mile from the northernmost point of the curved perimeter. Daniels was driving, with Van Eyck beside him and García manning the Madsen machine-gun. Aletti and Hills, who had left the overhang much earlier with Riordan and Frenchie, were lying in wait with their machine-pistols at a point exactly opposite, two hundred yards from the southern half of the perimeter.

'OK,' Van Eyck said. 'It's time. You can drive up to the fence the next time one patrol comes around. One suppresses the lights, no? And then, José Manuel and Art, you dispose of the crew. Only two guys after all.'

They could hear the engine of the approaching patrol. Daniels shoved the Hanomag into gear and eased out the clutch. Very slowly they breasted the rise. The three lights, two headlamps and the spot, were three hundred yards away. The long, probing pencil of the spotlight beam swept towards them over the rough ground. 'Stop!' Van Eyck called. He was standing up behind the windshield with his Dragunov.

Daniels braked.

Van Eyck shot out, coolly and calmly, first the spot and then the two headlights. The car screeched to a halt.

At once García opened up with the machine-gun, a stream of slugs smashing through the fence to rake the open body of the scout. Daniels switched on the headlights. They saw in the twin beams that the gunner beside the driver was slumped over the low-cut passenger door, but the driver himself was shouting into the hand-held microphone of the scout's radio. They could hear the harsh crackle of the base's response over the idling of the Hanomag's engine.

Daniels picked up a Garand and pumped several shots through the wire, and García fed through another short burst from the Madsen. The driver's head vanished in a cloud of blood and bone splinters.

In the distance now, dead on cue, they heard the lethal rattle of Schmeissers in the hands of Hills and Aletti. They would be shooting up a second patrol car, then dashing further west to enfilade a third from a rise in the ground. The fourth and last should be coming the Hanomag's way, in the opposite direction, at any moment. It didn't matter whether or not the cars were put out of action, the crews wounded or killed. The sole aim of the operation was to convince the Germans that the base was under attack from several different points at the same time. It was for this reason that the small charges prepared by Frenchie and lodged in place earlier were due to explode on the eastern perimeter at any time.

Daniels had swung the Hanomag west, away from the

stalled scout car, bucking and bouncing over the uneven terrain towards a new position. As soon as they saw the approaching lights, he stopped again and the three of them spilled out on to the ground. This time the crew had three different kinds of gunfire to report: a heavy machine-gun, rifles and a Schmeisser. Van Eyck had already shot out the lights. The patrol car lurched away and took up position two hundred yards inside the perimeter. Machine-gun fire now hammered through the fence from two directions. The patrol radio was quite loud: a voice barking orders. Presumably they were being told to stay put until reinforcements arrived.

The Hanomag, after a final volley, was speeding back down the far side of the rise. Before they dropped out of sight, a third patrol car appeared, swung away from the perimeter, and parked by the second. The driver killed the lights. There was a quick babble of German voices, and then the radio again. One of Frenchie's charges exploded with a dull thump at the eastern extremity of the site.

'Alex and Hills must have missed that one,' Daniels said. 'The third patrol car, I mean.'

'Doesn't matter,' Van Eyck said, 'as long as it draws the soldiery outside the perimeter. They can't bloody search for attackers inside the fence.'

Three minutes later, García dropped off the Hanomag, taking the Schmeisser and the Garand with him. He hurried up the slope and approached the base where the fence curved south towards the entrance gates. He fired three short bursts from the Schmeisser at nothing in particular and then, just to underline the point, lobbed in a hand-grenade – one of three clipped to his belt. Immediately after the livid flash and the cracking thump of the explosion, the second of Frenchie's charges detonated in the distance.

From here, García could see the entrance, the shrouded light above the gates, the glow of the floodlit concourse reflected off the horizontal ledges of the great cliff.

The sound of the Hanomag's modified engine died away

to the west. At any moment the trusty scout car would have the quickest quick-change in history, before returning to play the star role in Riordan's definitive plan.

Two half-track troop carriers, each crammed with armed soldiers, thundered out of the base entrance and turned, one north, the other south, to circle the outside of the perimeter fence.

Abruptly, the floodlights faded and died, and then every light on the base was extinguished.

The sudden darkness took Riordan and Frenchie completely by surprise. But they weren't as astonished as the three soldiers who had the drop on them. And the mercenaries were tougher, with faster reactions, apart from which they had become used for many days to doing most of the day's work in the darkness of the short Arctic night.

As if controlled by a single switch, the two men dropped and dived. Frenchie's huge hands wrapped around the ankles of the nearest German, jerking him off the ground. His weapon clattered away across the tarmac. At the same time the powerful French-Canadian, straightening up and still grabbing the man by the ankles, swung him around in a ferocious circle and cracked his head lethally against the wall of the ablutions block.

Riordan, falling fast and speeding in beneath the gun barrel, had snatched the holstered knife from his left ankle and stabbed upwards at a second man as he knocked him off balance. The razor-sharp blade seared through greatcoat and uniform to bury itself in the soldier's belly. He fell on his back with a strangled groan, dropping the machine-pistol to clamp both hands over the blood spurting from the wound.

Frenchie's first victim had collapsed lifeless to the ground as the French-Canadian whirled to hurl himself at the remaining soldier, who was attempting to distance himself enough to bring his gun into play. Steely fingers fastened themselves over his left hand, forcing the stubby barrel up and imprisoning the right hand with the pistol grip. Face to face, the two of them heaved and struggled, sweating with the effort as each strained to master the other. It was Riordan who settled the encounter. Using the knife again, he stabbed viciously upwards to bury the blade under the point of the German's chin, driving it up through the mouth and palate into the brain. The man died silently, choking on his own blood, but muscular spasms shuddering from the shock tightened his finger on the trigger, and the machine-pistol emptied its magazine into the air with a thundering roar.

They dragged the bodies into the block. 'Too much time lost because of them,' Riordan muttered. 'We'd better split up and divide the charges. I'll take the workshops and chemical plant; you do the big one in the hangar.'

'OK,' Frenchie said. 'And the timing?'

'Search me,' Riordan replied. 'But not less than thirteen minutes . . .'

Three hundred yards in front of Aletti and Hills, the fourth patrol car was stalled on the far side of the perimeter fence. The driver was dead. The front tyres – sprayed by the Italian's Schmeisser when the mercs were in their original position – were in ribbons. Hills had shot out the spotlight and one of the headlamps. Now, with the vehicle slewed sideways, the remaining lamp cast a long finger of light up the lower slopes of the hill.

The surviving crewman was sheltering behind the armoured panels of the bodywork on the far side of the car, waiting for reinforcements to arrive.

'No point wasting any more rounds now,' Hills murmured. 'He's radioed for help; it's on the way – probably outside the wire. That was the aim of the operation: draw the buggers out of the jolly old base to let Frenchie and Himself their magic charms display.'

'Tell me something,' Aletti said. They were lying in a hollow overlooking the perimeter, waiting for the deadline:

the precise time at which they were to run for the track approaching the base. 'It's a question I always wanted to ask, but somehow never got around to.'

'Fire away, old son,' Hills said warmly.

'It's . . . well, maybe a man in a hazardous situation he shouldn't put personal questions to a fellow victim, but it's this: is your name *really* Beverley Hills?'

'Absolutely,' Hills said. 'Or, rather, not entirely.'

'Say again?'

'Beverley's the genuine article. On the birth certificate and all that. Actually, though, the family name is Hills-Loumis-Fazackerlay . . .'

'Good God!'

'. . . and I decided to limit myself to the first bit. Deuced inconvenient otherwise, you see, when it comes to one's visiting cards,' Hills said gravely. 'One has to have the bally things made especially wide.'

Light fell on them from behind. 'It's a tiny hand,' a voice said, 'but it's not frozen. And it's holding a Walther automatic. If you'd like to get up very quietly, very slowly, I think it would be nice if we took a walk together.'

They spun around. The gun was held by Sigurd Hasso.

Van Eyck's part in the final stages of the raid was capital. He spoke perfect German. Physically, with his upright carriage, pale hair and regular features, he could pass as ideal Master Race material – and it was because of this that Riordan, overriding protests from Daniels, had insisted on two unexpected items being included within their supplies. The two items were a high-crowned, shiny-peaked, German army officer's cap, and a replica of the high-collared uniform jacket that would be worn with it. Replica because, although it looked thick and heavy, the garment was made from a special lightweight, uncrushable material that could be rolled into a small bundle. Worn with a half-open parka, the jacket and cap were entirely convincing.

Standing up in the Hanomag dressed in this way, with one hand on top of the windshield and a monocle jammed into his left eye, Van Eyck looked Nazi enough to fool Goebbels, Goering and Himmler all at once.

Circling out of sight of the base, the scout car had been stripped of the modifications and mufflers improvised by García and Aletti once it reached the approach track used by the supply tankers. Now, once again emitting its normal harsh racket, the Hanomag was grinding up the rise leading to the site entrance.

To strengthen the illusion that its arrival had nothing to do with the attackers, García, who had worked his way around to within two hundred yards of the gates, opened fire with his Schmeisser as the Hanomag approached. Superbly unconcerned, still ramrod erect, Van Eyck would not deign even to turn in the direction of the shots — reasonably enough, since he knew very well that they would be fired well wide of the scout car.

Daniels, indistinguishable with goggles and a hooded parka, squealed the Hanomag to a halt, scattering gravel. Two sentries ran out from behind a striped barrier pole, opening the steel gates wide enough for the scout car to pass through and halt by the pole. An NCO emerged from the guardroom.

'What the devil is going on here? What is this nonsense?' Van Eyck shouted in his best *gauleiter* manner. 'Guns firing! Bombs exploding! One had imagined this to be a *secret* installation. I have a message of the highest importance, the very highest importance, for SS Obersturmbannführer Höhner-Lanz. Where is he to be found?'

'Yes, sir. Of course.' The NCO snapped into a crisp salute. 'There appears to be some kind of terrorist attack aimed at the base, and the . . .'

'I can see that, man. Where is the Chief of Security?'

'Doubtless in the military command post, opposite the operations room. Two squads of Feldgendarmerie, have already been sent out to neutralize the attackers. Already the gunfire has greatly diminished.'

In the distance, the third and largest of Frenchie's prepositioned charges on the eastern perimeter exploded.

'I see what you mean,' Van Eyck said drily. 'Now be a good fellow and raise that damn pole.'

'Yes, sir.' The NCO swallowed. 'If the Herr Oberst would be so good as to show his papers . . .'

Van Eyck choked off an exclamation of impatience. 'Damn-fool formalities. Franzel!' He tapped Daniels on the shoulder.

The Romany plunged a languid hand inside his parka, produced a number of documents, and held them out to the NCO without looking at him. These included the fruits of Frenchie's genius as a forger: a *laissez-passer* relevant to this particular base, made out in the name of Oberst Heinz Benckendorff, military ID papers in the same name, a soldier's pay book (taken from one of the Germans killed in the ambush, with Franzel substituted for the original name), the Hanomag's own identification document with the military registration number changed, and a letter to Hönner-Lanz identifying the bearer, Oberst Benckendorff, as a messenger from the headquarters of General Erich Heinemann's 66th Corps. The officer's ID was on a blank from Frenchie's forgery kit; the other headings, titles and stamps were copied from the papers Riordan had removed from Germans killed or wounded in the ambush.

The dimmed lamp above the guardhouse – the only light source now visible from the outside on the entire base was not bright enough for the papers to be read. 'If the Herr Oberst will be patient for one moment,' the NCO said, 'I have to take these inside.' Saluting again, he disappeared into the building. The light from an electric lamp outlined the doorway.

'Hurry, you dolt!' Van Eyck shouted. 'The message I have concerns the man who may lead these terrorists.'

The NCO reappeared. 'That will be quite all right,

sir. About one hundred and fifty metres. On the left. There is a sign.' He signalled to someone inside the guardhouse. The hydraulically operated barrier pole rose on its counterweight.

'And my papers?'

The guard handed back the letter. 'It is regretted, Herr Oberst, but we have to retain the others. They will be returned to you when you leave. Orders of the General Commanding the Military Area.'

'So be it,' Van Eyck grunted. There was nothing else he could say. He raised an arm. '*Heil Hitler!*'

'*Heil Hitler!*'

Daniels put the Hanomag in gear and drove slowly into the compound.

Riordan was placing the last of several small charges in a welding shop when the light penetrating the serrated glass roof was extinguished. He unclipped the small torch from his belt. The sounds of battle outside were diminishing. The troop carriers had left. The gunfire had died away. In the distance, he heard a single explosion.

So far, so good. Everything was going according to plan ... and everything now depended upon Frenchie and himself. The fight with the three soldiers had wrecked their timetable, but the charges still had to be placed. He hoped Van Eyck and Daniels had managed to bluff their way into the base. And that the four of them could get clear before the troop carriers returned to report that there was *no* attack, that the perimeter was *not* surrounded by hostile 'terrorists'.

The final charge in this shop was placed among a stack of triangular panels leaning against one wall, which could have been part of the finned lower end of the missile. Beside them were sets of graphite vanes intended, Riordan thought, to defect the exhaust gases and thus 'steer' the rocket – presumably under radio control.

He had stepped back, directing the narrow torch beam

downward to check that the charge was invisible from above, when a door behind him was flung violently open and a heavy body lunged into him with such force that he was thrown to the floor and the torch flew from his grasp.

Before he could twist around or make any attempt to rise, he was himself caught in the brilliant beam of a much more powerful light – a beam in whose upper extremity a black-gloved hand holding a Walther automatic was visible. 'Mr Riordan, I assume,' the sneering voice of Höhner-Lanz drawled. He stepped quickly forward and snatched the Balaclava from the mercenary leader's head. '*Ach, so!* I thought as much. I was expecting some kind of foolish intrusion, which is why I did not go out with the troops. Well, this time, my friend, you will not so easily escape. I have every right to shoot you down here and now – a saboteur, a cheap hired terrorist caught in the act! But not to kill you, just to wound. For there are questions still to be asked. Who exactly does the hiring, for example. *Stand up, man. Now!*'

Riordan struggled to his feet, as near to the German as he could. Höhner-Lanz stepped back and away, the torch beam steady. The barrel of the Walther was angled down, pointing at the lower part of Riordan's belly. 'You should have remembered,' he said, 'that even a faint light demands attention when everything else is dark – and that a glass roof allows light *out* as well as in!' He shifted his feet slightly, steadying his aim.

Riordan followed his own advice. The simplest way is the best. 'I should watch where you step,' he said conversationally. 'The charge at the bottom of those panels is actuated by a trembler coil: the slightest movement can set it off.'

Höhner-Lanz fell for it, the oldest ruse in the world. Surprise added to uncertainty, in a situation itself unplanned. Instinctively, he glanced down.

Riordan leapt, striking the gun hand down with the

ACTION IN THE ARCTIC

iron-hard outside edge of his own left. The weapon fell to
the floor. He kicked it away as the two of them closed.

The wide reflector head of the torch struck him a
stunning blow on the shoulder. It was followed by a heavy
diaphragm punch from the German's steel fist. Riordan
gagged, bringing a knee up to his adversary's crotch.
Höhner-Lanz twisted away – but left the hand holding
the torch momentarily vulnerable. Riordan, fighting for
breath, flailed out with one arm. The torch shot away to
land on a workbench.

In the shaft of intense light blazing from there to the shop
wall, the two men lurched into a titanic struggle, huge shadows racing over the galvanized surface. Riordan moved in
close to wrap powerful arms into a bear-hug, for the German was immensely strong, and as soon as he had distanced
himself enough to swing that lethal steel fist, the mercenary
was in danger. Locked together, heaving and groaning with
the effort, they swayed across the floor, cannoning into a
workbench, crashing against a control panel. Glass tinkled
to the ground, a Bakelite cover split and fell.

Riordan butted with all his force, smashing his opponent's nose. Höhner-Lanz broke free, blood streaming
over his mouth and chin, and landed a haymaker that
sent Riordan reeling against the wall. A second punch
to the head felled him to the floor. Höhner-Lanz leapt.
With lightning speed, Riordan drew up his knees, allowed
the German to land on the soles of his feet, then fiercely
straightened his legs.

Höhner-Lanz flew through the air. He thumped against
the workbench, the thick iron edge catching him across the
small of the back, and was still gasping from this crippling
blow when Riordan in his turn piled in tigerishly.

Behind the bench was the control panel. The cover which
had been damaged and knocked off was the housing for
a 360-volt plug used to power some of the welding
equipment. Now, minus the safety shield, the two naked
terminals inside gleamed in the bright light.

Riordan had worn rubber gloves to place the charges. Bending Höhner-Lanz backwards over the bench, he seized the struggling man's arm and forced it, inch by inch, towards the electrical socket. With a final heave, he jammed the back of the steel hand hard against the exposed terminals, and held it there.

A hole opened in the German's bloodied face and he screamed. The body jerked, convulsed, thrashed against the bench in long shudders, then went limp.

Riordan allowed it to sag to the floor. He ran out of the workshop.

Frenchie was waiting where he said he would be. 'What happened?' he whispered. 'I thought I heard . . .'

'Later,' Riordan replied. 'What's that?'

Somewhere over by the workshops there were shouts, the sounds of running feet.

'I think they found the guys we shoved into the lats,' Frenchie said.

Apart from that distant hubbub, the base was unnaturally quiet. The scientists and technicians would have been sent back to their quarters; the duty officers and those who had not gone out with the troop carriers would be in the military command post. But the troops themselves would be back at any minute with a negative report, and . . .

Lights all over the camp, including the floods over the concourse, blazed to life with sudden brilliance.

'Shit!' Riordan swore. 'That means they *already* radioed back an all-clear. We'll have two squads to deal with if we don't get out of here!'

'Look!' Frenchie said, clutching his arm.

Above the entrance, brightly lit now, a heavily insulated electricity supply line was looped between a row of posts stretching away towards the overhang. And on the section nearest the guardroom, silhouetted with outstretched arms like the circus slack-wire performer he once was, Daniels – minus his parka – wobbled and swayed his way in the direction of the gates.

When he was directly behind the gatehouse and guardroom, he dropped, hanging from the line at the full stretch of his arms. A moment later, he vanished, falling fifteen feet to the canvas roof of a patrol car, landing in a combat roll and then jumping nimbly to the ground. He stole around the corner of the building and crept up to the entrance.

Voices, cigarette smoke, the stifling reek of an oil heater. 'There's something wrong here,' one of the men said. 'That Hanomag – the military registration numbers don't agree with the engine and chassis numbers on these papers.'

'Let me see.' Another voice. 'Wait a minute . . . four-oh-nine-*six-seven*? But that's the number of . . . Hell, that's *our* Hanomag, the one they stole after the ambush! Holy shit, pass me that phone . . .'

Daniels removed a shallow box from beneath his belt. Carefully, he removed from inside it two glass capsules identical to those used by Riordan and Frenchie at the bunker. Carefully, he lobbed them, one after the other, in through the open door of the guardroom.

Very soon afterwards, the barrier pole rose.

The silence was broken by the engine of a Hanomag grinding suddenly to life. With Van Eyck at the wheel, the scout car careered out from under the overhang, paused for Riordan and his partner to climb aboard, and raced for the gates. Behind them, someone shouted. A shot rang out.

Daniels had the gates open. He hurled himself aboard as Van Eyck slowed again, then leaned out to help García, who had materialized from the darkness. The Hanomag sped away down the track as the first of the troop carriers appeared around the northern curve of the perimeter fence.

It was then that the first of the demolition charges exploded.

23

The phosphor bomb among the secret papers in the operations room was, as planned, the first to explode.

A discreet, hollow detonation, not unlike the popping of a huge cork. Strong enough nevertheless to blow out the windows and shutters. And then, through the splintered gaps in the wall, to release this magnesium dazzle of unbelievably bright light, a livid, greenish glare to start with, rapidly, blindingly brightening still further to an aching orange-crimson.

Brown smoke boiled out through the windows as the papers were incinerated. Flames burst through the wooden roof. Within seconds the interior of the low building was an inferno.

From the far end of the site the bell of a fire engine clanged. Men ran from the command post, spilled from the troop carrier, which had halted by the gates. A confused shouting could be heard over the roar and crackle of flames.

Frenchie's plastic bomb detonated with an ear-shattering thump, flattening the outer wall of the operations room to scatter blazing debris across the roadway. The smoke was now black – a writhing dark tower, leaning away from the wind, the lower surfaces marbled with reflections from the fire.

The fire engine had arrived and the hoses were adding steam to the conflagration when a flicker of crimson and a thumping explosion from the northern quarter of the base announced the destruction of the control hut beside the launching pad. This was followed within seconds by five other detonations, of varying strength, wreaking havoc in assembly shops, laboratories and work sheds. Flames and smoke belched through shattered roofs; burning fragments showered to the ground; alarm bells shrilled.

Now there was chaos on the concourse. Soldiers, scientists, engineers and technicians, milled and wheeled, retreating before the scorching fury of the original blaze, advancing in futile attempts to help the fire-fighters, busy as the inhabitants of a disturbed ant-heap.

But the most impressive of Frenchie Delorme's pyrotechnic surprises was left – was it a Gallic sense of the theatrical? – to the end of the display.

It started with a throaty growling behind the huge sliding doors of the hangar and the escape around those doors of violet smoke in accelerating wisps. Two small charges then erupted inside the hangar, shaking the structure on its steel frame.

Riordan never knew whether the explosion wrecking the control hut inadvertently triggered some firing mechanism, or Frenchie's strategically placed miniature bombs did the trick. The saboteur himself would only smile cryptically and mutter: 'Like I say – use the enemy's strength against him!' What was certain was that, somewhere amidst the multiple explosions, a rocket motor ignited: the turbine turned, the pump pumped, the two fuels were forced under pressure into the jet chamber . . . and the rocket readied itself for lift-off. Horizontally.

The missile, scheduled for a trial the following day, was attached to the ladder-frame of a *Meillerwagen* facing the hangar doors.

The motor fired up with a thunderous roar. The jet pressure, blasting backwards, buckled the hulls of two other V-2s and started a colossal fire. The *Meillerwagen*, helpless beneath the immense force of the beast on its back, lurched forward and burst open the hangar doors. Steel frames and savaged woodwork went spinning off sideways as the great truck and its flaming burden careered away, zigzagging wildly across the concourse with terrified soldiers scattering before its awesome advance.

Surviving witnesses disagreed. Some said the rocket burst the shackles tethering it to the ladder; others swore that it literally took off and streaked through the air with the vehicle hanging beneath it – the steel prey of a jet-propelled eagle. There was not enough left of either to say which was right.

The rocket flashed in beneath the overhang and burst against the rock wall at the cavern's innermost extremity. The cataclysmic explosion of the one-ton warhead, dwarfing any detonation which had preceded it, flattened every wooden building on the site that was still standing and destroyed the entire motor pool. Sixty-five people died.

Seconds after the earth-shaking reverberations had died away, there was an ominous, menacing rumble from above. In the flickering light of burning ruins, a whole section of the hundred-foot cliff was seen to move. Dozens of rows of the horizontal strata slipped, slid relentlessly downwards and then separated to drop into the void. Hundreds, thousands of tons of rock smashed down on the decimated base with a roar that sounded like the end of creation.

When daylight returned, there was nothing left beneath the raw wound scarring the cliff but a stone wilderness, blackened by charred debris, steaming in the cold sun.

Riordan and Van Eyck clapped one another on the shoulder when the rogue V-2 exploded behind them, splashing the underside of racing clouds with carmine. 'Man,' the Dutchman said to Frenchie, 'you're a real wizard!'

'Fucking genius,' Daniels said.

The pulsing glow in the sky was still visible when they reached the ambush ravine. 'Slow down,' Riordan said to Van Eyck. 'This is where we have to pick up the others.' So far, there had been no sign of pursuit.

When the Hanomag rounded the corner at the head of

the ravine, Van Eyck jammed on the brakes. The narrowest part of the track, where it rounded the bluff, was blocked by a vehicle. Reaching for a Schmeisser, he switched the headlights on full.

It was a strange sight: a dun-coloured, four-year-old Renault Primaquatre, with a laid-back 'V' radiator and sloping tall, a 2.5-litre sports saloon standing oddly high on much-modified, raised springs, with small wheels and ribbed heavy-duty tyres. Standing in front of it was a familiar figure in a furred parka.

Sigurd Hasso.

Riordan was holding one of the SIG-Sauer automatics loosely in his lap. The young woman walked towards them, long legs lithely striding. She was unarmed. 'This would be a good place to change cars,' she said, 'now that your work is over.'

Riordan stared. Behind her, Hills and Aletti climbed out of the car and waved.

'My God,' Riordan said. 'So it *was* you!'

'I beg your pardon?'

'This.' He pulled the empty Beretta from his pocket and held it out towards her. 'I believe this may be yours.'

'Thank you. Please hurry now. I will explain later.'

They transferred the rest of their gear, which had been stowed in the Hanomag. It was only when this was done that they realized something was very wrong. García, who had not spoken a word since they left the base, was slumped in the rear seat, his breath like snoring and the front of his parka sodden with blood.

'Afraid I caught a couple,' he said weakly when Riordan tried to rouse him. 'One of the patrols . . . firing through the wire.'

'But . . . why didn't you say?'

García shook his head. 'No use . . . hold up the rest of you. I know that I'm on . . . my way.' He coughed up some blood. 'There is one thing . . .'

'Tell me.' Riordan looked with agonized eyes at Daniels.

The Romany in turn shook his head. He mouthed the words: 'Seen too many. Ten minutes, not more.'

'My sister Incarnita . . . in Lyons,' García whispered. 'I would like . . .'

'She'll receive your full share. I will attend to it personally.'

'Good.' García smiled. 'It is nice, at the last, to have been concerned with . . . something . . . worthwhile,' he said in a stronger voice. And then, still smiling, quietly died.

'My brief,' Sigurd said, 'was basically to keep an eye on you, help if necessary and when possible, avoid compromising my own position – and report back any successes you had.'

'Of course,' Riordan said. 'That short-wave radio! But why? I don't . . .'

'Because I was here, in place, already. They thought they might as well row me in on the periphery, as it were.'

'Why didn't you say?'

'Instructions. They want to keep me here. I can be useful. The Germans know me, as you have seen. I really am a naturalist: the work I do is genuine: I *am* connected with the university at Vaasa. But I must not be connected . . .'

'In case we fuck up! Yes, I understand. But why the tip-off to the SS?'

'I was determined to get you inside the base, by any means possible, so that you could find out what they were doing – and then get you out again, so that you could take any action you thought necessary. This seemed the best way.'

'Well, thank you very much,' Riordan said, fingering his split cheek.

'And you, of course,' Aletti said, 'are the lady she upsets our culinary arrangements, stuffing messages into our mess tins?'

Sigurd laughed. 'I'm afraid so.'

'But why pull a gun on us, when at last you come clean, when you bring us here?'

278

'I was afraid you might not believe me. I had to tell the whole story first.'

'Darling,' Beverley Hills said, 'the way you look, you could make me believe the tundra up there was the Garden of bloody Eden.'

The girl flashed him an approving look.

Typical younger son, Riordan thought with an irrational surge of irritation. Self-centred, conceited, determined to succeed at any cost. The boy might be a good shot, but he was irresponsible, amoral, with the fecklessness of those with a cushioned background. He recalled the affair of the ptarmigans, the cold-blooded execution of the man on the float-plane, the eagerness to cash in on Zabrisky's share of the proceeds . . . Still, in his line of work you were thrown together with all types of people. And that was the least of his problems. It's a dirty job but someone's got to do it, he thought – not for the first time.

'What I can't understand,' he said to Sigurd, shaking off the uncharacteristic attack of spleen, 'is how you got about so quickly. Do you use this buggy all the time – and why didn't we see it?'

'I drove up from Vaasa in it. I don't use it during my nature research. Too frightening for the creatures I study. But it's helpful when I'm babysitting.'

'Babysitting?'

She smiled. 'Professional jargon. It's not pejorative.'

They had already reached the gravelled highway which led to Ivalo. Driving in shifts the following day, they were to go south to Laanila and then west through the forests of Katkatunturi to the Swedish border, well clear of the German military presence in Lapland.

At Muonio, the frontier town, a civilized place with neat wooden buildings, a lake, petrol pumps and a public garden, they even took rooms in a hotel and ate a restaurant meal. Arrangements had been made to convey them secretly across the border the following day, after which they were to take a Swedish bus to Pajala, where a representative of

Monsieur Huefer by the name of Lang would take delivery of their films and documents and evaluate Riordan's personal report.

During the previous twenty-four hours, Riordan had been increasingly aware of the light in Sigurd's blue eyes, the laughter in her voice, the satisfyingly ripe contours discernible when the sweater was no longer hidden by a parka. Perhaps it was because of the vividness of that dream – how long ago now? – that he cherished a hope of future meetings, a row, even today perhaps, on the lake, a quiet walk together in the spring sunshine.

But when he awoke, Sigurd had already left. Beverley Hills's room was empty too. There was a note pushed under Riordan's door.

He stood by the open window, breathing in the sharp, satisfying scent of spruce and pine. Green branches swayed in a pleasant breeze. The note read: 'Frightfully sorry to leave the rest of the chaps as it were in the lurch, old son. But, ignoramus as I am, the lure of a short course at the University of Vaasa, and the opportunity of learning a smattering of the lingo, has proved too much for yours truly. B.H. P.S. Thanks for the trip. You know the number of my Swiss bank account.

Riordan stared at the trees. 'Oh, well,' he murmured, 'especially with women, you can't win 'em all!'

He tore the note up into very small pieces, held out his hand, and watched the fragments carried away by the wind.

Epilogue

Subsequently, the partly destroyed Finland station was abandoned. Assembly and test-firing of the V-2 was transferred to Peenemunde on the Baltic coast, where the V-1 flying bomb was already being evaluated. Having experienced further difficulties, the V-2 design team decided to reduce the effective range to two hundred miles. Manufacture of the 1000-hp pump which forced the fuels into the jet chamber, and of the hydrogen-peroxide-powered turbine which drove the pump, was transferred at that time to the Harz Mountains.

Captain Seamus McPhee O'Kelly, RN,
Director, CO(S)E

Although we could do little against the rockets once they were perfected and launched, we succeeded in postponing and substantially reducing the expected weight of the onslaught.

Winston Churchill

If the German had succeeded in perfecting and using this new V weapon six months earlier than he did, our invasion of Europe would have proved exceedingly difficult, perhaps impossible.

General Dwight Eisenhower

OTHER TITLES IN SERIES FROM 22 BOOKS

Available now at newsagents and booksellers
or use the order form opposite

SOLDIER A SAS: Behind Iraqi Lines
SOLDIER B SAS: Heroes of the South Atlantic
SOLDIER C SAS: Secret War in Arabia
SOLDIER D SAS: The Colombian Cocaine War
SOLDIER E SAS: Sniper Fire in Belfast
SOLDIER F SAS: Guerrillas in the Jungle
SOLDIER G SAS: The Desert Raiders
SOLDIER H SAS: The Headhunters of Borneo
SOLDIER I SAS: Eighteen Years in the Elite Force
SOLDIER J SAS: Counter-insurgency in Aden
SOLDIER K SAS: Mission to Argentina
SOLDIER L SAS: The Embassy Siege
SOLDIER M SAS: Invisible Enemy in Kazakhstan
SOLDIER N SAS: The Gambian Bluff
SOLDIER O SAS: The Bosnian Inferno
SOLDIER P SAS: Night Fighters in France
SOLDIER Q SAS: Kidnap the Emperor!
SOLDIER R SAS: Death on Gibraltar

*   *   *   *   *

SOLDIER OF FORTUNE 1:   Valin's Raiders
SOLDIER OF FORTUNE 2:   The Korean Contract
SOLDIER OF FORTUNE 3:   The Vatican Assignment
SOLDIER OF FORTUNE 4:   Operation Nicaragua
SOLDIER OF FORTUNE 6:   The Khmer Hit

All at £4.99 net

22 Books offers an exciting list of titles in this series. All the books are available from:

    Little, Brown and Company (UK) Limited,
    PO Box 11,
    Falmouth,
    Cornwall TR10 9EN.

Alternatively you may fax your order to the above address. Fax number: 0326 376423.

Payments can be made by cheque or postal order (payable to Little, Brown and Company) or by credit card (Visa/Access). Do not send cash or currency. UK customers and BFPO please allow £1.00 for postage and packing for the first book, plus 50p for the second book, plus 30p for each additional book up to a maximum charge of £3.00 (seven books or more). Overseas customers, including customers in Ireland, please allow £2.00 for the first book, plus £1.00 for the second book, plus 50p for each additional book.

NAME (BLOCK LETTERS PLEASE) ....

....

ADDRESS ....

....

....

☐ I enclose my remittance for £_____

☐ I wish to pay by Access/Visa

Card number

☐☐☐☐☐ ☐☐☐☐☐ ☐☐☐☐☐ ☐☐☐☐☐

Card expiry date

☐☐ ☐☐